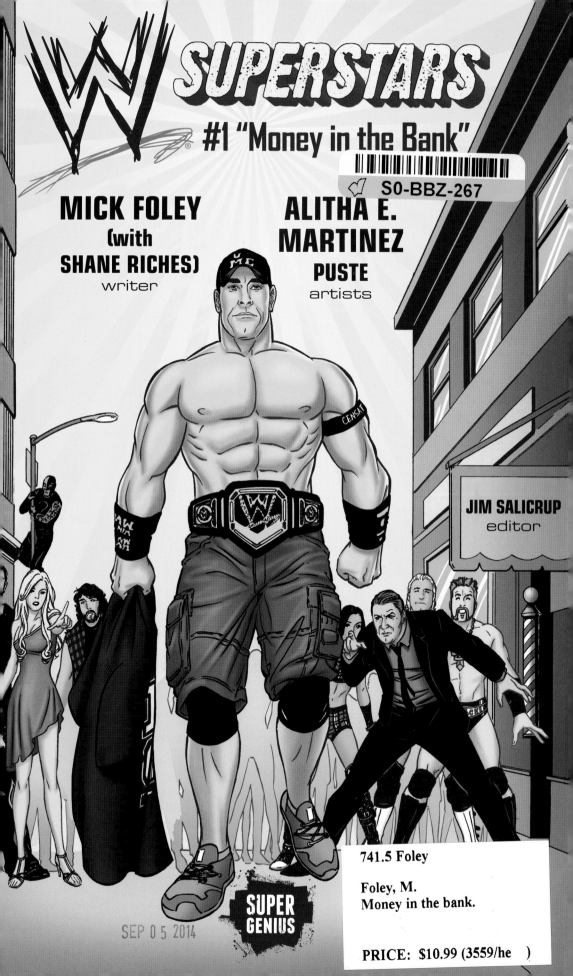

W SUPERSTARS

#1 "Money in the Bank"

MICK FOLEY
(with
SHANE RICHES)
writer

ALITHA E. MARTINEZ
PUSTE
artists

JIM SALICRUP
editor

SUPER GENIUS

SEP 0 5 2014

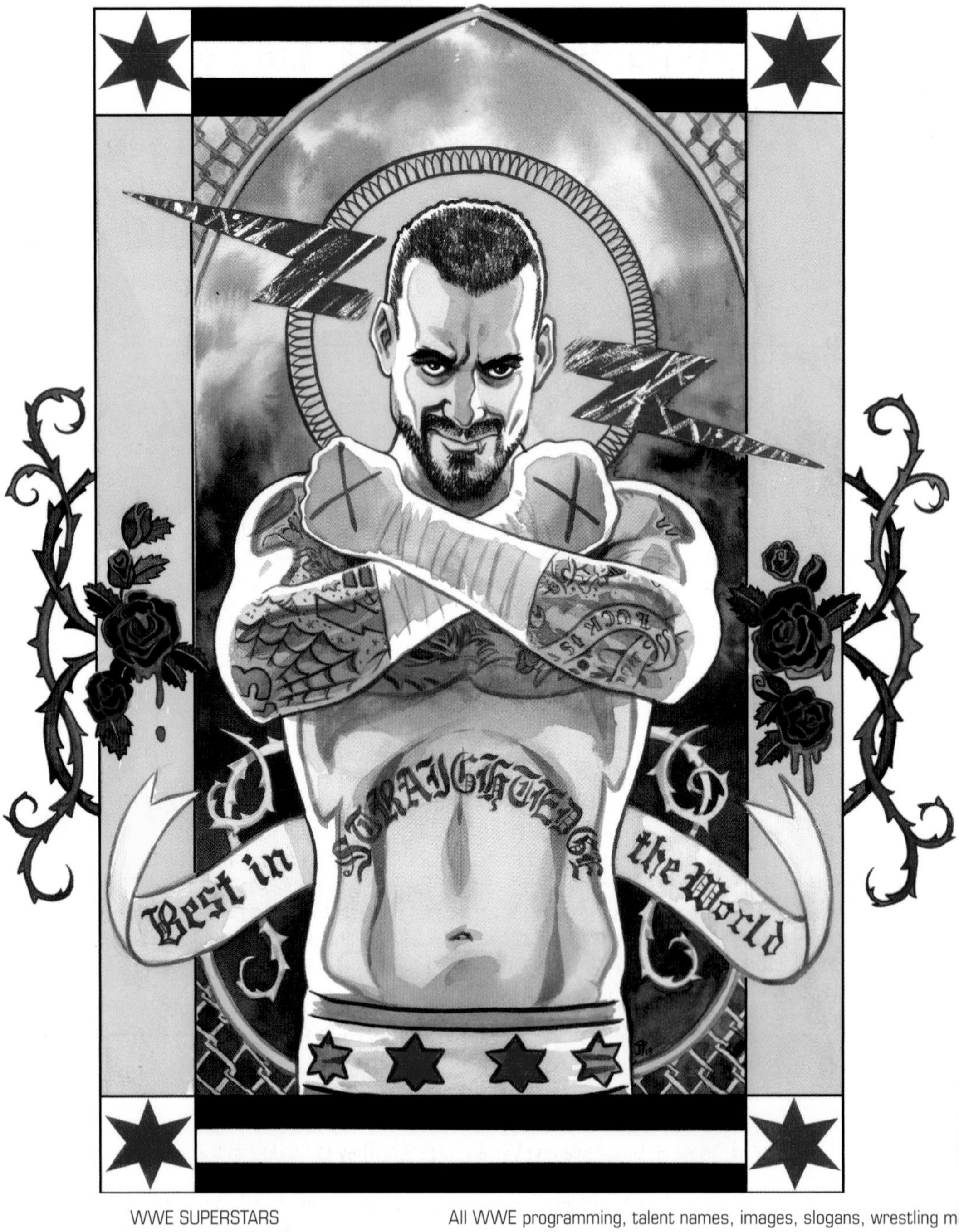
Best in
STRAIGHTEDGE
the World

WWE SUPERSTARS
#1 "Money in the Bank"

Mick Foley (with Shane Riches) – writer
Alitha E. Martinez – artist (pages 1, 16-89, 94, & 95)
Puste – artist (pages 4-15, 90-93)
Jill Thompson – artist (page 2)
Puste – cover artist
JayJay Jackson – colorist (cover & pages 1, 4-89, 94, & 95)
Laurie E. Smith – colorist (pages 90-93)
Tom Orzechowski – letterer
Jim Salicrup – Editor
Dawn K. Guzzo – Production
Beth Scorzato – Production Coordinator
Michael Petranek – Associate Editor
Jim Salicrup
Editor-in-Chief

Originally published as WWE SUPERSTARS #0-4 comics,
by Super Genius, an imprint of Papercutz,
160 Broadway, Suite 700, East Wing, New York, NY 10038.

ISBN: 978-1-59707-720-0

Printed in the US
June 2014 by Avenue 4 Communications
2901 Byrdhill Road
Richmond, VA 23228

Super Genius books may be purchased for business or promotional
For information on bulk purchases please contact Macmillan Corpo
and Premium Sales Department at (800) 221-7945 x5442.

Distributed by Macmillan
First Printing

Welcome to Titan City...

A metropolis where everyone's hiding secrets. A concrete jungle where there's no one to trust. From the scheming south side to the infamous wrestling gyms and tattoo parlors to the barren desert no man's land where even the law refuses to go. The powerful factions of Titan City are locked in a battle for control. With tensions and treaties, animosity and alliances, it's a thrilling world filled with a riveting and unforgettable landscape. In a corrupt world where everyone is looking to cash in, we'll follow the journey of three men...

John Cena[1]: Ex-cop and former WWE World Champion. John was the pride of the city. Hailed as a future police commissioner or D.A. – the sky was the limit. Everyone loved him. The mobsters couldn't touch him. Then a literal money in the bank – a briefcase with $10,000,000.00 – went missing on a sting operation Cena was in charge of... John was framed for a crime he didn't commit. Now, he's both loved and hated by the citizens at large. To some he's just one more good guy screwed by the system. To others, he's their last hope who betrayed them. Practically friendless with little money and failing hope, John's desperate to prove his innocence and be the hero he knows he can be to the people of Titan City.

Randy Orton[2]: This apex predator leads the ultimate double-life – scheming in private as the ultimate mob ruler while preaching law and order – even running for DA against **Alberto Del Rio**[9] – in his public life. This viper finds himself in constant conflict with one of the few honest cops in Titan City – the relentless **Captain Christian**[10] (whom the public has dubbed "Captain Charisma") who is Cena's former best friend and partner. Beyond the ongoing investigation from Christian, Randy must also deal with ambitious underlings like Ryback and opportunistic enemies like **Daniel Bryan**[11].

CM Punk[3]: An urban vigilante of sorts who's sick of the people of Titan City suffering under corrupt rule. Punk is determined to bring down the system that controls Titan City. Almost an anarchist, the people love him but the authorities – both the law and the mobsters – hate him. He operates completely outside of the system and gives little regard to those in power. Punk's arranged a massive demonstration – a "Take Back the City" rally. And he will help free the people of Titan City... By any means necessary.

Who's really in control of Titan City?

With the release of Cena and Punk's rising popularity the city is about to explode...

The factions...

The Authority: Triple H, Stephanie and Vince McMahon. They like to lurk in the shadows, but events may quickly bring them out.

The Brothers: Kane[4] and **Undertaker**[5]. Not corrupt but not on the up-and-up either. Everyone wants them on their side but winning over one of them doesn't necessarily guarantee the cooperation of the other.

The Shield[8]: Three cops born and raised in Titan City. They want power not for themselves but to return the city into their idealized version of what it used to be. But they will do whatever it takes to accomplish their goal -- even betraying Captain Christian[10].

The Wyatt Family[12]: Sadistic, cult-like family that lives in the barren wastelands outside the city.

Other...

Daniel Bryan[11]: A loose cannon. Not good for goodness sake, but good to destroy Orton who has wronged him the past.

Paul Heyman[13]: The madman. Public enemy #1. Will make hell for anyone who crosses him – along with his men – **Brock Lesnar** and **Curtis Axel**.

Alberto del Rio[9]: A man of privilege who will take whatever he wants by whatever means he wants.

Big Show[14]: His own man. Old guard who wants to go legit but will maintain power by whatever means necessary.

Hornswoggle[6]: Who knows what he's plotting. Partnered with the beloved gentle giant **Great Khali**[7] but don't trust the mischievous Hornswoggle.

Rey Mysterio[15]: a heroic vigilante who wears a mask while bringing justice to Titan City.

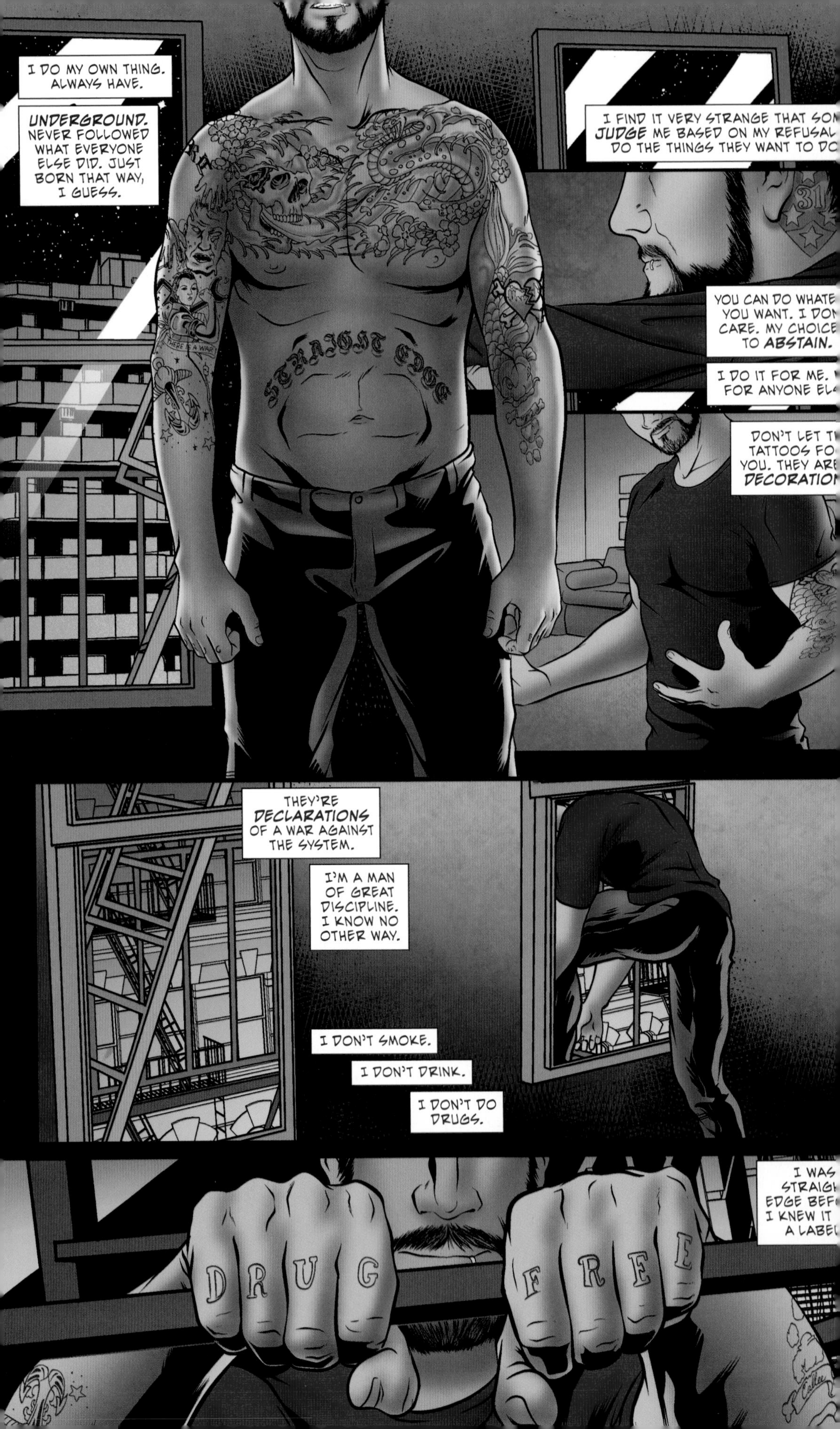

I DO MY OWN THING. ALWAYS HAVE.
UNDERGROUND. NEVER FOLLOWED WHAT EVERYONE ELSE DID. JUST BORN THAT WAY, I GUESS.
STRAIGHT EDGE
I FIND IT VERY STRANGE THAT SOM *JUDGE* ME BASED ON MY REFUSAL DO THE THINGS THEY WANT TO DO
YOU CAN DO WHATE YOU WANT. I DON CARE. MY CHOICE TO **ABSTAIN.**
I DO IT FOR ME. FOR ANYONE EL
DON'T LET T TATTOOS FO YOU. THEY ARE *DECORATION*
THEY'RE *DECLARATIONS* OF A WAR AGAINST THE SYSTEM.
I'M A MAN OF GREAT DISCIPLINE. I KNOW NO OTHER WAY.
I DON'T SMOKE.
I DON'T DRINK.
I DON'T DO DRUGS.
DRUG FREE
I WAS STRAIG EDGE BEF I KNEW IT A LABE

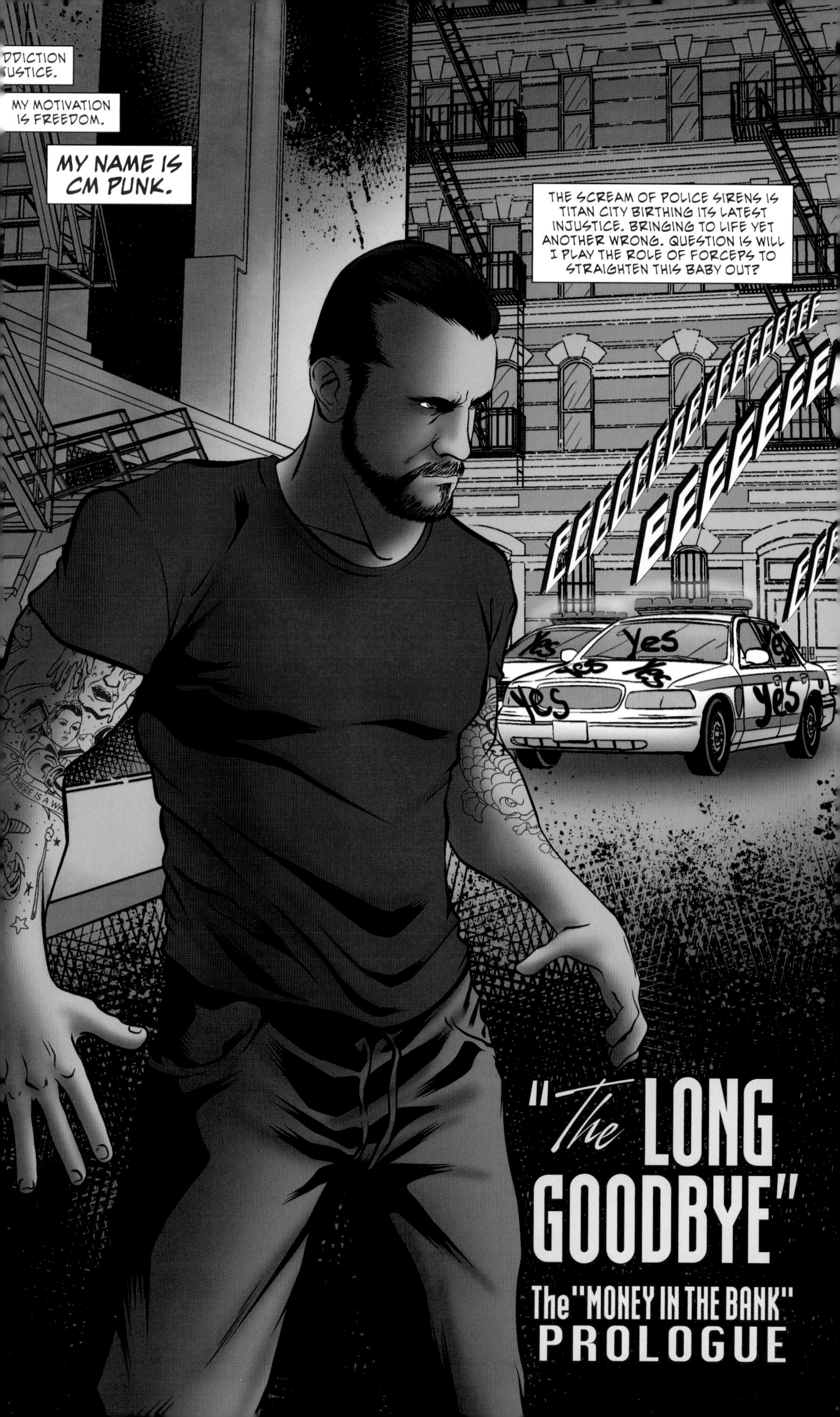

DDICTION
USTICE.
MY MOTIVATION IS FREEDOM.
MY NAME IS CM PUNK.
THE SCREAM OF POLICE SIRENS IS TITAN CITY BIRTHING ITS LATEST INJUSTICE. BRINGING TO LIFE YET ANOTHER WRONG. QUESTION IS WILL I PLAY THE ROLE OF FORCEPS TO STRAIGHTEN THIS BABY OUT?
"The LONG GOODBYE"
The "MONEY IN THE BANK" PROLOGUE

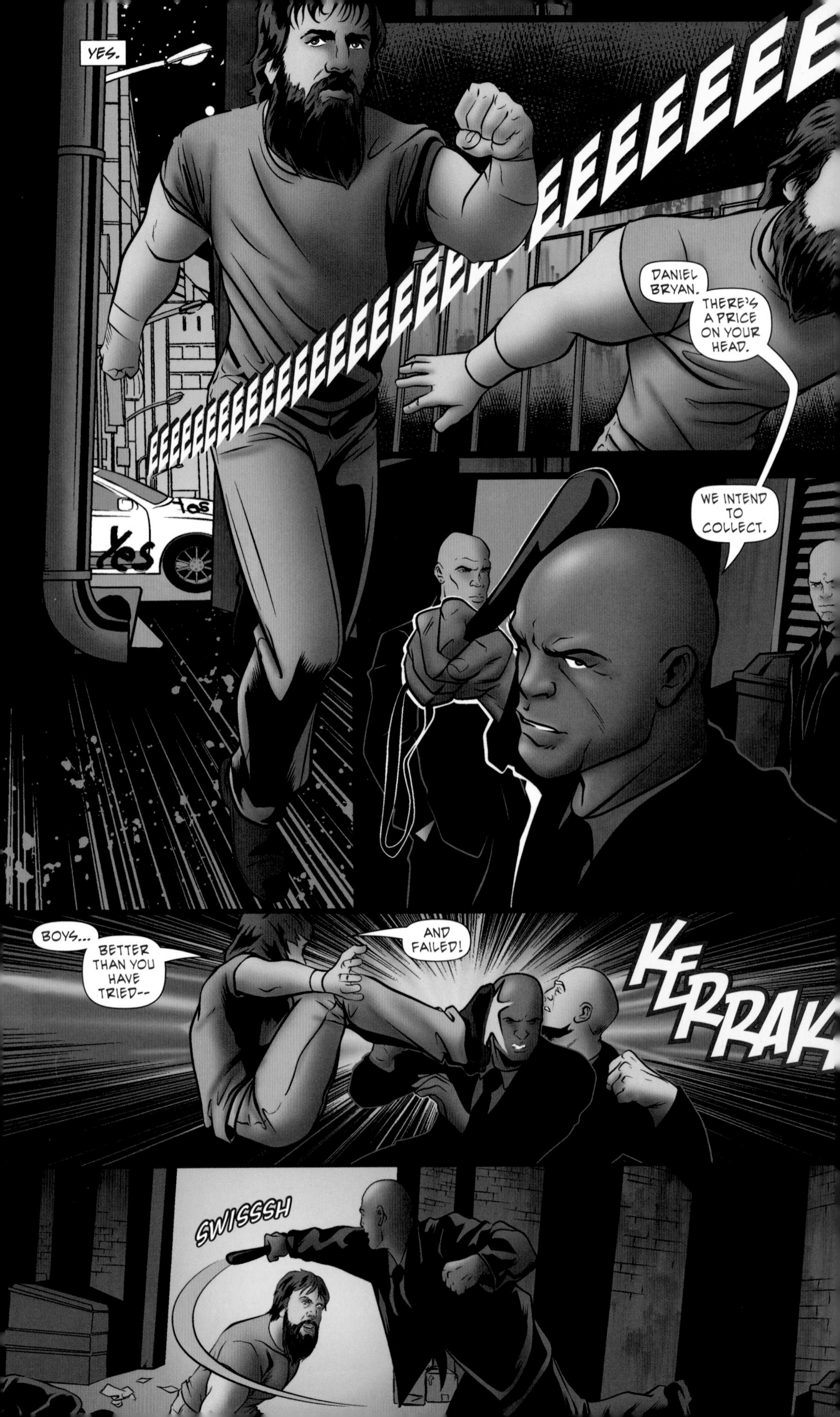
YES.
EEEEEEEEEEEEEEEEEEEEEEEEEEEEEE
DANIEL BRYAN.
THERE'S A PRICE ON YOUR HEAD.
WE INTEND TO COLLECT.
YES
BOYS... BETTER THAN YOU HAVE TRIED--
AND FAILED!
KERRAK
SWISSSH

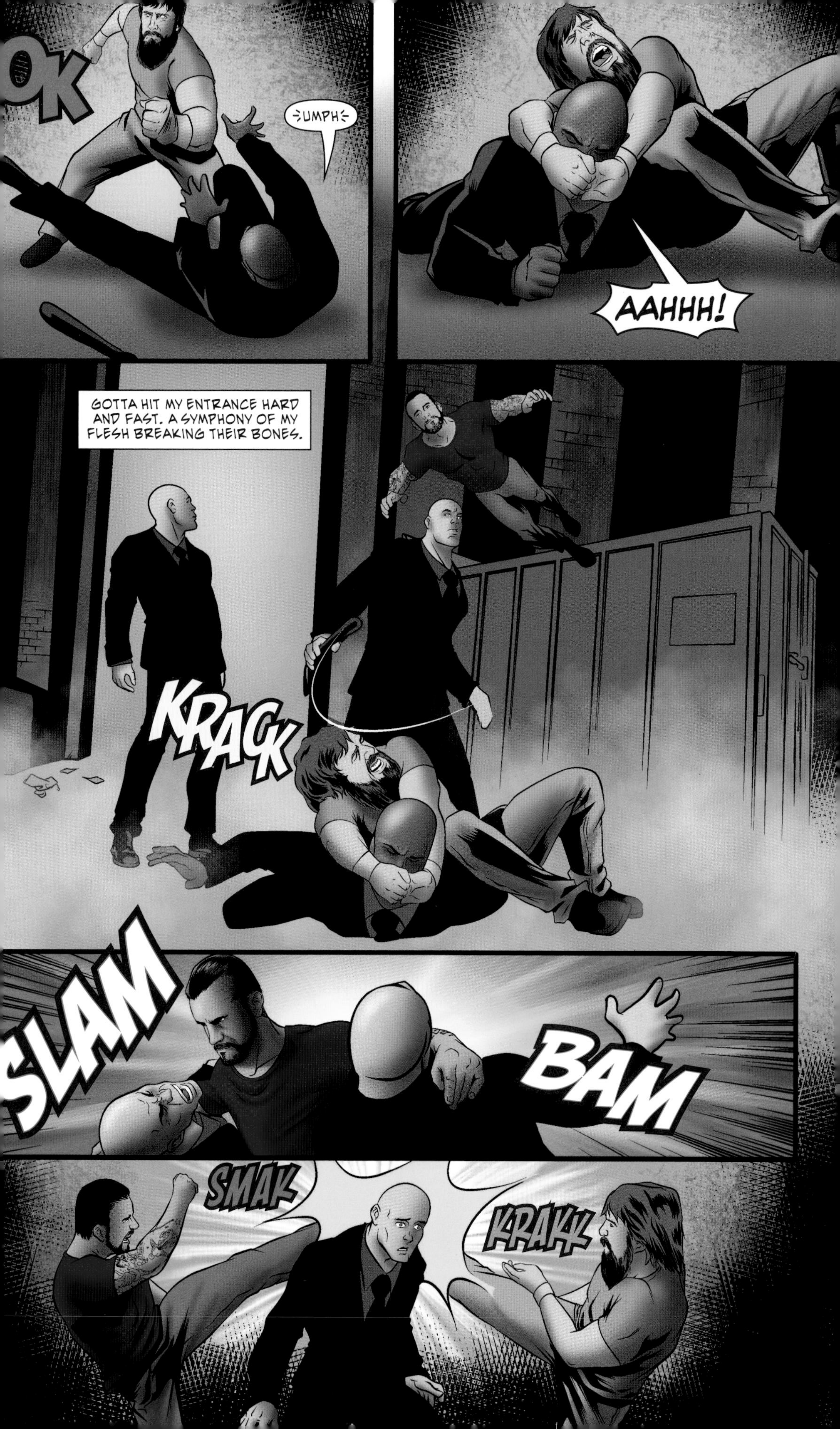
OK
UMPH
AAHHH!
GOTTA HIT MY ENTRANCE HARD AND FAST. A SYMPHONY OF MY FLESH BREAKING THEIR BONES.
KRACK
SLAM
BAM
SMAK
KRAKK

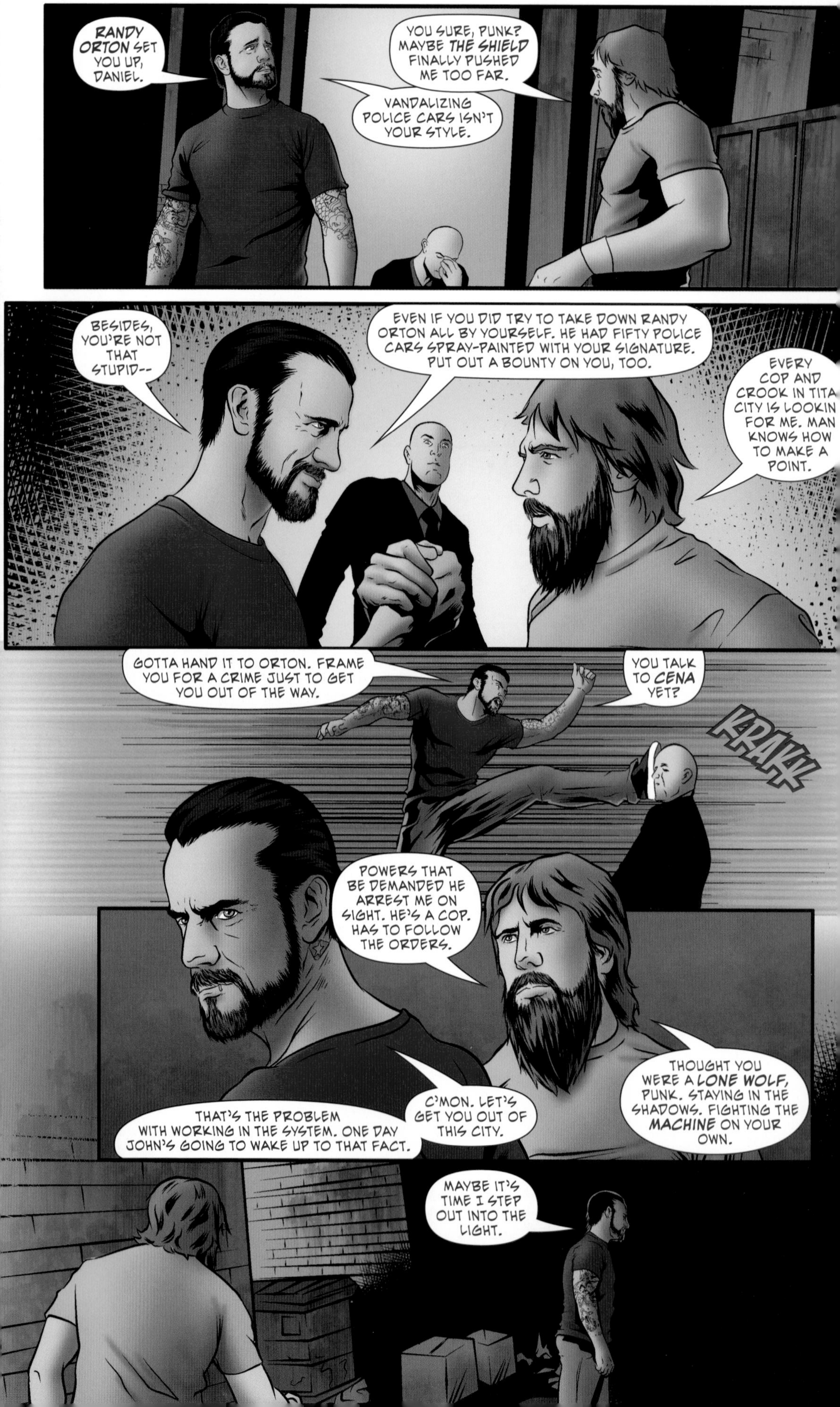
RANDY ORTON SET YOU UP, DANIEL.
YOU SURE, PUNK? MAYBE THE SHIELD FINALLY PUSHED ME TOO FAR.
VANDALIZING POLICE CARS ISN'T YOUR STYLE.
BESIDES, YOU'RE NOT THAT STUPID--
EVEN IF YOU DID TRY TO TAKE DOWN RANDY ORTON ALL BY YOURSELF. HE HAD FIFTY POLICE CARS SPRAY-PAINTED WITH YOUR SIGNATURE. PUT OUT A BOUNTY ON YOU, TOO.
EVERY COP AND CROOK IN TITA CITY IS LOOKIN FOR ME. MAN KNOWS HOW TO MAKE A POINT.
GOTTA HAND IT TO ORTON. FRAME YOU FOR A CRIME JUST TO GET YOU OUT OF THE WAY.
YOU TALK TO CENA YET?
KRAKK!
POWERS THAT BE DEMANDED HE ARREST ME ON SIGHT. HE'S A COP. HAS TO FOLLOW THE ORDERS.
THAT'S THE PROBLEM WITH WORKING IN THE SYSTEM. ONE DAY JOHN'S GOING TO WAKE UP TO THAT FACT.
C'MON. LET'S GET YOU OUT OF THIS CITY.
THOUGHT YOU WERE A LONE WOLF, PUNK. STAYING IN THE SHADOWS. FIGHTING THE MACHINE ON YOUR OWN.
MAYBE IT'S TIME I STEP OUT INTO THE LIGHT.

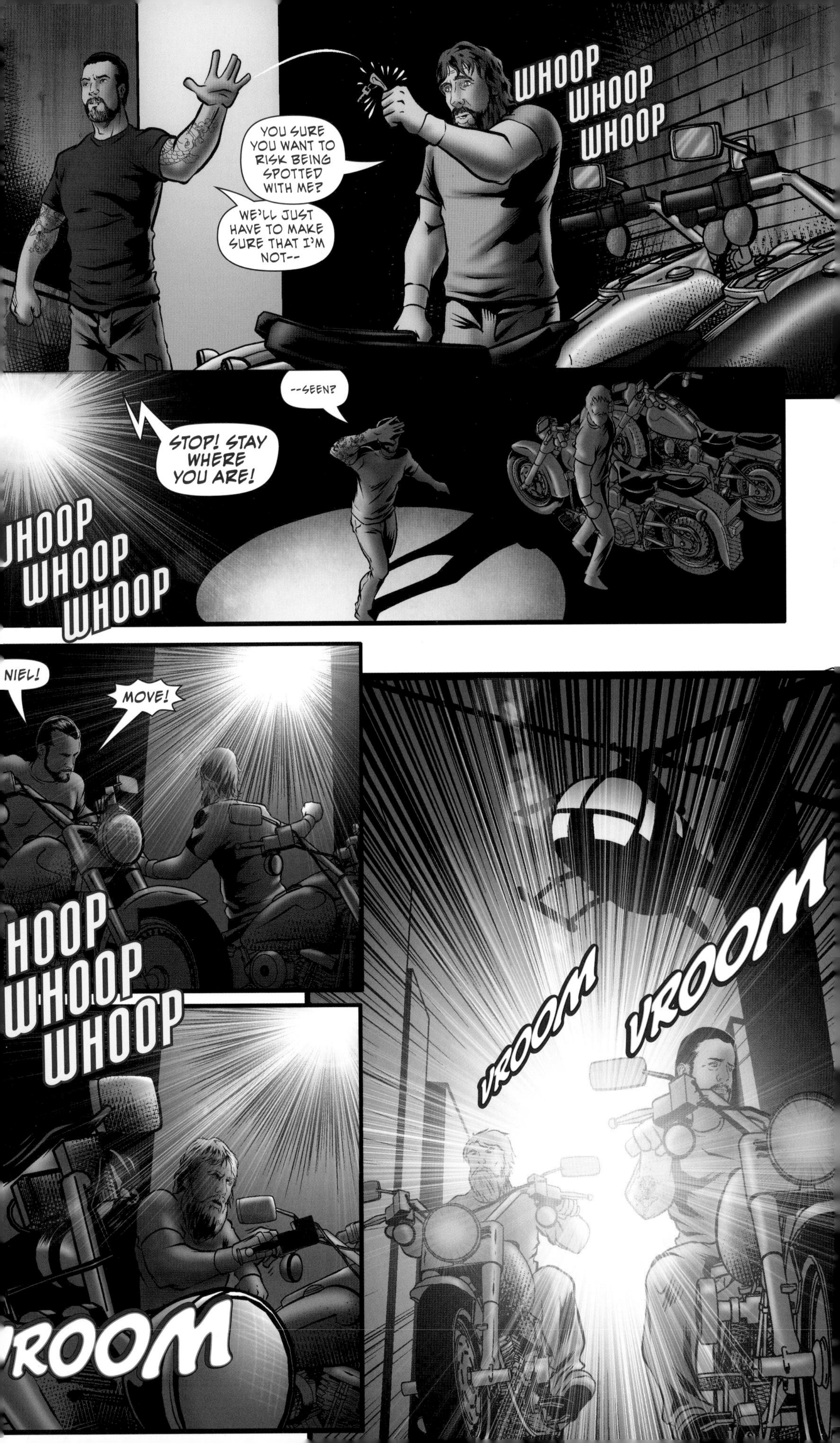
YOU SURE YOU WANT TO RISK BEING SPOTTED WITH ME?
WE'LL JUST HAVE TO MAKE SURE THAT I'M NOT--
WHOOP WHOOP WHOOP
--SEEN?
STOP! STAY WHERE YOU ARE!
WHOOP WHOOP WHOOP
NIEL!
MOVE!
HOOP WHOOP WHOOP
ROOM
VROOM
VROOM

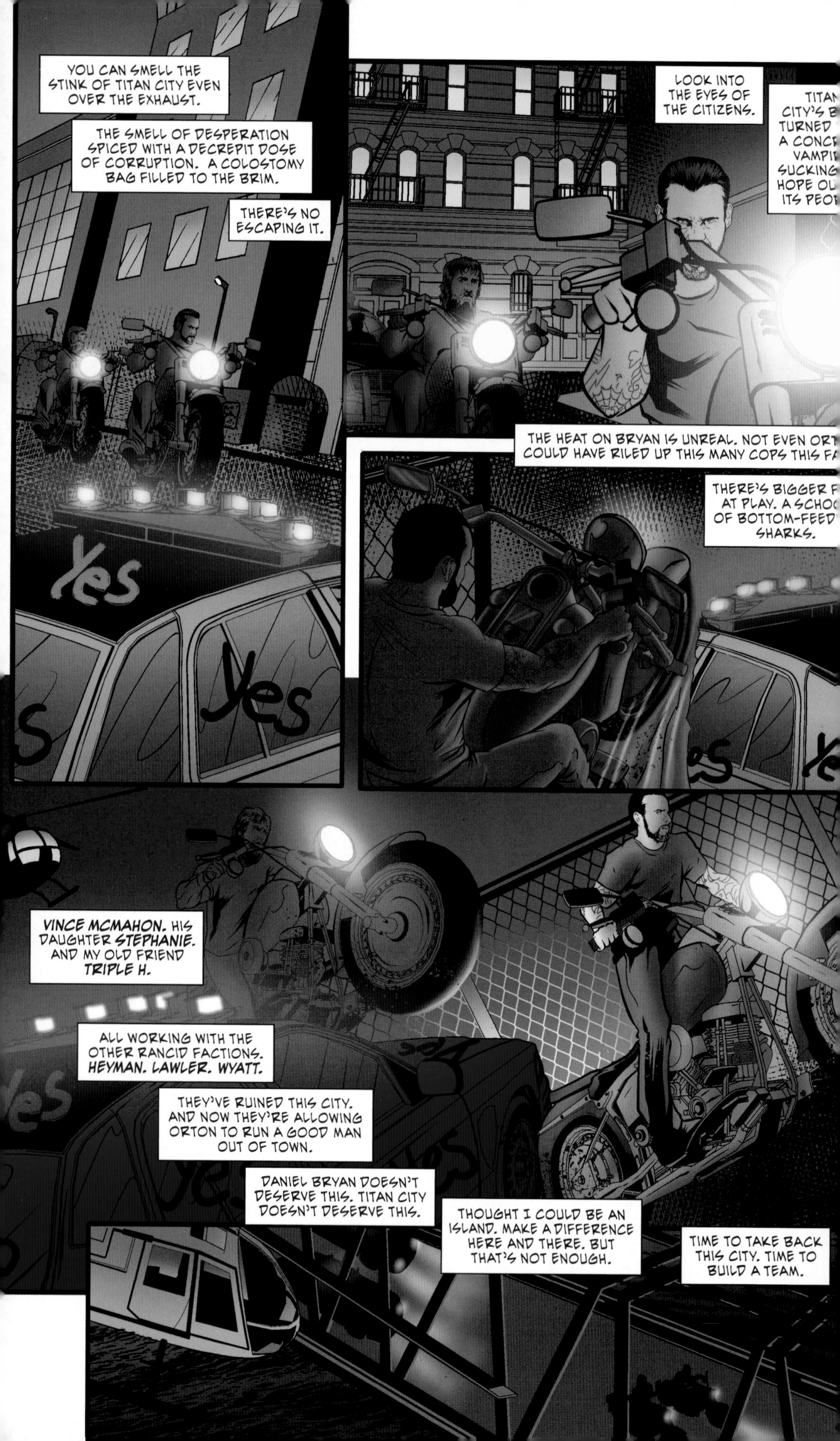
YOU CAN SMELL THE STINK OF TITAN CITY EVEN OVER THE EXHAUST.
THE SMELL OF DESPERATION SPICED WITH A DECREPIT DOSE OF CORRUPTION. A COLOSTOMY BAG FILLED TO THE BRIM.
THERE'S NO ESCAPING IT.
Yes
LOOK INTO THE EYES OF THE CITIZENS.
TITAN CITY'S B TURNED A CONCR VAMPI SUCKING HOPE OU ITS PEOP
THE HEAT ON BRYAN IS UNREAL. NOT EVEN ORT COULD HAVE RILED UP THIS MANY COPS THIS FA
THERE'S BIGGER F AT PLAY. A SCHOO OF BOTTOM-FEED SHARKS.
VINCE MCMAHON. HIS DAUGHTER STEPHANIE. AND MY OLD FRIEND TRIPLE H.
ALL WORKING WITH THE OTHER RANCID FACTIONS. HEYMAN. LAWLER. WYATT.
THEY'VE RUINED THIS CITY. AND NOW THEY'RE ALLOWING ORTON TO RUN A GOOD MAN OUT OF TOWN.
DANIEL BRYAN DOESN'T DESERVE THIS. TITAN CITY DOESN'T DESERVE THIS.
THOUGHT I COULD BE AN ISLAND. MAKE A DIFFERENCE HERE AND THERE. BUT THAT'S NOT ENOUGH.
TIME TO TAKE BACK THIS CITY. TIME TO BUILD A TEAM.

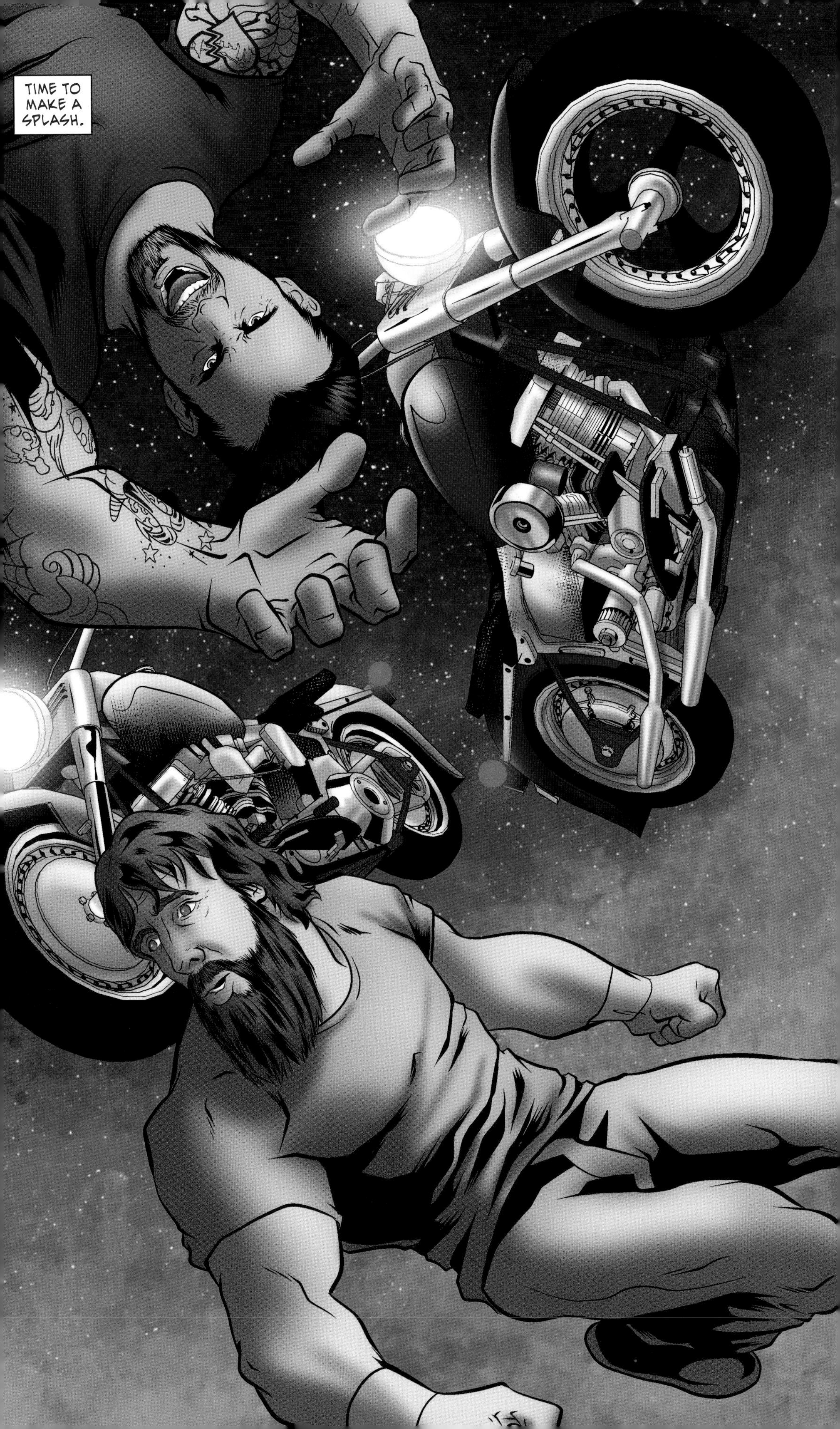
TIME TO MAKE A SPLASH.

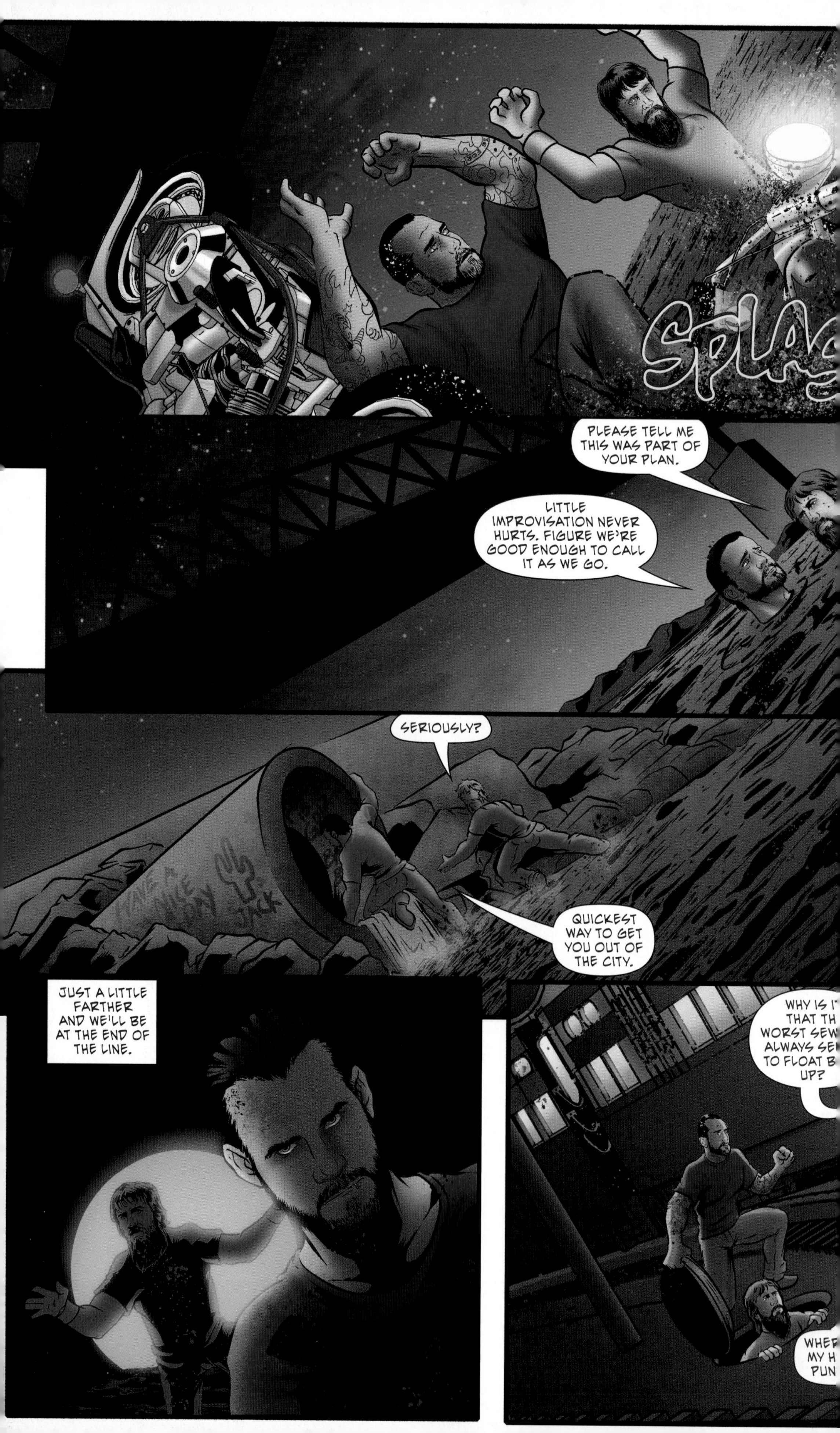

SPLAS
PLEASE TELL ME THIS WAS PART OF YOUR PLAN.
LITTLE IMPROVISATION NEVER HURTS. FIGURE WE'RE GOOD ENOUGH TO CALL IT AS WE GO.
SERIOUSLY?
HAVE A NICE DAY
JACK
QUICKEST WAY TO GET YOU OUT OF THE CITY.
JUST A LITTLE FARTHER AND WE'LL BE AT THE END OF THE LINE.
WHY IS IT THAT TH WORST SEW ALWAYS SE TO FLOAT B UP?
WHER MY H PUN

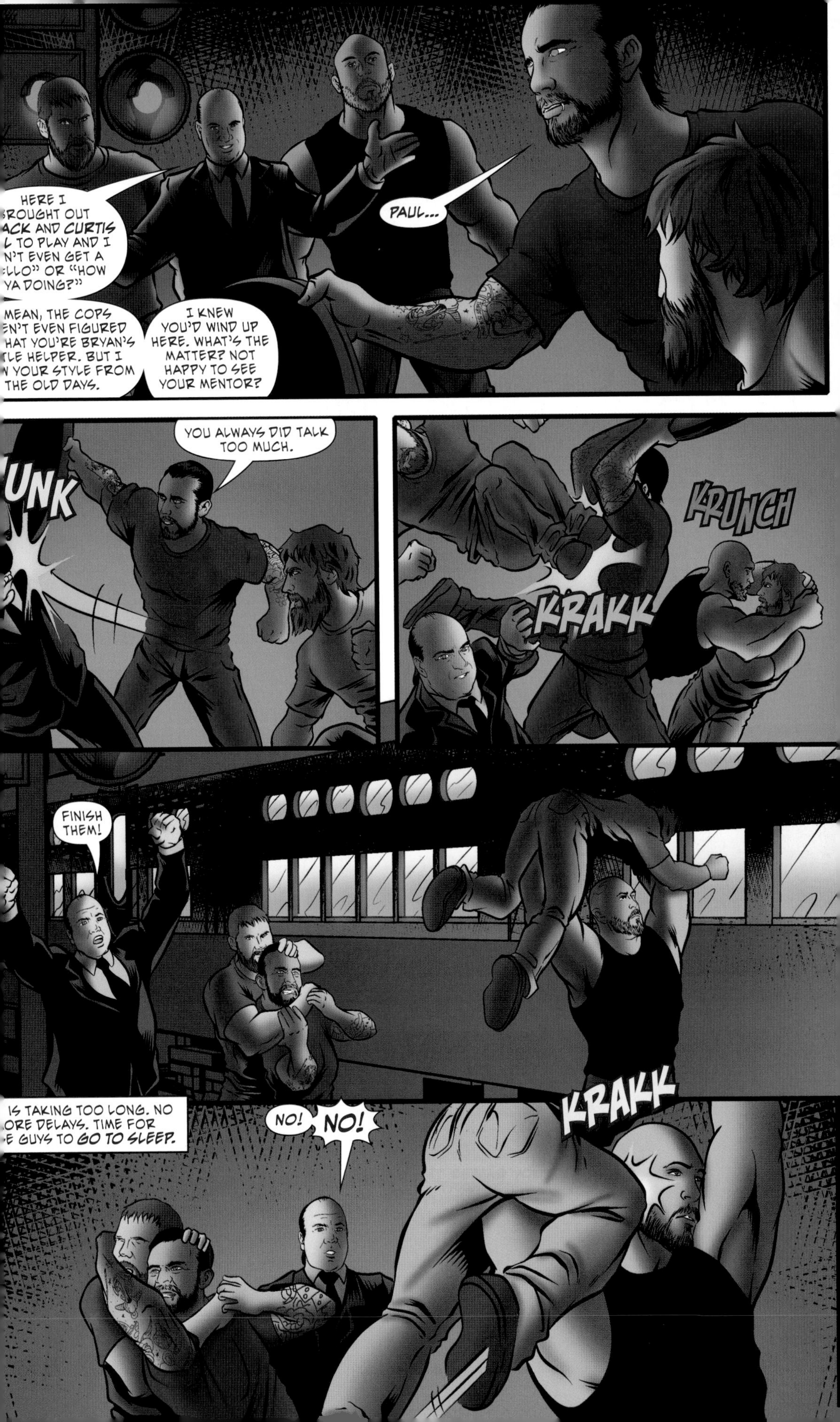

HERE I
BROUGHT OUT
ACK AND CURTIS
L TO PLAY AND I
N'T EVEN GET A
LLO" OR "HOW
YA DOING?"
PAUL...
MEAN, THE COPS
EN'T EVEN FIGURED
HAT YOU'RE BRYAN'S
TLE HELPER. BUT I
W YOUR STYLE FROM
THE OLD DAYS.
I KNEW YOU'D WIND UP HERE. WHAT'S THE MATTER? NOT HAPPY TO SEE YOUR MENTOR?
YOU ALWAYS DID TALK TOO MUCH.
UNK
KRUNCH
KRAKK
FINISH THEM!
KRAKK
IS TAKING TOO LONG. NO
ORE DELAYS. TIME FOR
E GUYS TO GO TO SLEEP.
NO!
NO!

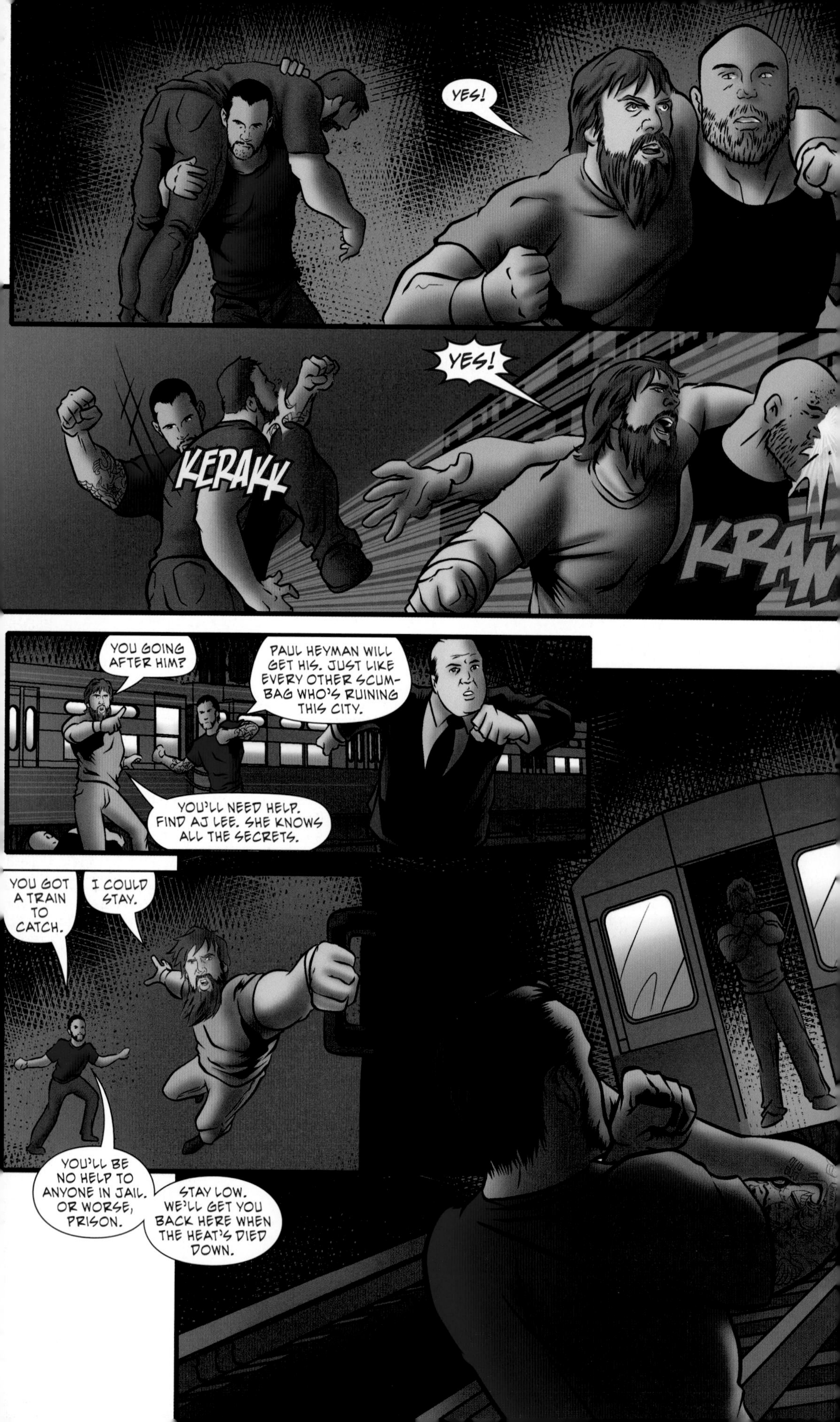
YES!
YES!
KERAKK
KRA
YOU GOING AFTER HIM?
PAUL HEYMAN WILL GET HIS. JUST LIKE EVERY OTHER SCUM-BAG WHO'S RUINING THIS CITY.
YOU'LL NEED HELP. FIND AJ LEE. SHE KNOWS ALL THE SECRETS.
YOU GOT A TRAIN TO CATCH.
I COULD STAY.
YOU'LL BE NO HELP TO ANYONE IN JAIL. OR WORSE, PRISON.
STAY LOW. WE'LL GET YOU BACK HERE WHEN THE HEAT'S DIED DOWN.

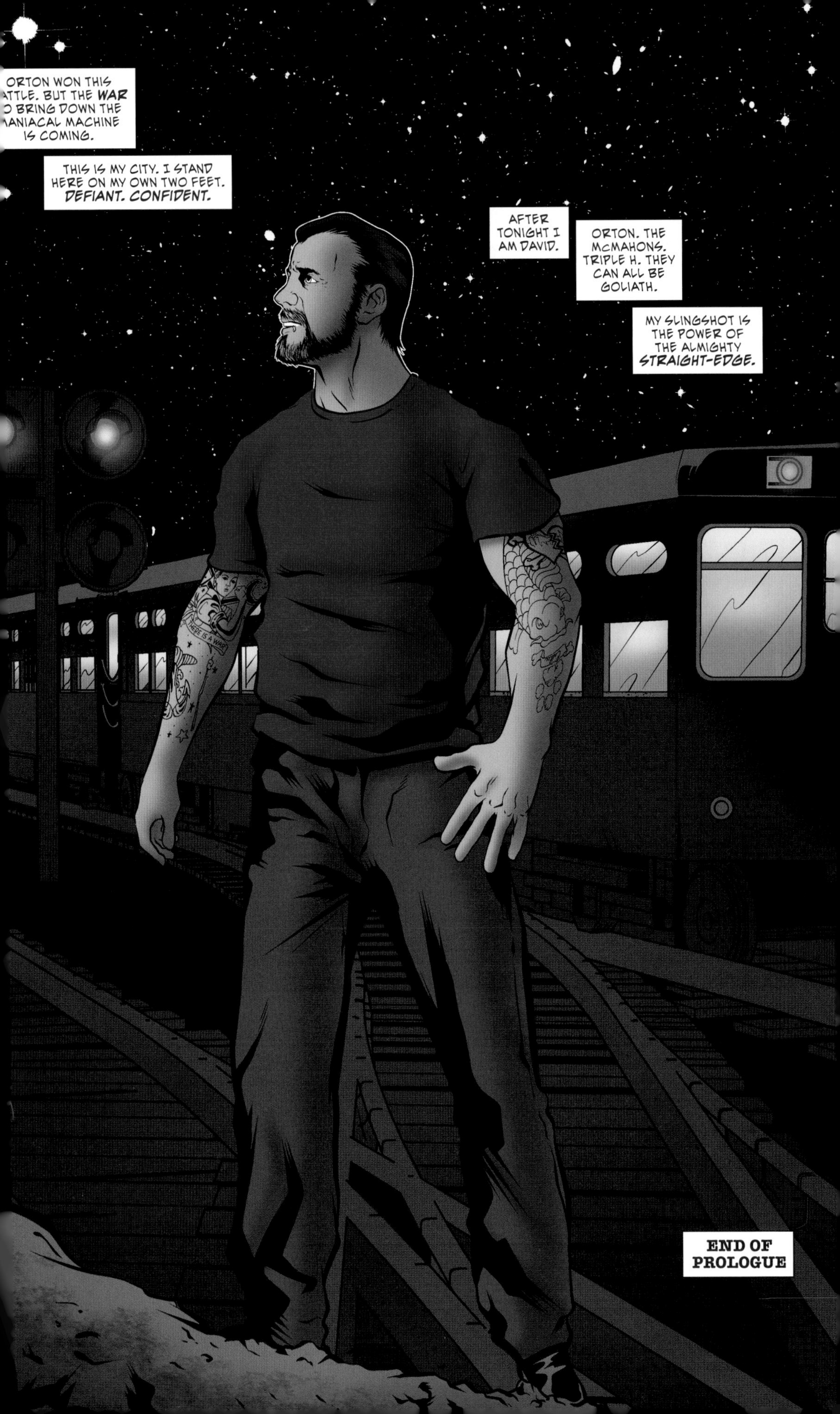
ORTON WON THIS ATTLE. BUT THE WAR O BRING DOWN THE ANIACAL MACHINE IS COMING.
THIS IS MY CITY. I STAND HERE ON MY OWN TWO FEET. DEFIANT. CONFIDENT.
AFTER TONIGHT I AM DAVID.
ORTON. THE McMAHONS. TRIPLE H. THEY CAN ALL BE GOLIATH.
MY SLINGSHOT IS THE POWER OF THE ALMIGHTY STRAIGHT-EDGE.
END OF PROLOGUE

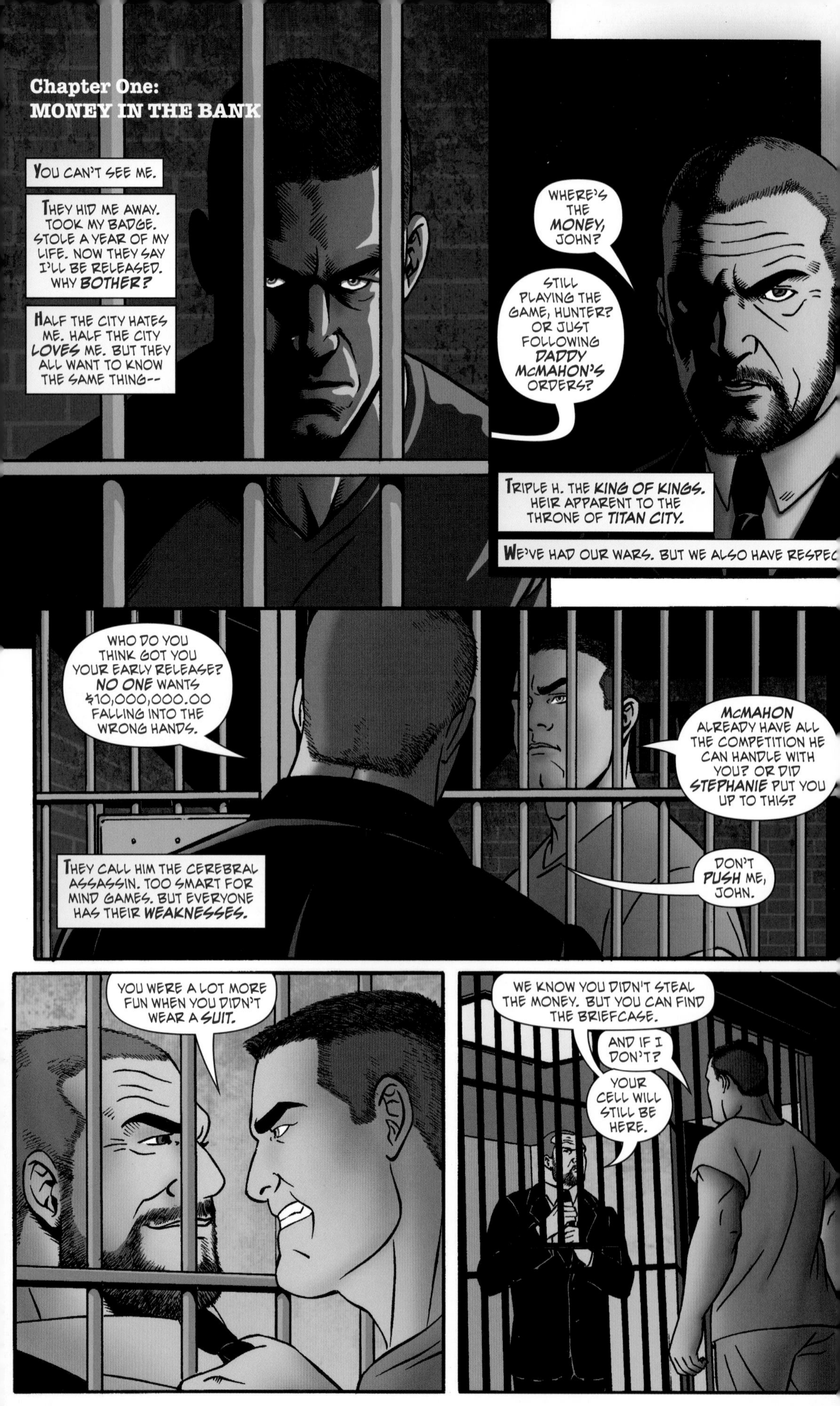
Chapter One:
MONEY IN THE BANK
YOU CAN'T SEE ME.
THEY HID ME AWAY. TOOK MY BADGE. STOLE A YEAR OF MY LIFE. NOW THEY SAY I'LL BE RELEASED. WHY BOTHER?
HALF THE CITY HATES ME. HALF THE CITY LOVES ME. BUT THEY ALL WANT TO KNOW THE SAME THING--
WHERE'S THE MONEY, JOHN?
STILL PLAYING THE GAME, HUNTER? OR JUST FOLLOWING DADDY McMAHON'S ORDERS?
TRIPLE H. THE KING OF KINGS. HEIR APPARENT TO THE THRONE OF TITAN CITY.
WE'VE HAD OUR WARS. BUT WE ALSO HAVE RESPEC
WHO DO YOU THINK GOT YOU YOUR EARLY RELEASE? NO ONE WANTS $10,000,000.00 FALLING INTO THE WRONG HANDS.
McMAHON ALREADY HAVE ALL THE COMPETITION HE CAN HANDLE WITH YOU? OR DID STEPHANIE PUT YOU UP TO THIS?
THEY CALL HIM THE CEREBRAL ASSASSIN. TOO SMART FOR MIND GAMES. BUT EVERYONE HAS THEIR WEAKNESSES.
DON'T PUSH ME, JOHN.
YOU WERE A LOT MORE FUN WHEN YOU DIDN'T WEAR A SUIT.
WE KNOW YOU DIDN'T STEAL THE MONEY. BUT YOU CAN FIND THE BRIEFCASE.
AND IF I DON'T?
YOUR CELL WILL STILL BE HERE.

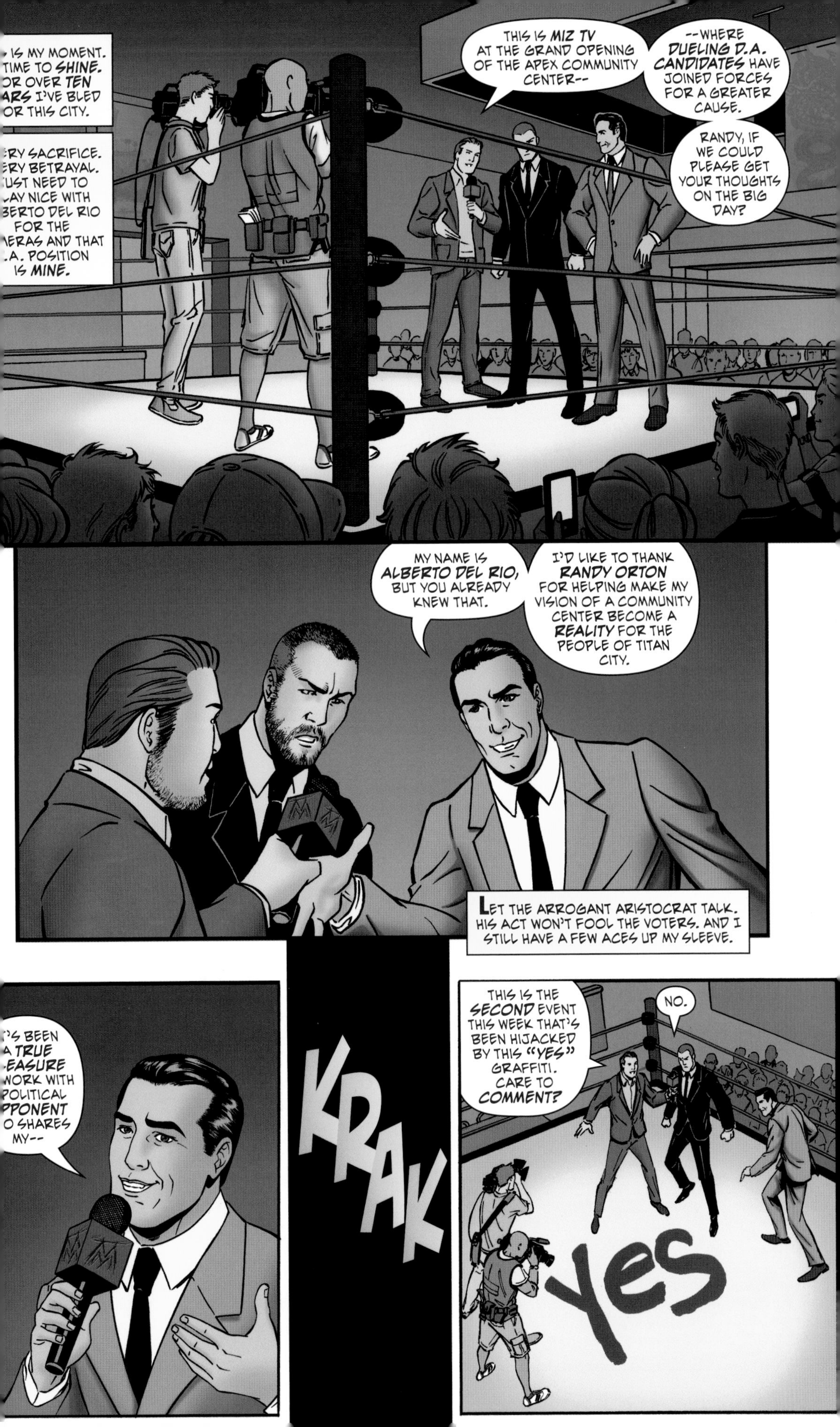

IS MY MOMENT. TIME TO SHINE. OR OVER TEN ARS I'VE BLED FOR THIS CITY.
ERY SACRIFICE. ERY BETRAYAL. JUST NEED TO LAY NICE WITH BERTO DEL RIO FOR THE MERAS AND THAT .A. POSITION IS MINE.
THIS IS MIZ TV AT THE GRAND OPENING OF THE APEX COMMUNITY CENTER--
--WHERE DUELING D.A. CANDIDATES HAVE JOINED FORCES FOR A GREATER CAUSE.
RANDY, IF WE COULD PLEASE GET YOUR THOUGHTS ON THE BIG DAY?
MY NAME IS ALBERTO DEL RIO, BUT YOU ALREADY KNEW THAT.
I'D LIKE TO THANK RANDY ORTON FOR HELPING MAKE MY VISION OF A COMMUNITY CENTER BECOME A REALITY FOR THE PEOPLE OF TITAN CITY.
LET THE ARROGANT ARISTOCRAT TALK. HIS ACT WON'T FOOL THE VOTERS. AND I STILL HAVE A FEW ACES UP MY SLEEVE.
'S BEEN A TRUE EASURE WORK WITH POLITICAL PPONENT O SHARES MY--
KRAK
THIS IS THE SECOND EVENT THIS WEEK THAT'S BEEN HIJACKED BY THIS "YES" GRAFFITI. CARE TO COMMENT?
NO.
YES

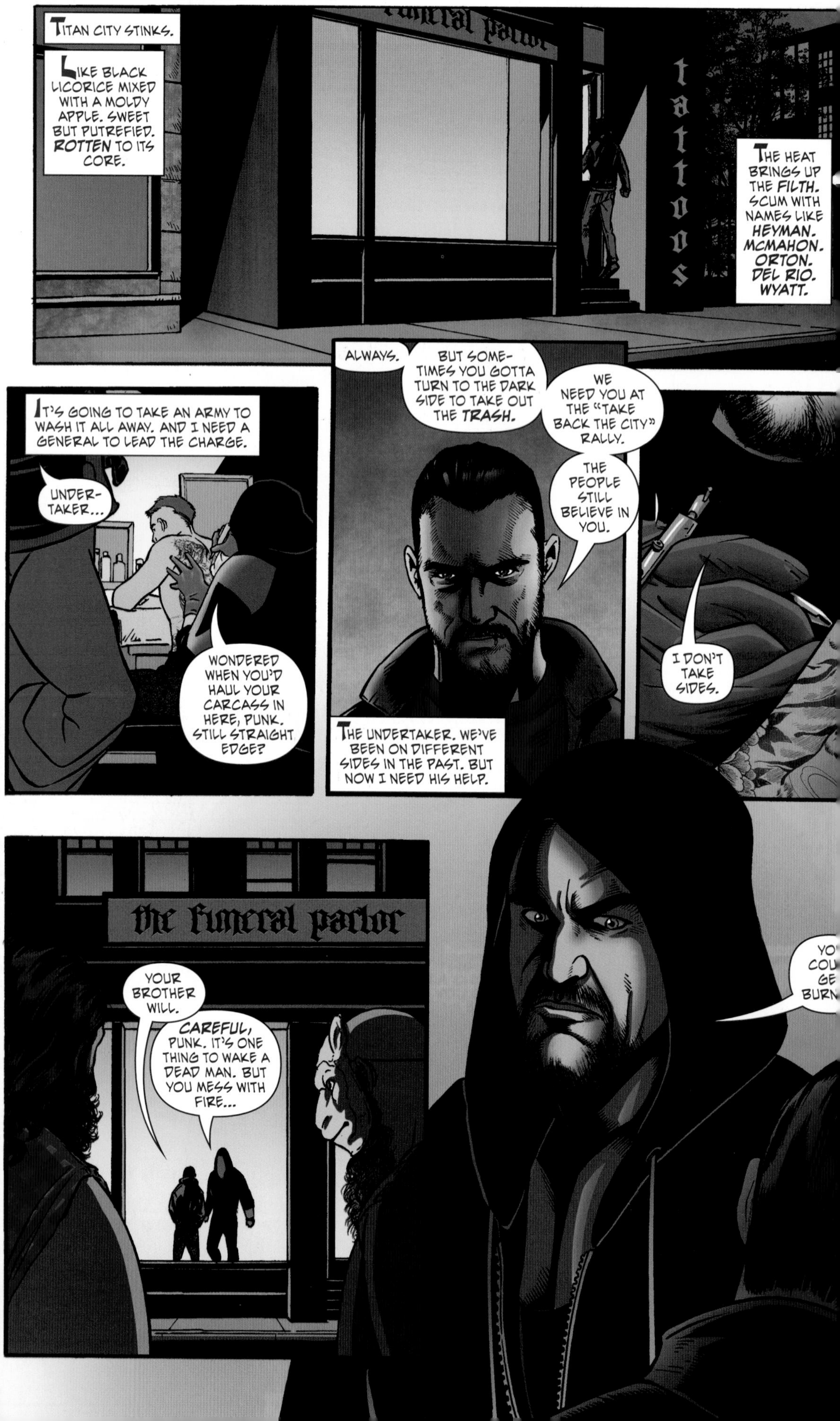
funeral parlor
tattoos
TITAN CITY STINKS.
LIKE BLACK LICORICE MIXED WITH A MOLDY APPLE. SWEET BUT PUTREFIED. ROTTEN TO ITS CORE.
THE HEAT BRINGS UP THE FILTH. SCUM WITH NAMES LIKE HEYMAN. MCMAHON. ORTON. DEL RIO. WYATT.
IT'S GOING TO TAKE AN ARMY TO WASH IT ALL AWAY. AND I NEED A GENERAL TO LEAD THE CHARGE.
UNDER-TAKER...
WONDERED WHEN YOU'D HAUL YOUR CARCASS IN HERE, PUNK. STILL STRAIGHT EDGE?
ALWAYS.
BUT SOME-TIMES YOU GOTTA TURN TO THE DARK SIDE TO TAKE OUT THE TRASH.
WE NEED YOU AT THE "TAKE BACK THE CITY" RALLY.
THE PEOPLE STILL BELIEVE IN YOU.
THE UNDERTAKER. WE'VE BEEN ON DIFFERENT SIDES IN THE PAST. BUT NOW I NEED HIS HELP.
I DON'T TAKE SIDES.
the funeral parlor
YOUR BROTHER WILL.
CAREFUL, PUNK. IT'S ONE THING TO WAKE A DEAD MAN. BUT YOU MESS WITH FIRE...

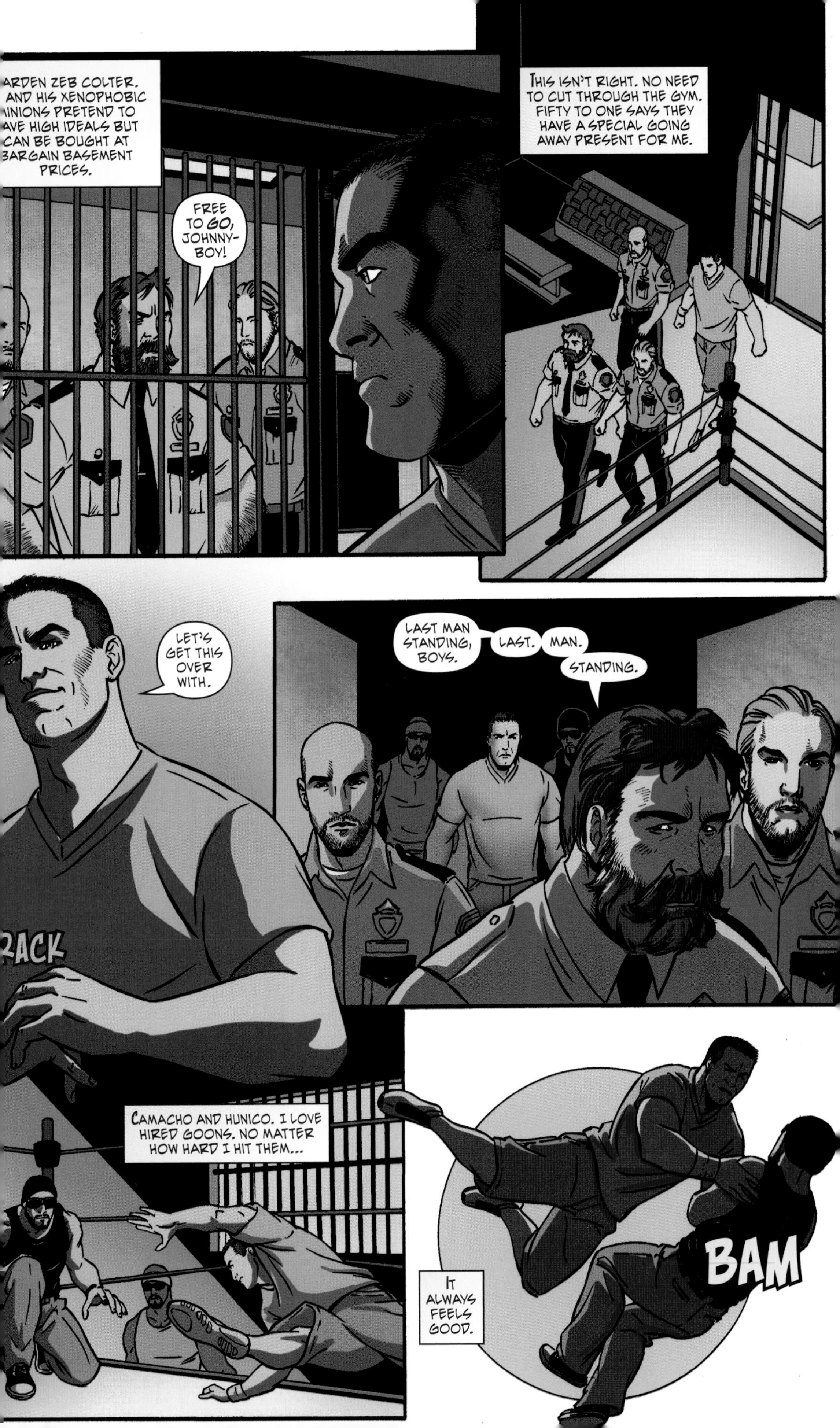
ARDEN ZEB COLTER. AND HIS XENOPHOBIC IINIONS PRETEND TO AVE HIGH IDEALS BUT CAN BE BOUGHT AT BARGAIN BASEMENT PRICES.
FREE TO GO, JOHNNY-BOY!
THIS ISN'T RIGHT. NO NEED TO CUT THROUGH THE GYM. FIFTY TO ONE SAYS THEY HAVE A SPECIAL GOING AWAY PRESENT FOR ME.
LET'S GET THIS OVER WITH.
LAST MAN STANDING, BOYS.
LAST.
MAN.
STANDING.
RACK
CAMACHO AND HUNICO. I LOVE HIRED GOONS. NO MATTER HOW HARD I HIT THEM...
IT ALWAYS FEELS GOOD.
BAM

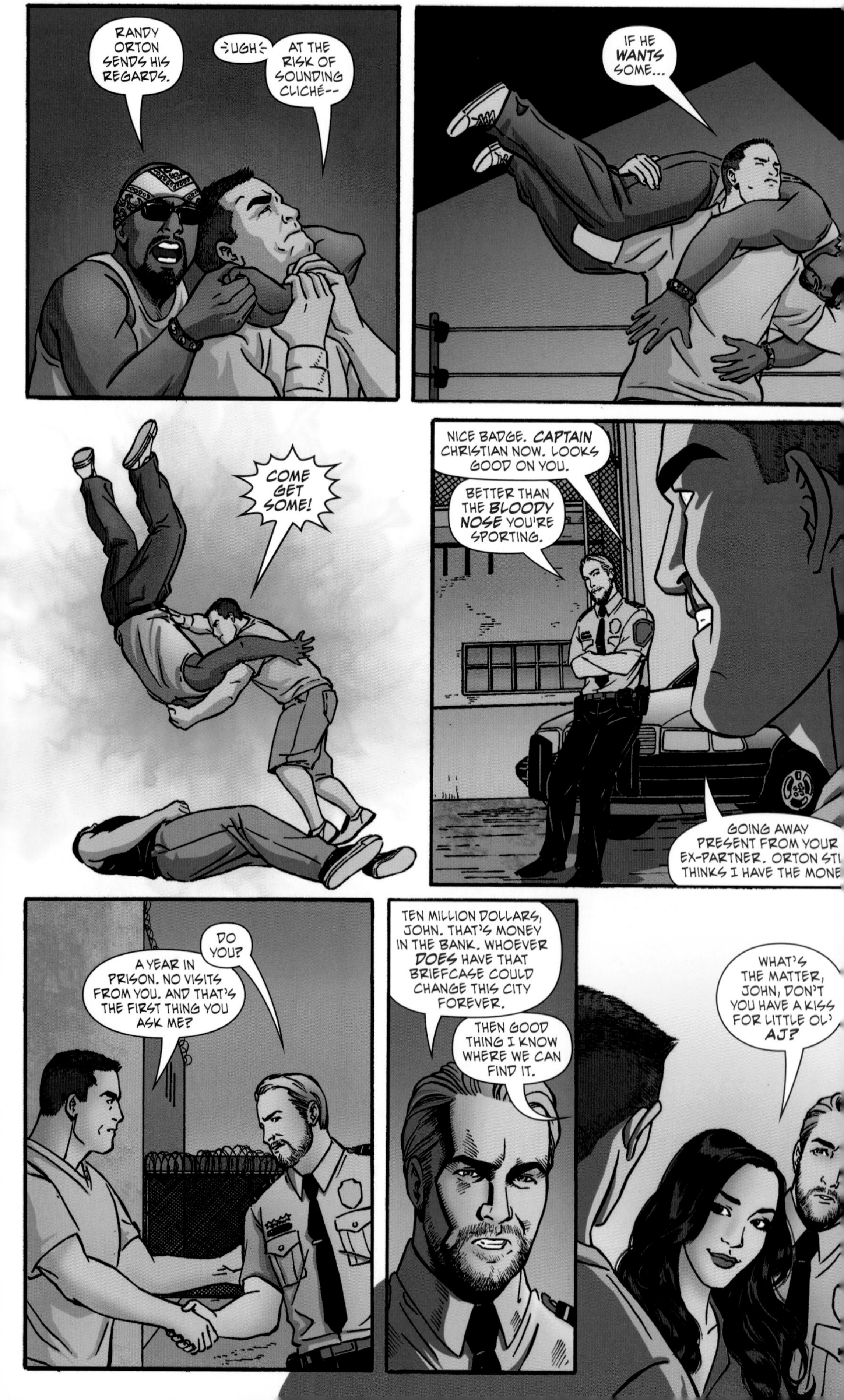

RANDY ORTON SENDS HIS REGARDS.
UGH
AT THE RISK OF SOUNDING CLICHÉ--
IF HE WANTS SOME...
COME GET SOME!
NICE BADGE. CAPTAIN CHRISTIAN NOW. LOOKS GOOD ON YOU.
BETTER THAN THE BLOODY NOSE YOU'RE SPORTING.
GOING AWAY PRESENT FROM YOUR EX-PARTNER. ORTON STI
THINKS I HAVE THE MONE
DO YOU?
A YEAR IN PRISON. NO VISITS FROM YOU. AND THAT'S THE FIRST THING YOU ASK ME?
TEN MILLION DOLLARS, JOHN. THAT'S MONEY IN THE BANK. WHOEVER DOES HAVE THAT BRIEFCASE COULD CHANGE THIS CITY FOREVER.
THEN GOOD THING I KNOW WHERE WE CAN FIND IT.
WHAT'S THE MATTER, JOHN, DON'T YOU HAVE A KISS FOR LITTLE OL' AJ?

YOU LET SOMEONE TRADE MY PLACE OF BUSINESS. EMBARRASS ME IN FRONT OF MY PUBLIC.

TELL ME, RYBACK, WHY SHOULDN'T I PUNT KICK YOUR SORRY SELF TO THE CURB?

I WAS TOLD MY SERVICES WERE NEEDED TO WATCH OUT FOR CENA. NOT PLAY BODYGUARD. BESIDES--

YOU'RE NOT MY BOSS.

I PAY HEYMAN! SO YOU DO WHAT YOU'RE TOLD! CENA'S NOT THE ONE SPRAY PAINTING "YES!" ALL OVER MY PROPERTIES.

BUT THAT WEASEL THE MIZ KNOWS SOMETHING. PAY HIM A VISIT. FIND OUT HOW MUCH HE KNOWS.

ANY IDEA WHO'S BEHIND THIS?

THAT'S EXACTLY WHAT I WAS GOING TO ASK.

ZIGGLER-- I DON'T NEED HELP FROM TITAN P.D.

C'MON, RANDY. WHAT SORT OF POLICE DETECTIVE WOULD I BE IF I DIDN'T WATCH OUT FOR THE CITY'S NEXT D.A.

SOMEONE'S VANDALIZING YOUR PROPERTY. I'M JUST HERE TO DO MY JOB.

EVEN FOR TRASH LIKE YOU.

OKAY, GOLDEN BOY. TITAN'S FINEST WANTS TO PLAY THE GOOD COP. FINE. I'VE GOT A NAME FOR YOU...

DANIEL BRYAN.

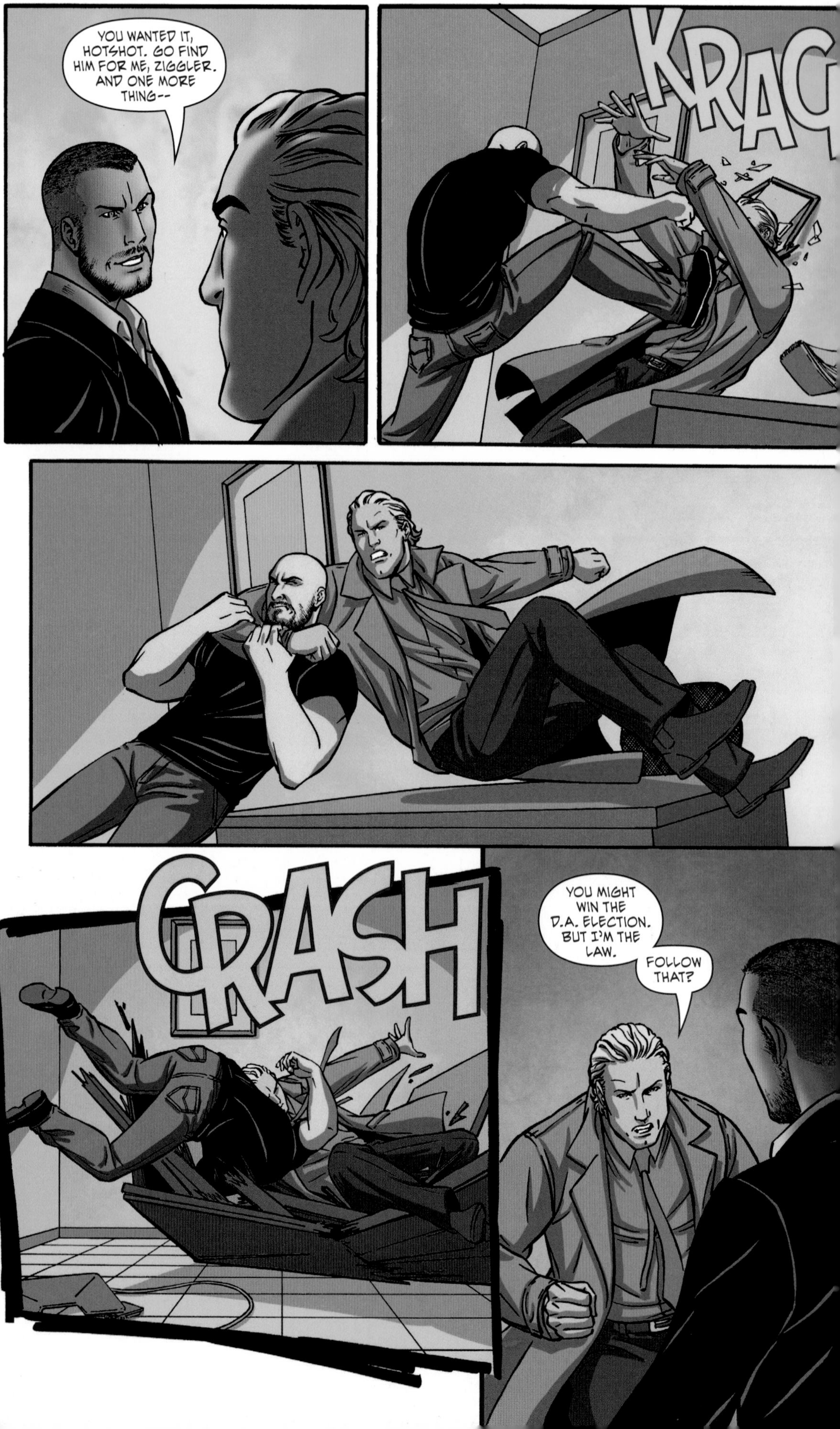
YOU WANTED IT, HOTSHOT. GO FIND HIM FOR ME, ZIGGLER. AND ONE MORE THING--
KRAG
CRASH
YOU MIGHT WIN THE D.A. ELECTION. BUT I'M THE LAW.
FOLLOW THAT?

EVEN UNDERTAKER WAS ON EDGE.

WE'RE ALL SITTING ON A POWDER KEG. THE BLOWBACK FROM CENA'S RELEASE HAS TENSIONS HIGH. TEN MILLION REASONS WHY EVERY IDIOT WITH ASPIRATIONS FOR POWER WILL BE GUNNING FOR HIM.

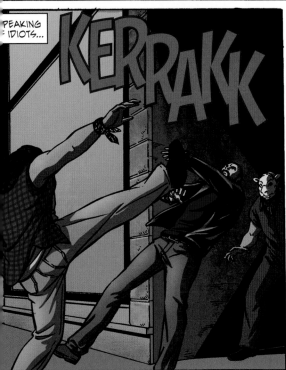

SPEAKING OF IDIOTS...

KERRAKK

THE WYATT FAMILY. LUKE HARPER AND ERICK ROWAN. A CULT OF THE WORST KIND FROM THE BARRENS OUTSIDE THE CITY.

WHEN THE MEN OF POWER WAGE WAR, ONLY THE INNOCENT SUFFER.

DOWN WITH THE MACHINE.

THUD

I RUN FROM NOBODY.

KRAKK

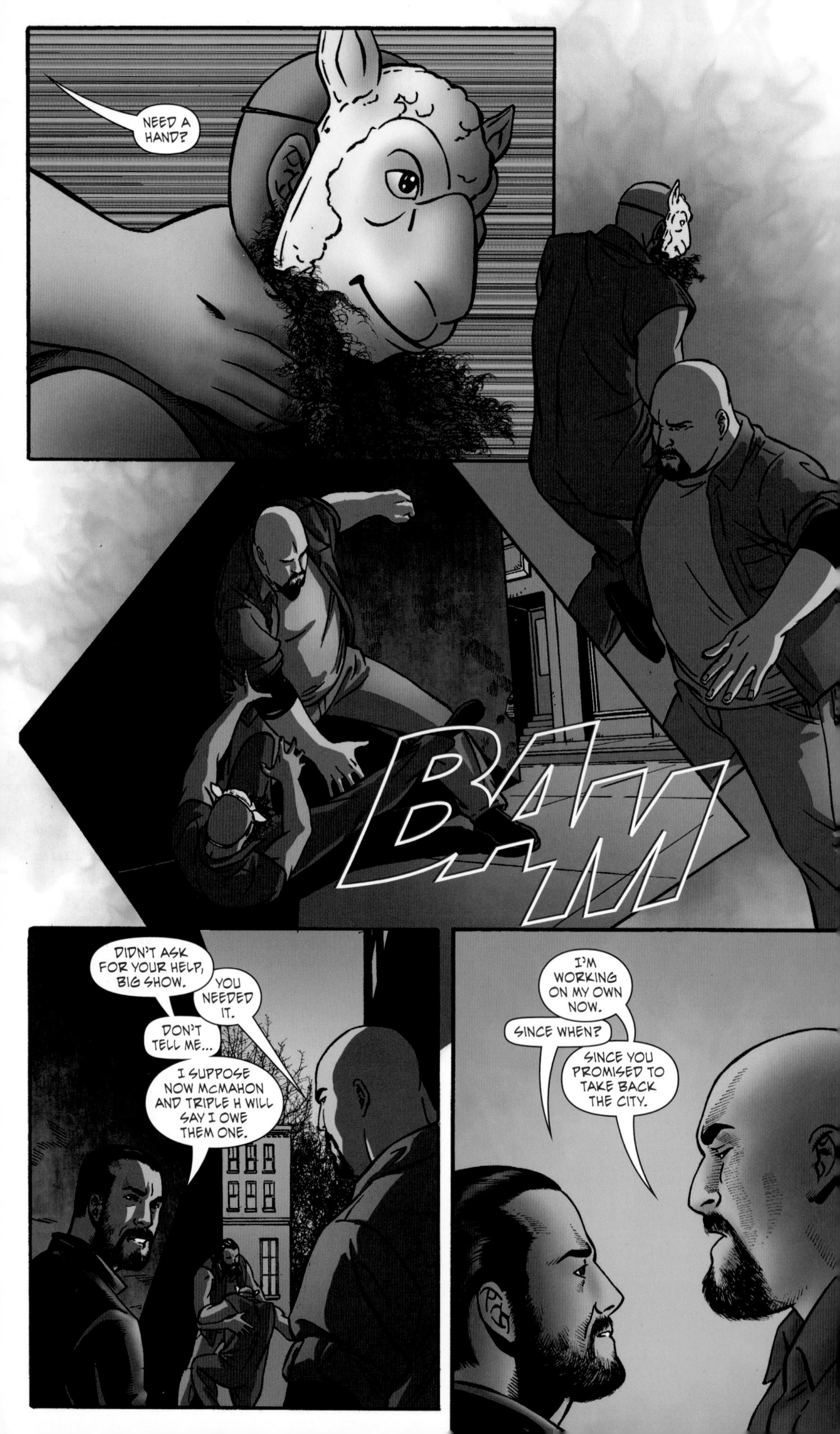
NEED A HAND?
BAM
DIDN'T ASK FOR YOUR HELP, BIG SHOW.
YOU NEEDED IT.
DON'T TELL ME...
I SUPPOSE NOW MCMAHON AND TRIPLE H WILL SAY I OWE THEM ONE.
I'M WORKING ON MY OWN NOW.
SINCE WHEN?
SINCE YOU PROMISED TO TAKE BACK THE CITY.

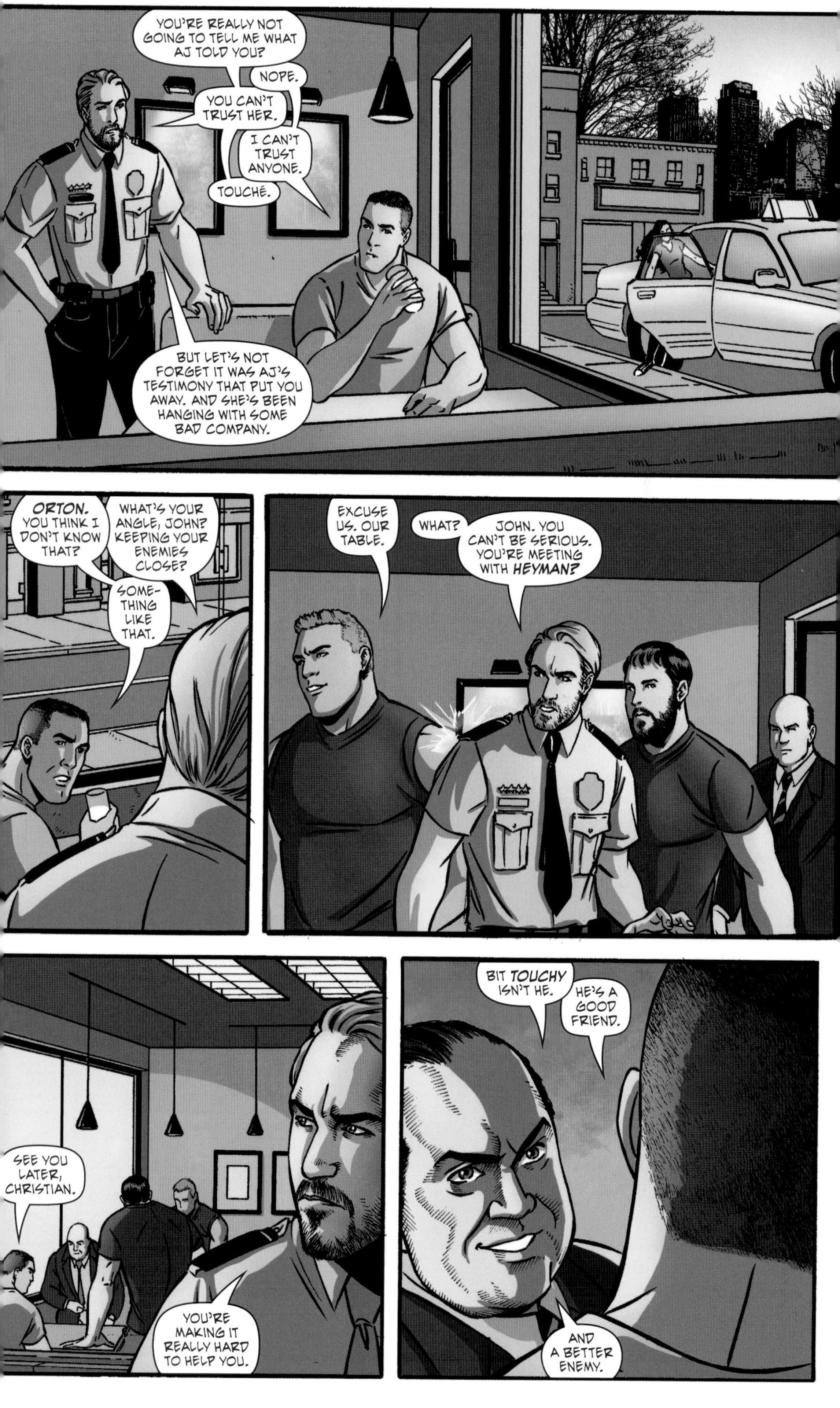
YOU'RE REALLY NOT GOING TO TELL ME WHAT AJ TOLD YOU?
NOPE.
YOU CAN'T TRUST HER.
I CAN'T TRUST ANYONE.
TOUCHÉ.
BUT LET'S NOT FORGET IT WAS AJ'S TESTIMONY THAT PUT YOU AWAY. AND SHE'S BEEN HANGING WITH SOME BAD COMPANY.
ORTON. YOU THINK I DON'T KNOW THAT?
WHAT'S YOUR ANGLE, JOHN? KEEPING YOUR ENEMIES CLOSE?
SOME-THING LIKE THAT.
EXCUSE US. OUR TABLE.
WHAT?
JOHN. YOU CAN'T BE SERIOUS. YOU'RE MEETING WITH HEYMAN?
SEE YOU LATER, CHRISTIAN.
YOU'RE MAKING IT REALLY HARD TO HELP YOU.
BIT TOUCHY ISN'T HE.
HE'S A GOOD FRIEND.
AND A BETTER ENEMY.

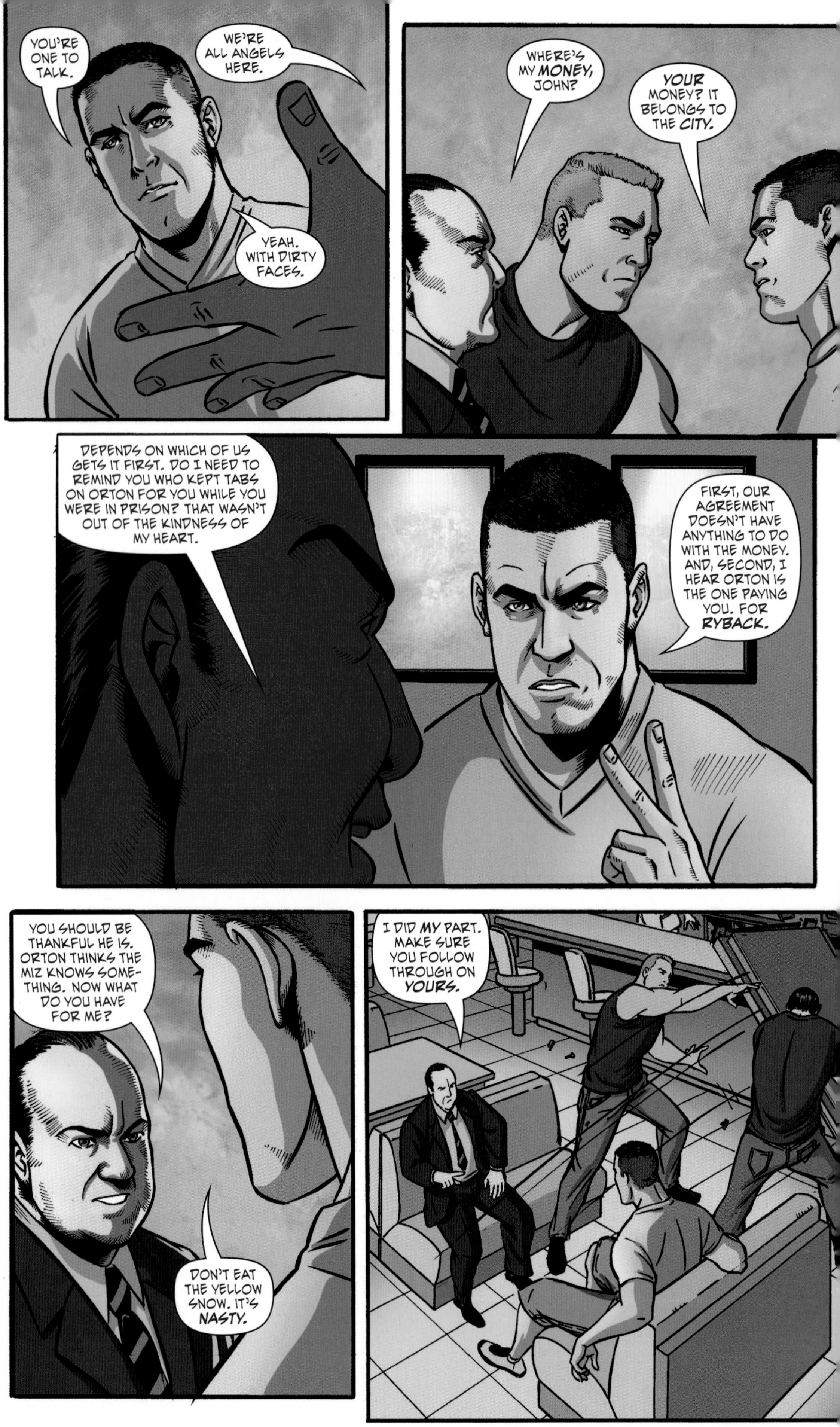

YOU'RE ONE TO TALK.
WE'RE ALL ANGELS HERE.
YEAH. WITH DIRTY FACES.
WHERE'S MY MONEY, JOHN?
YOUR MONEY? IT BELONGS TO THE CITY.
DEPENDS ON WHICH OF US GETS IT FIRST. DO I NEED TO REMIND YOU WHO KEPT TABS ON ORTON FOR YOU WHILE YOU WERE IN PRISON? THAT WASN'T OUT OF THE KINDNESS OF MY HEART.
FIRST, OUR AGREEMENT DOESN'T HAVE ANYTHING TO DO WITH THE MONEY. AND, SECOND, I HEAR ORTON IS THE ONE PAYING YOU. FOR RYBACK.
YOU SHOULD BE THANKFUL HE IS. ORTON THINKS THE MIZ KNOWS SOME-THING. NOW WHAT DO YOU HAVE FOR ME?
DON'T EAT THE YELLOW SNOW. IT'S NASTY.
I DID MY PART. MAKE SURE YOU FOLLOW THROUGH ON YOURS.

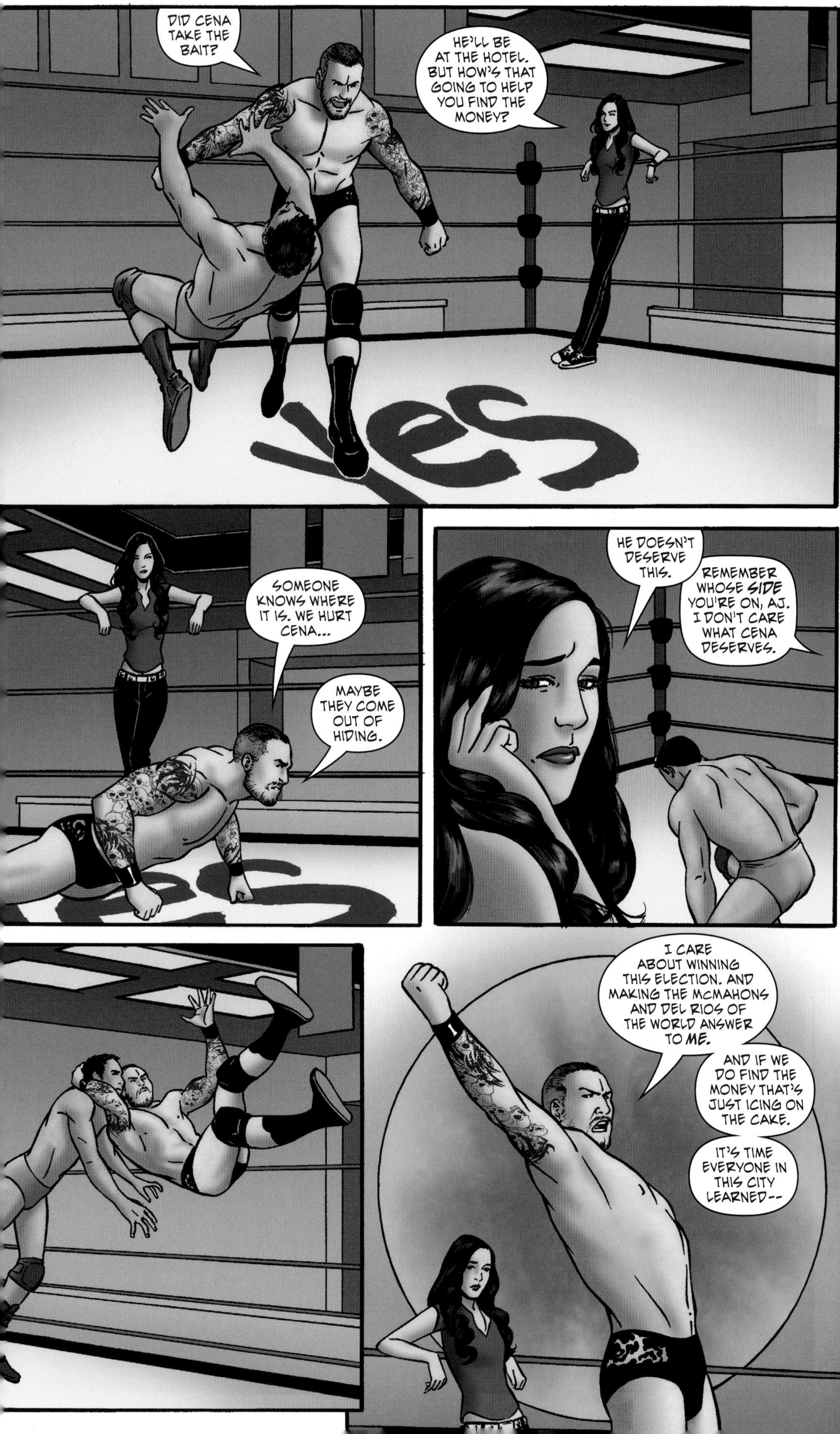
DID CENA TAKE THE BAIT?
HE'LL BE AT THE HOTEL. BUT HOW'S THAT GOING TO HELP YOU FIND THE MONEY?
SOMEONE KNOWS WHERE IT IS. WE HURT CENA...
MAYBE THEY COME OUT OF HIDING.
HE DOESN'T DESERVE THIS.
REMEMBER WHOSE SIDE YOU'RE ON, AJ. I DON'T CARE WHAT CENA DESERVES.
I CARE ABOUT WINNING THIS ELECTION. AND MAKING THE MCMAHONS AND DEL RIOS OF THE WORLD ANSWER TO ME.
AND IF WE DO FIND THE MONEY THAT'S JUST ICING ON THE CAKE.
IT'S TIME EVERYONE IN THIS CITY LEARNED--

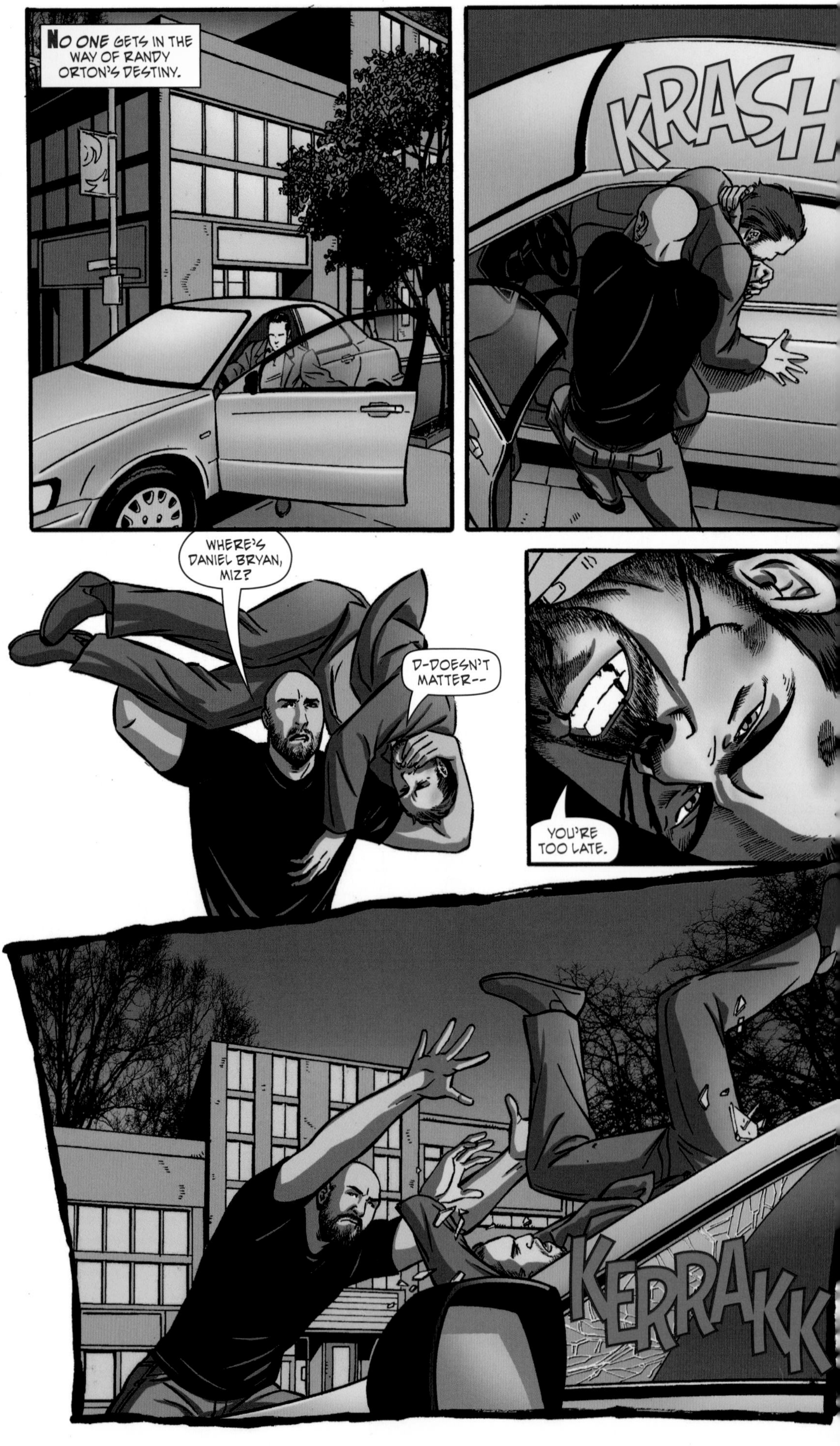
NO ONE GETS IN THE WAY OF RANDY ORTON'S DESTINY.
KRASH
WHERE'S DANIEL BRYAN, MIZ?
D-DOESN'T MATTER--
YOU'RE TOO LATE.
KERRAKK

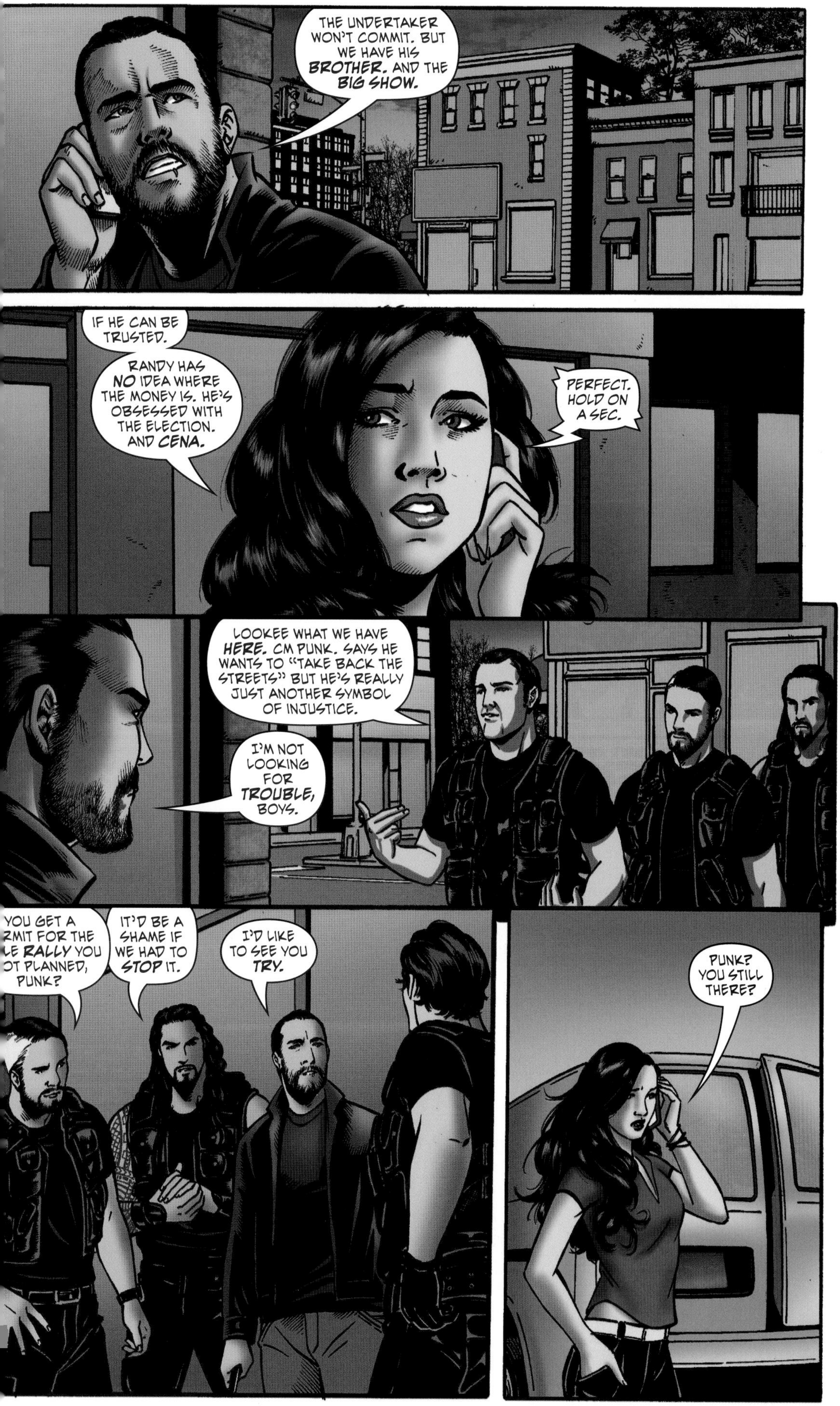
THE UNDERTAKER WON'T COMMIT. BUT WE HAVE HIS BROTHER. AND THE BIG SHOW.
IF HE CAN BE TRUSTED.
RANDY HAS NO IDEA WHERE THE MONEY IS. HE'S OBSESSED WITH THE ELECTION. AND CENA.
PERFECT. HOLD ON A SEC.
LOOKEE WHAT WE HAVE HERE. CM PUNK. SAYS HE WANTS TO "TAKE BACK THE STREETS" BUT HE'S REALLY JUST ANOTHER SYMBOL OF INJUSTICE.
I'M NOT LOOKING FOR TROUBLE, BOYS.
YOU GET A RMIT FOR THE LE RALLY YOU OT PLANNED, PUNK?
IT'D BE A SHAME IF WE HAD TO STOP IT.
I'D LIKE TO SEE YOU TRY.
PUNK? YOU STILL THERE?

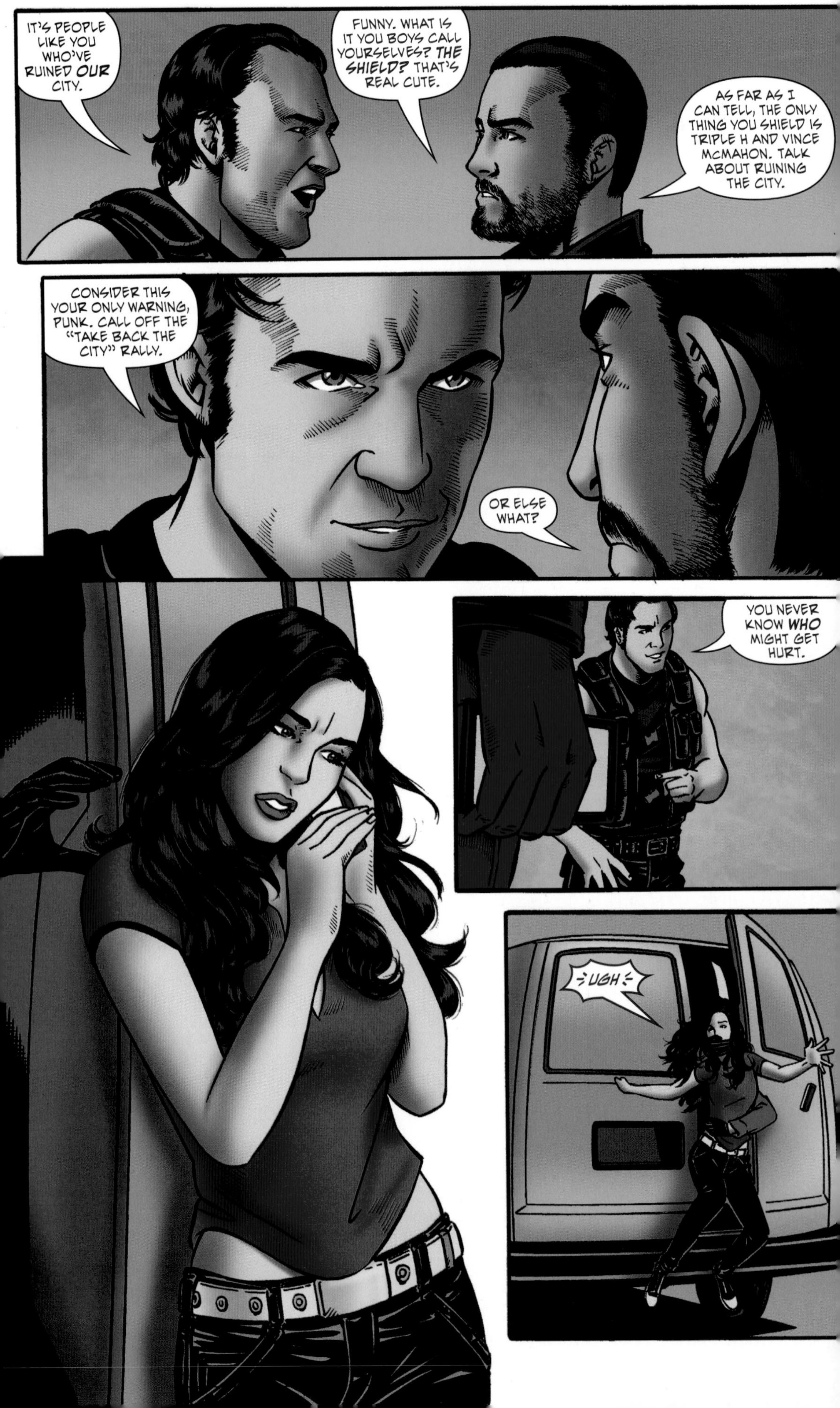
IT'S PEOPLE LIKE YOU WHO'VE RUINED **OUR** CITY.
FUNNY. WHAT IS IT YOU BOYS CALL YOURSELVES? ***THE SHIELD?*** THAT'S REAL CUTE.
AS FAR AS I CAN TELL, THE ONLY THING YOU SHIELD IS TRIPLE H AND VINCE McMAHON. TALK ABOUT RUINING THE CITY.
CONSIDER THIS YOUR ONLY WARNING, PUNK. CALL OFF THE "TAKE BACK THE CITY" RALLY.
OR ELSE WHAT?
YOU NEVER KNOW **WHO** MIGHT GET HURT.
UGH

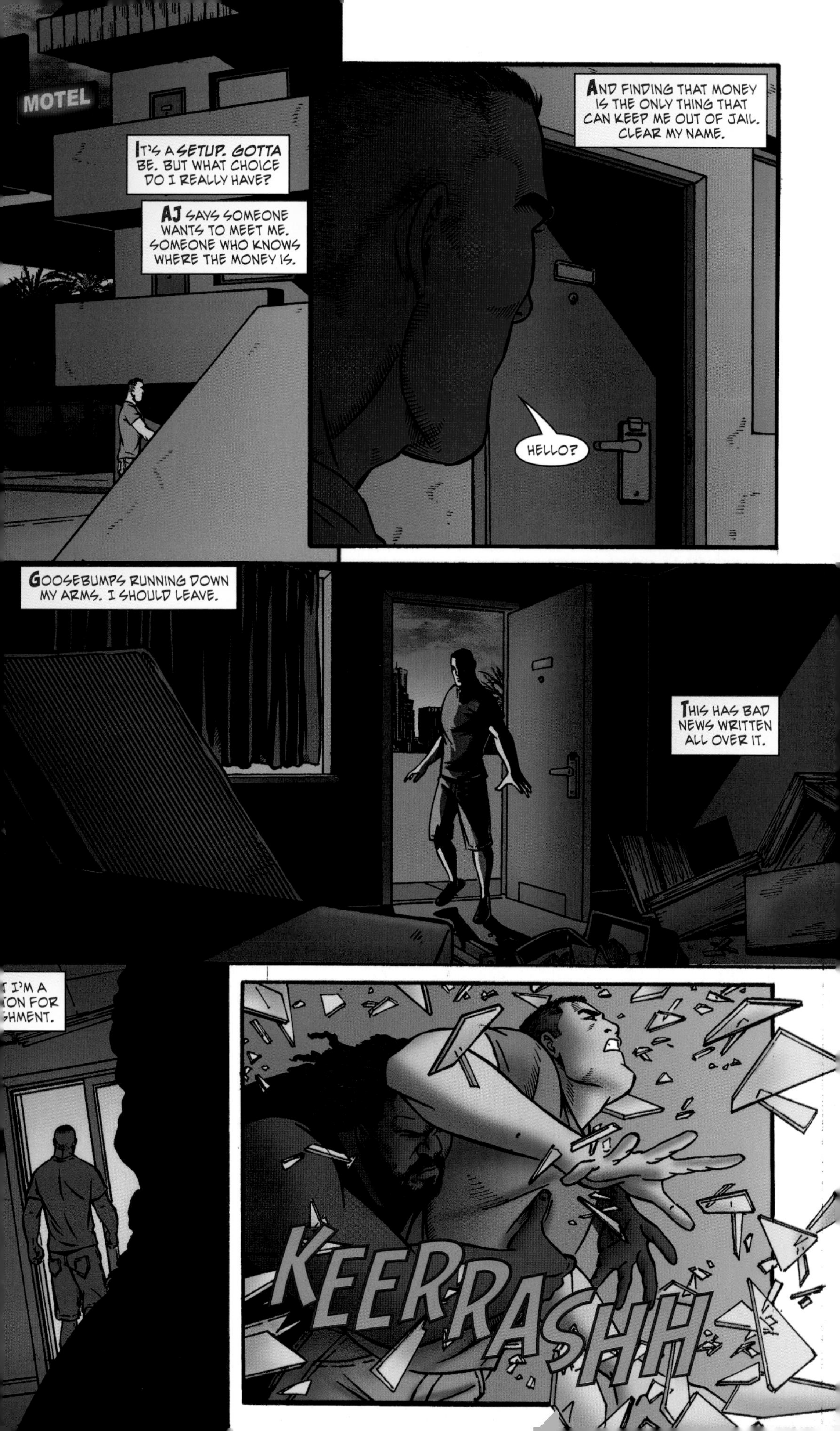
IT'S A SETUP. GOTTA BE. BUT WHAT CHOICE DO I REALLY HAVE?
AJ SAYS SOMEONE WANTS TO MEET ME. SOMEONE WHO KNOWS WHERE THE MONEY IS.
MOTEL
AND FINDING THAT MONEY IS THE ONLY THING THAT CAN KEEP ME OUT OF JAIL. CLEAR MY NAME.
HELLO?
GOOSEBUMPS RUNNING DOWN MY ARMS. I SHOULD LEAVE.
THIS HAS BAD NEWS WRITTEN ALL OVER IT.
T I'M A
ION FOR
GHMENT.
KEERRASHH

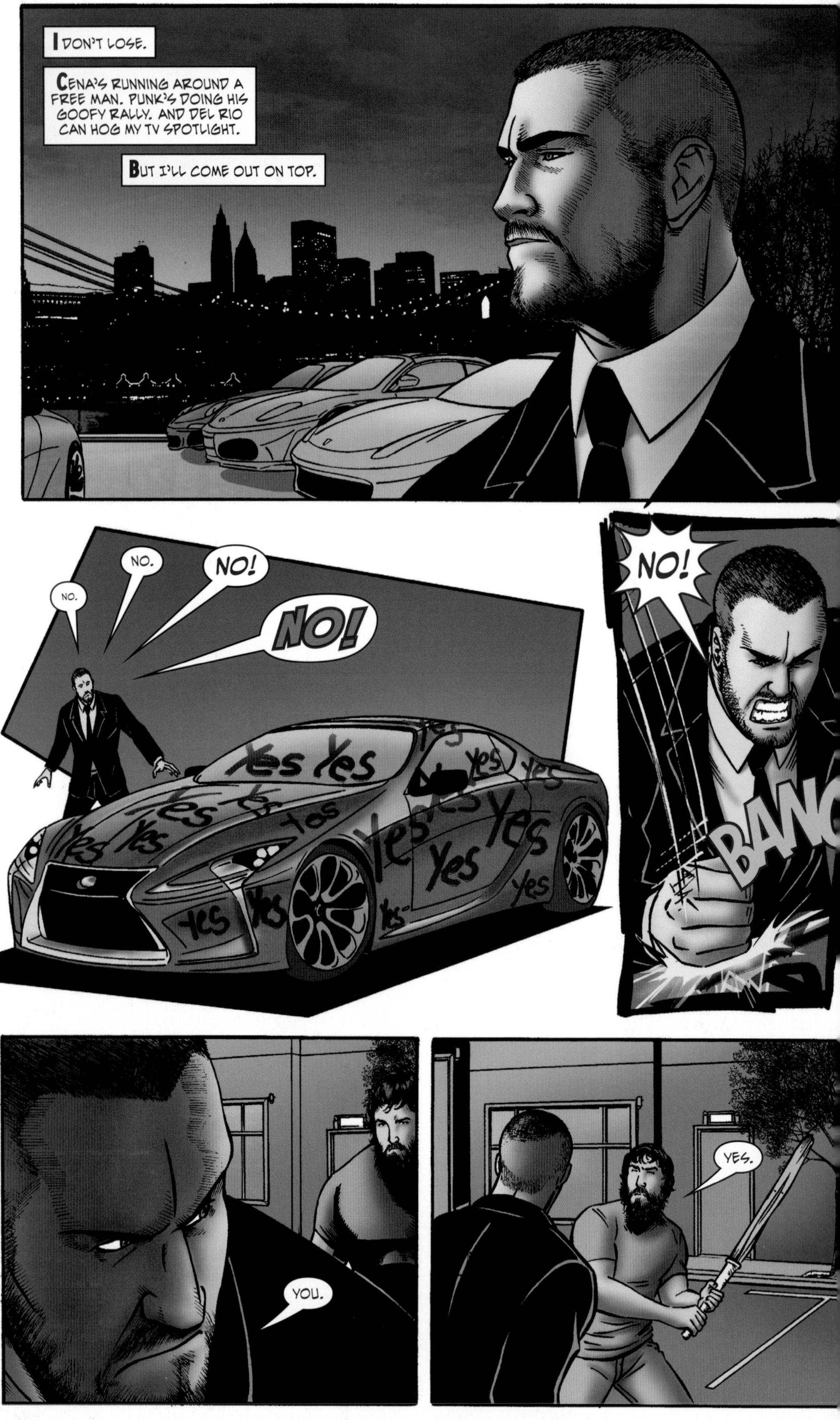
I DON'T LOSE.
CENA'S RUNNING AROUND A FREE MAN. PUNK'S DOING HIS GOOFY RALLY. AND DEL RIO CAN HOG MY TV SPOTLIGHT.
BUT I'LL COME OUT ON TOP.
NO.
NO.
NO!
NO!
NO!
BANG
YOU.
YES.

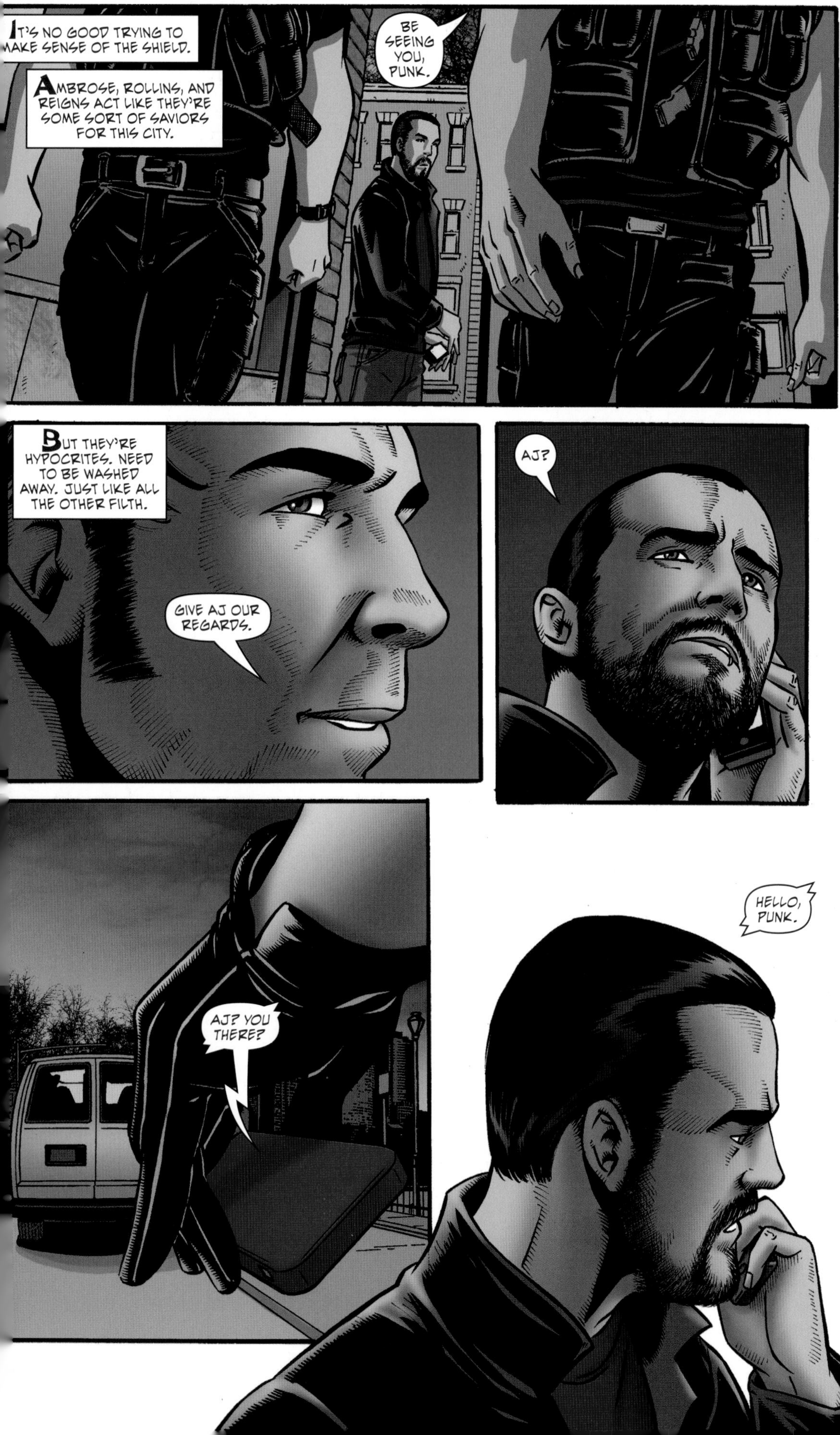
IT'S NO GOOD TRYING TO MAKE SENSE OF THE SHIELD.
AMBROSE, ROLLINS, AND REIGNS ACT LIKE THEY'RE SOME SORT OF SAVIORS FOR THIS CITY.
BE SEEING YOU, PUNK.
BUT THEY'RE HYPOCRITES. NEED TO BE WASHED AWAY. JUST LIKE ALL THE OTHER FILTH.
GIVE AJ OUR REGARDS.
AJ?
AJ? YOU THERE?
HELLO, PUNK.

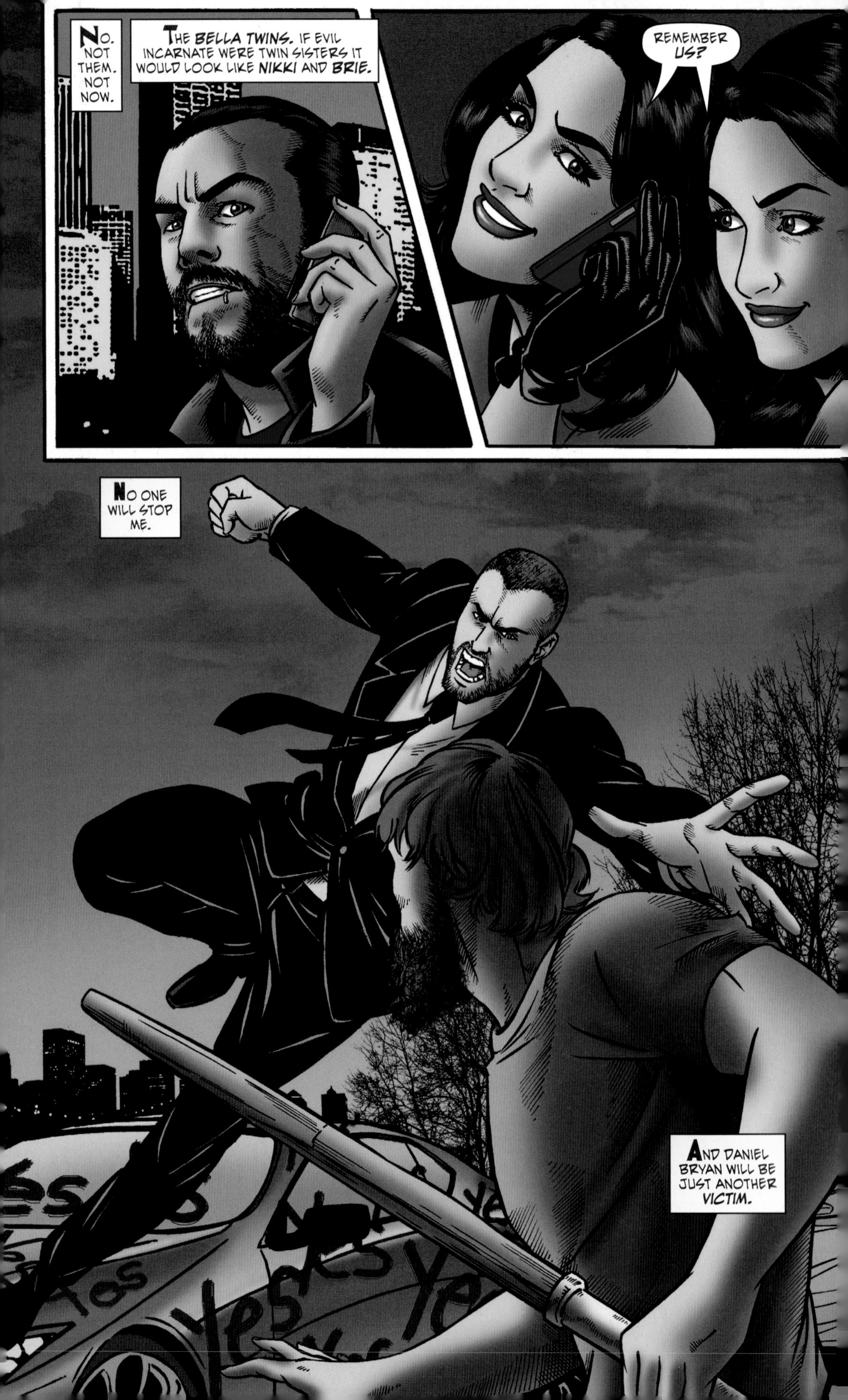

No. Not them. Not now.
The Bella Twins. If evil incarnate were twin sisters it would look like Nikki and Brie.
Remember us?
No one will stop me.
And Daniel Bryan will be just another victim.

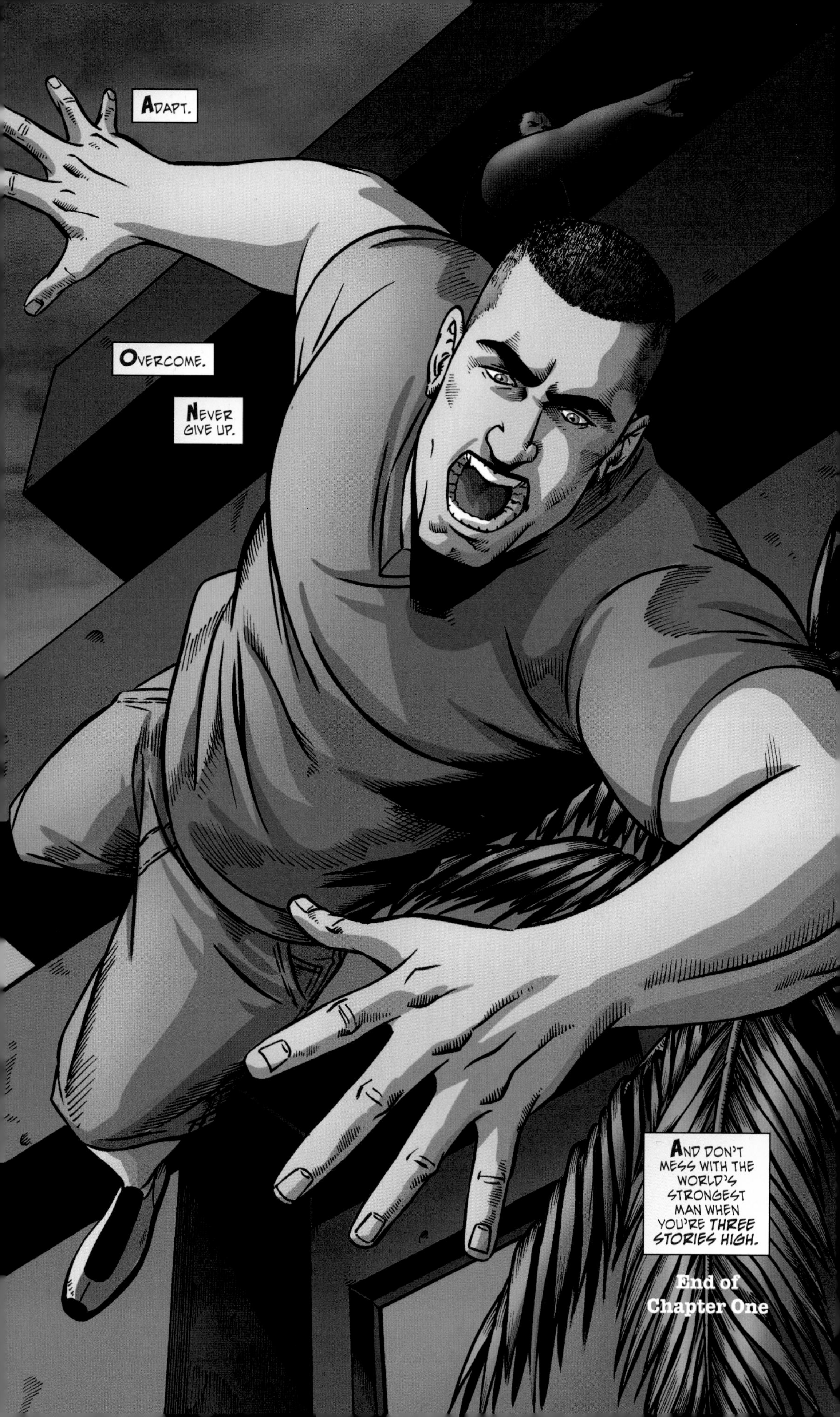
ADAPT.
OVERCOME.
NEVER GIVE UP.
AND DON'T MESS WITH THE WORLD'S STRONGEST MAN WHEN YOU'RE THREE STORIES HIGH.
End of Chapter One

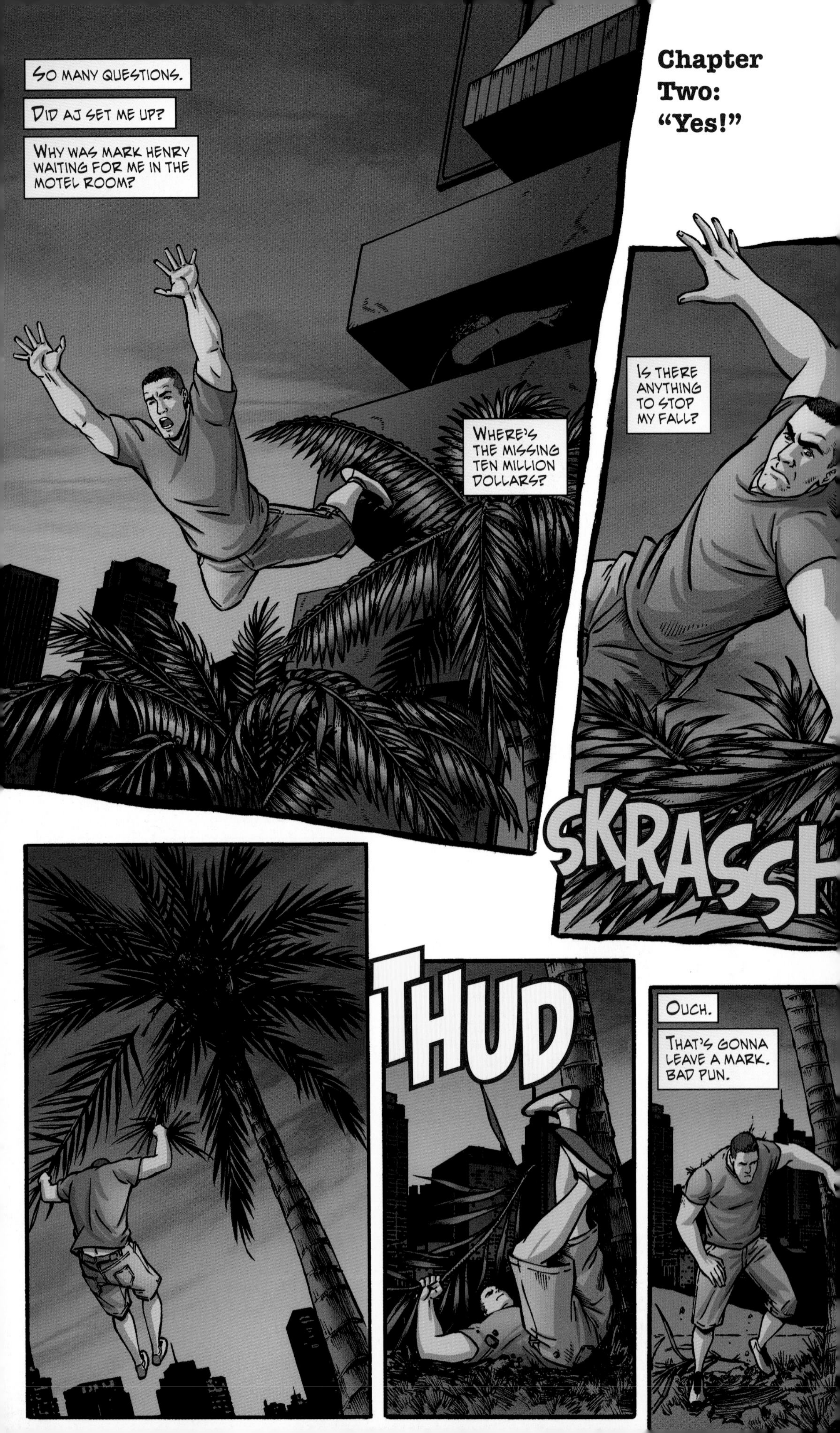

Chapter Two: "Yes!"
So many questions.
Did AJ set me up?
Why was Mark Henry waiting for me in the motel room?
Where's the missing ten million dollars?
Is there anything to stop my fall?
SKRASSH
THUD
Ouch.
That's gonna leave a mark. Bad pun.

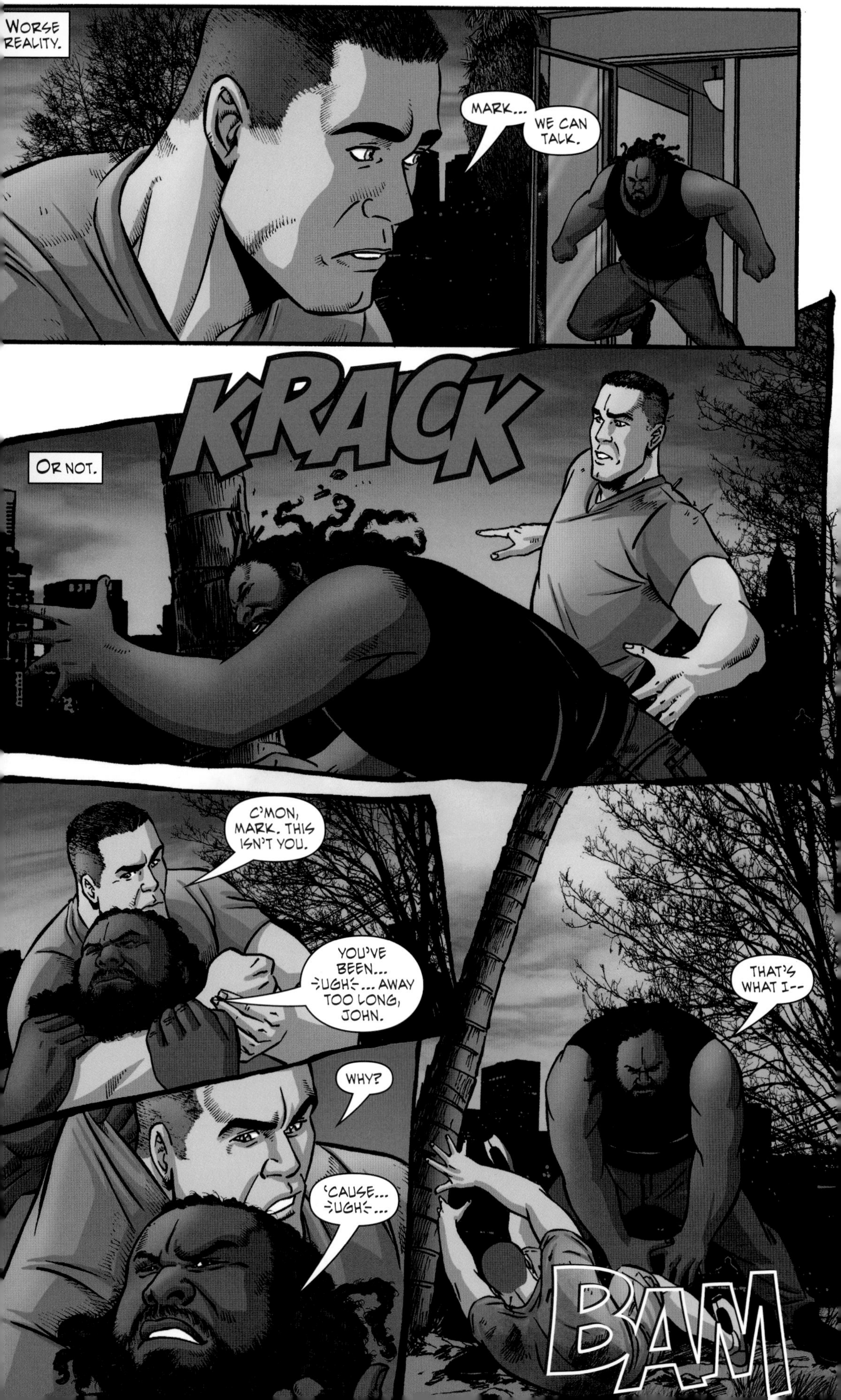
WORSE REALITY.
MARK...
WE CAN TALK.
KRACK
OR NOT.
C'MON, MARK. THIS ISN'T YOU.
YOU'VE BEEN... -UGH-... AWAY TOO LONG, JOHN.
WHY?
'CAUSE... -UGH-...
THAT'S WHAT I--
BAM

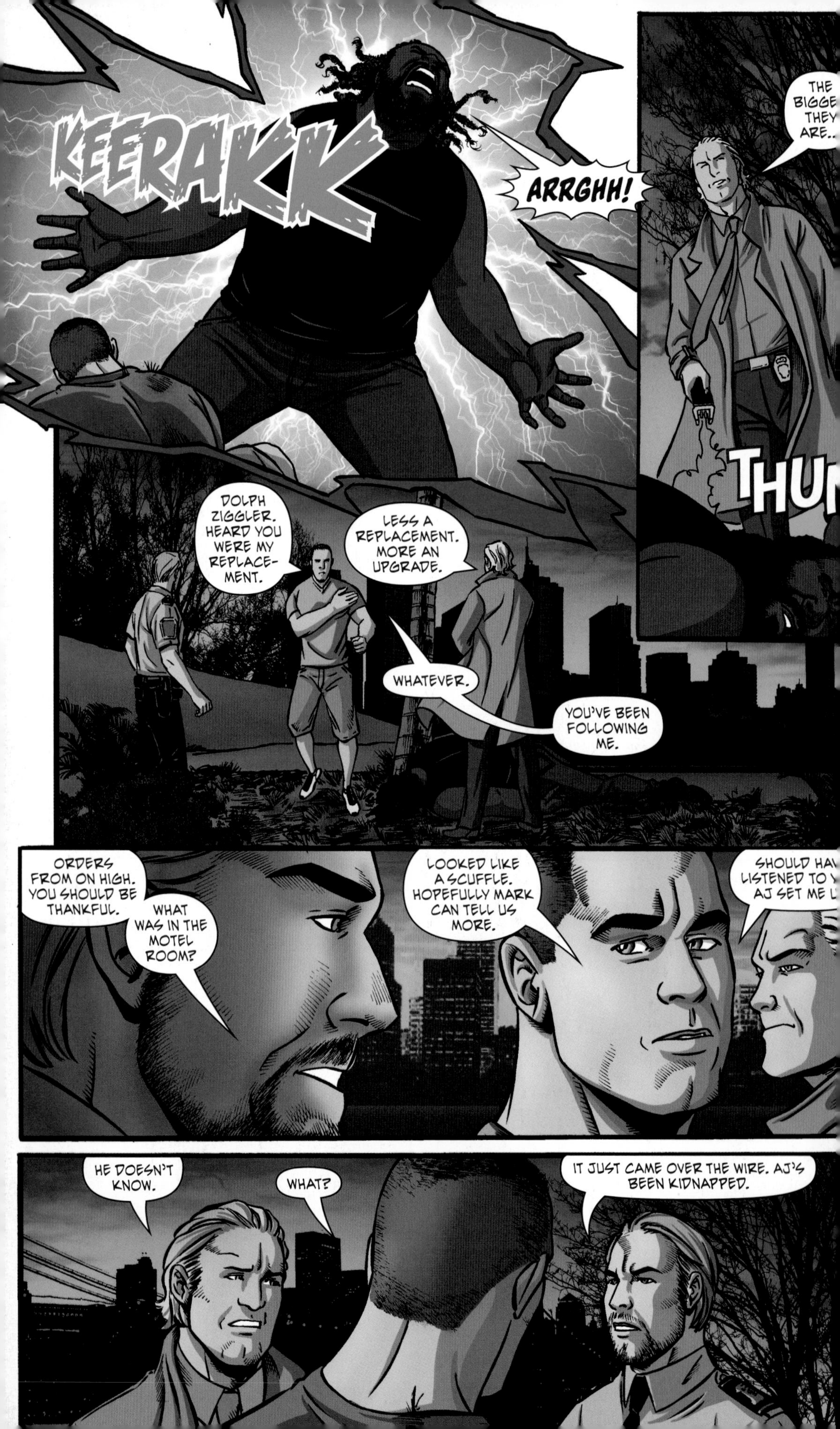
KEERAKK
ARRGHH!
THE BIGGE THEY ARE..
THUN
DOLPH ZIGGLER. HEARD YOU WERE MY REPLACE-MENT.
LESS A REPLACEMENT. MORE AN UPGRADE.
WHATEVER.
YOU'VE BEEN FOLLOWING ME.
ORDERS FROM ON HIGH. YOU SHOULD BE THANKFUL.
WHAT WAS IN THE MOTEL ROOM?
LOOKED LIKE A SCUFFLE. HOPEFULLY MARK CAN TELL US MORE.
SHOULD HAV LISTENED TO Y AJ SET ME L
HE DOESN'T KNOW.
WHAT?
IT JUST CAME OVER THE WIRE. AJ'S BEEN KIDNAPPED.

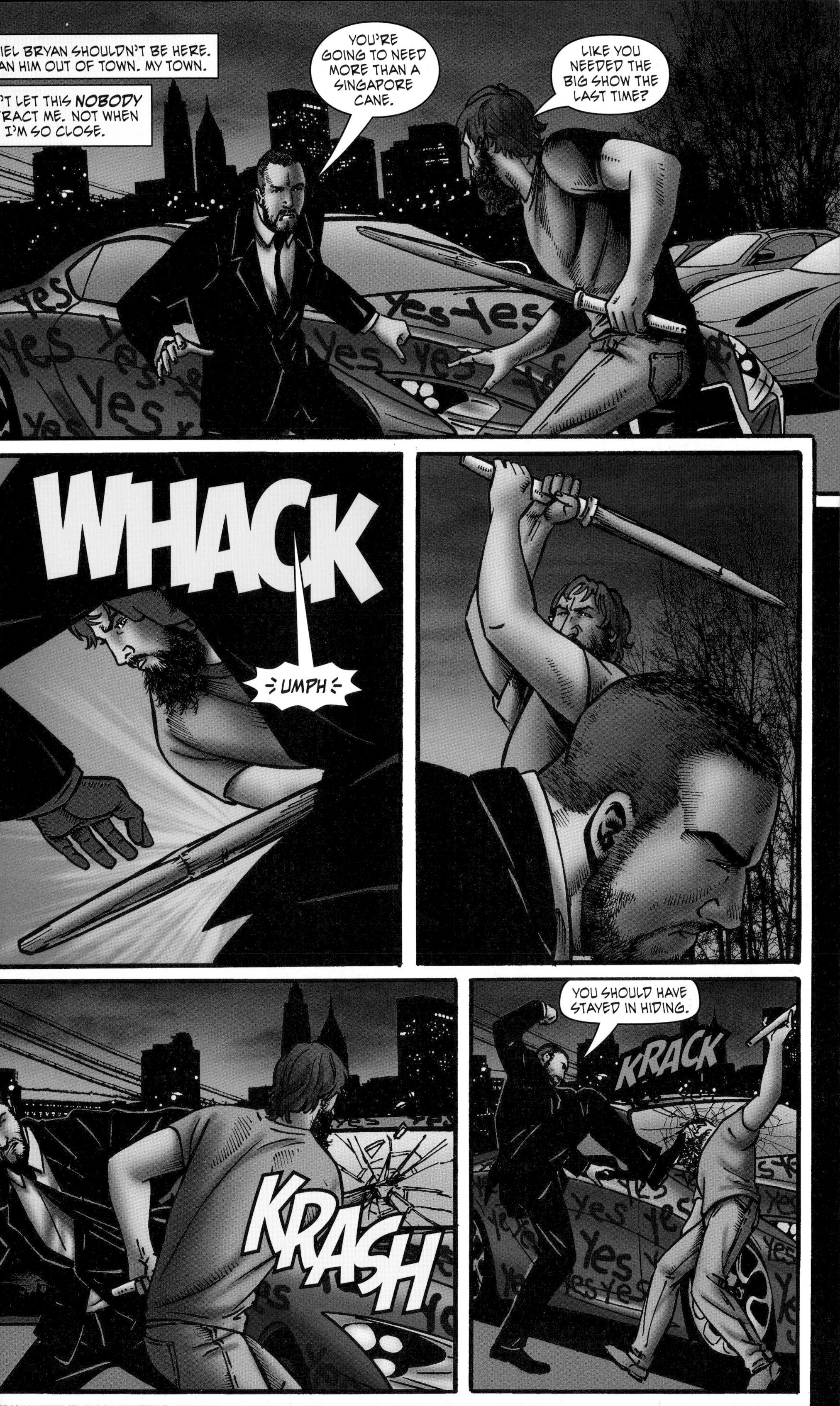
IEL BRYAN SHOULDN'T BE HERE. AN HIM OUT OF TOWN. MY TOWN.
'T LET THIS NOBODY TRACT ME. NOT WHEN I'M SO CLOSE.
YOU'RE GOING TO NEED MORE THAN A SINGAPORE CANE.
LIKE YOU NEEDED THE BIG SHOW THE LAST TIME?
WHACK
UMPH
KRASH
YOU SHOULD HAVE STAYED IN HIDING.
KRACK

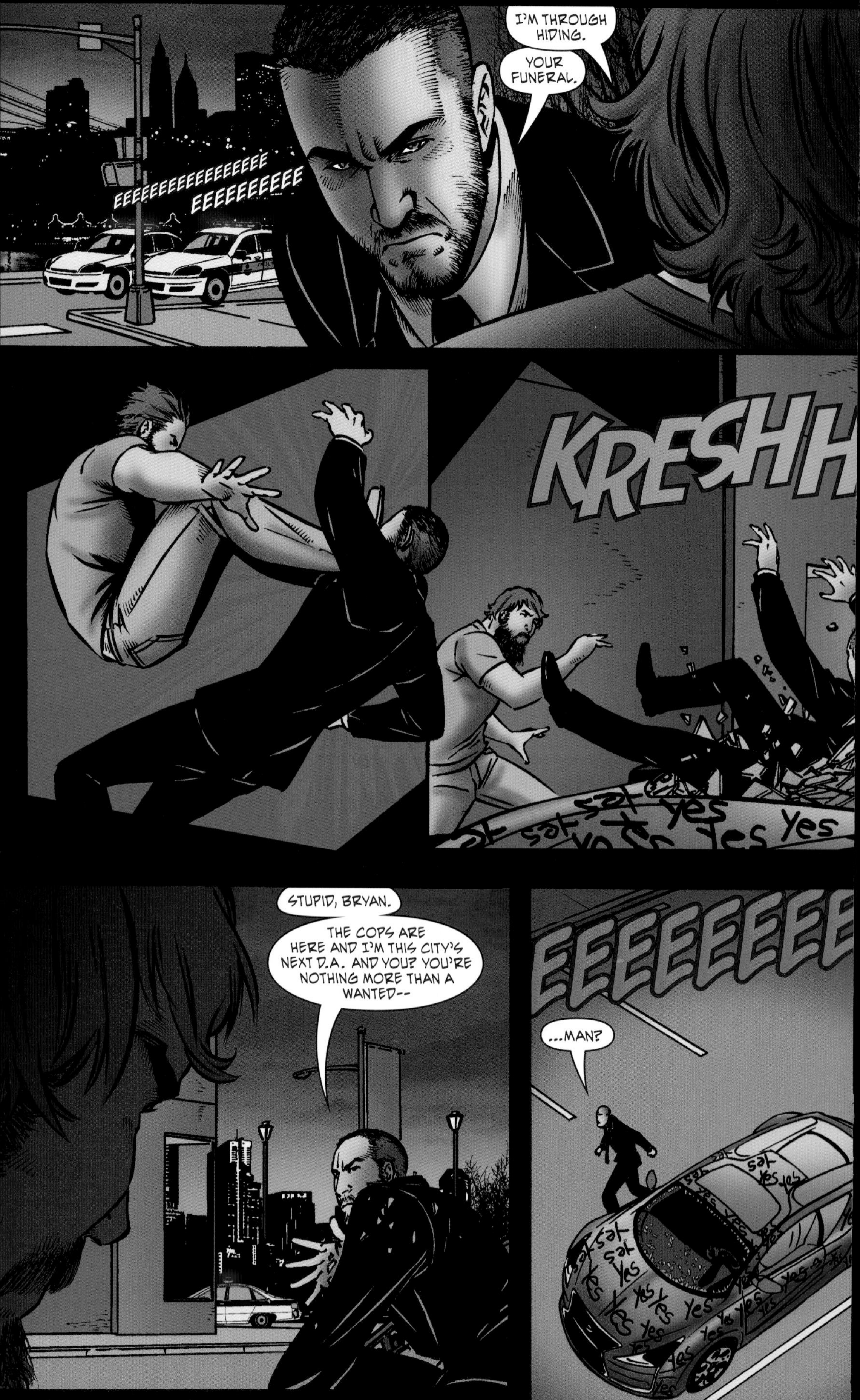
I'M THROUGH HIDING.
YOUR FUNERAL.
EEEEEEEEEEEEEEEEE
EEEEEEEEE
KRESHH
yes yes yes yes yes yes yes
STUPID, BRYAN.
THE COPS ARE HERE AND I'M THIS CITY'S NEXT D.A. AND YOU? YOU'RE NOTHING MORE THAN A WANTED--
EEEEEEEEE
...MAN?
yes yes yes yes yes yes yes yes

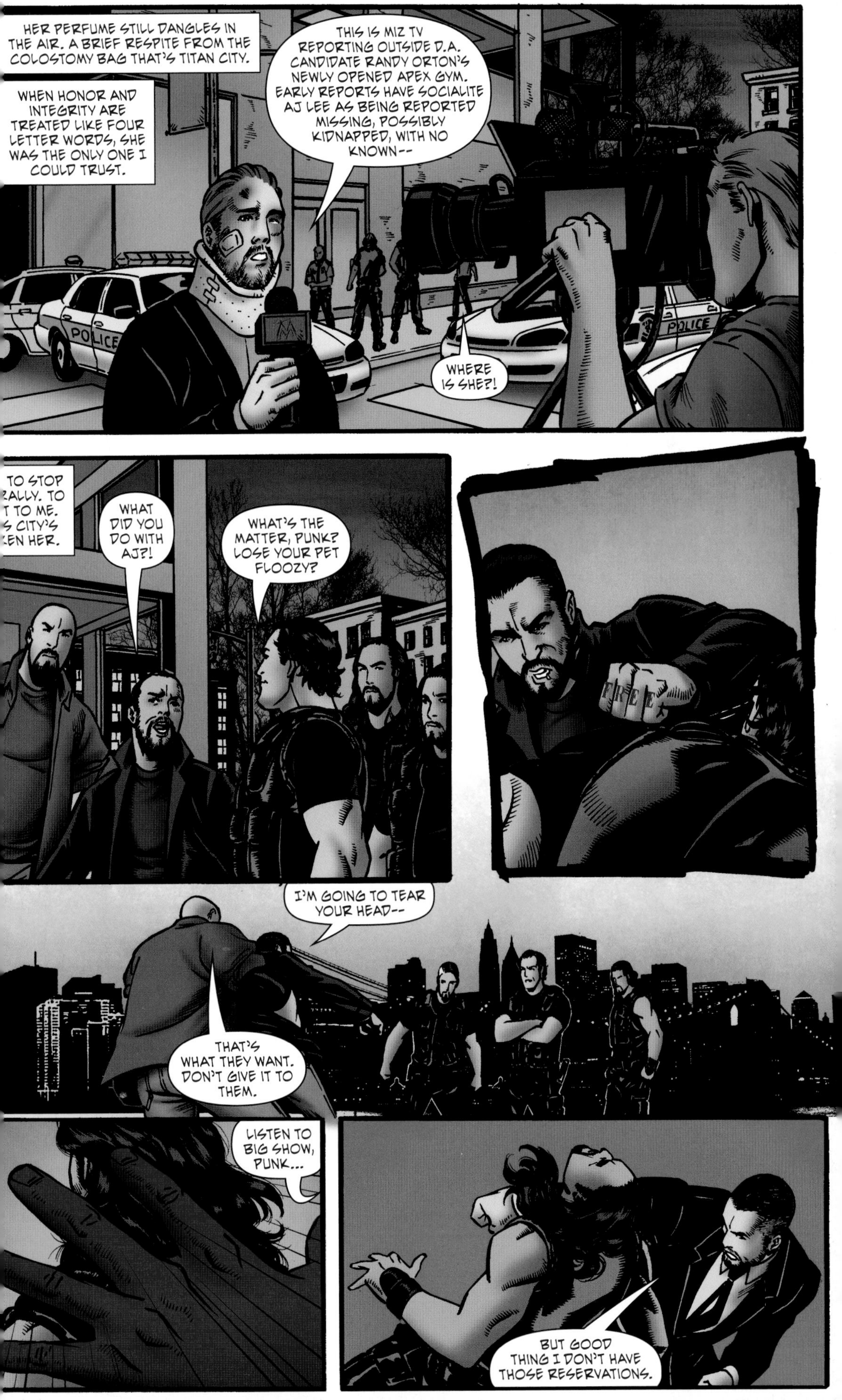
HER PERFUME STILL DANGLES IN THE AIR. A BRIEF RESPITE FROM THE COLOSTOMY BAG THAT'S TITAN CITY.
WHEN HONOR AND INTEGRITY ARE TREATED LIKE FOUR LETTER WORDS, SHE WAS THE ONLY ONE I COULD TRUST.
THIS IS MIZ TV REPORTING OUTSIDE D.A. CANDIDATE RANDY ORTON'S NEWLY OPENED APEX GYM. EARLY REPORTS HAVE SOCIALITE AJ LEE AS BEING REPORTED MISSING, POSSIBLY KIDNAPPED, WITH NO KNOWN--
POLICE
POLICE
WHERE IS SHE?!
WHAT DID YOU DO WITH AJ?!
WHAT'S THE MATTER, PUNK? LOSE YOUR PET FLOOZY?
I'M GOING TO TEAR YOUR HEAD--
THAT'S WHAT THEY WANT. DON'T GIVE IT TO THEM.
LISTEN TO BIG SHOW, PUNK...
BUT GOOD THING I DON'T HAVE THOSE RESERVATIONS.

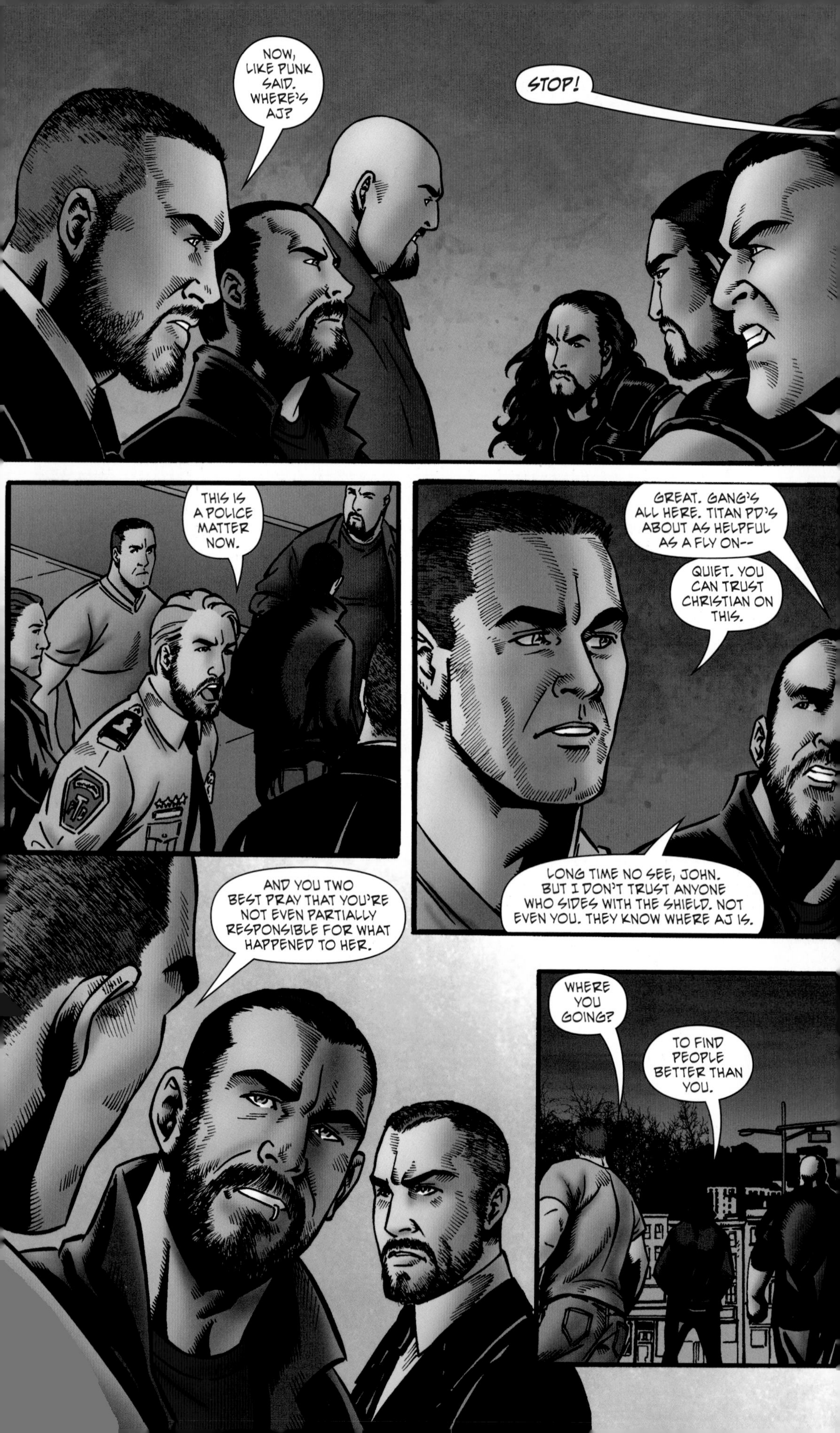
NOW, LIKE PUNK SAID. WHERE'S AJ?
STOP!
THIS IS A POLICE MATTER NOW.
GREAT. GANG'S ALL HERE. TITAN PD'S ABOUT AS HELPFUL AS A FLY ON--
QUIET. YOU CAN TRUST CHRISTIAN ON THIS.
LONG TIME NO SEE, JOHN. BUT I DON'T TRUST ANYONE WHO SIDES WITH THE SHIELD. NOT EVEN YOU. THEY KNOW WHERE AJ IS.
AND YOU TWO BEST PRAY THAT YOU'RE NOT EVEN PARTIALLY RESPONSIBLE FOR WHAT HAPPENED TO HER.
WHERE YOU GOING?
TO FIND PEOPLE BETTER THAN YOU.

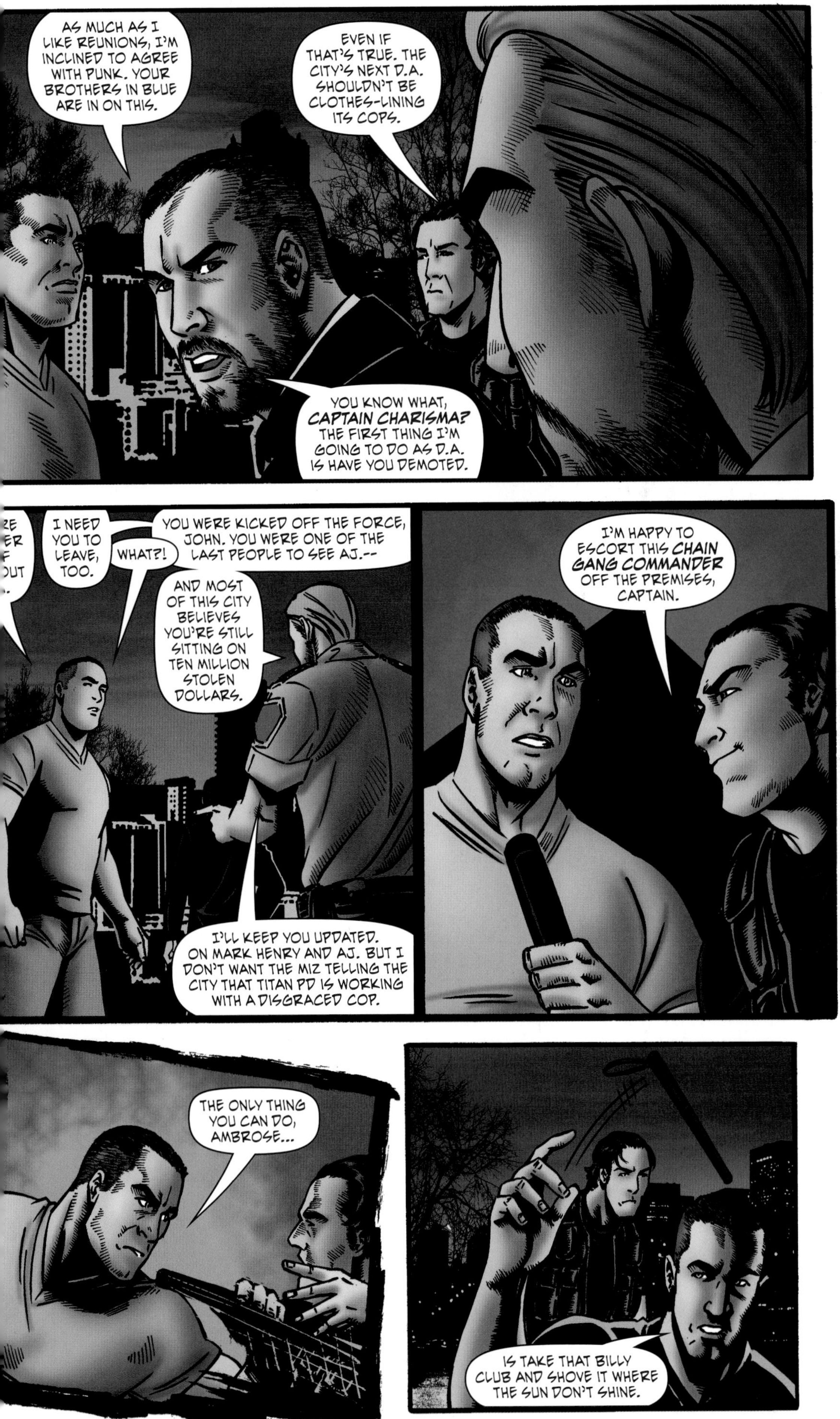
AS MUCH AS I LIKE REUNIONS, I'M INCLINED TO AGREE WITH PUNK. YOUR BROTHERS IN BLUE ARE IN ON THIS.
EVEN IF THAT'S TRUE. THE CITY'S NEXT D.A. SHOULDN'T BE CLOTHES-LINING ITS COPS.
YOU KNOW WHAT, CAPTAIN CHARISMA? THE FIRST THING I'M GOING TO DO AS D.A. IS HAVE YOU DEMOTED.
I NEED YOU TO LEAVE, TOO.
WHAT?!
YOU WERE KICKED OFF THE FORCE, JOHN. YOU WERE ONE OF THE LAST PEOPLE TO SEE AJ.--
AND MOST OF THIS CITY BELIEVES YOU'RE STILL SITTING ON TEN MILLION STOLEN DOLLARS.
I'LL KEEP YOU UPDATED. ON MARK HENRY AND AJ. BUT I DON'T WANT THE MIZ TELLING THE CITY THAT TITAN PD IS WORKING WITH A DISGRACED COP.
I'M HAPPY TO ESCORT THIS CHAIN GANG COMMANDER OFF THE PREMISES, CAPTAIN.
THE ONLY THING YOU CAN DO, AMBROSE...
IS TAKE THAT BILLY CLUB AND SHOVE IT WHERE THE SUN DON'T SHINE.

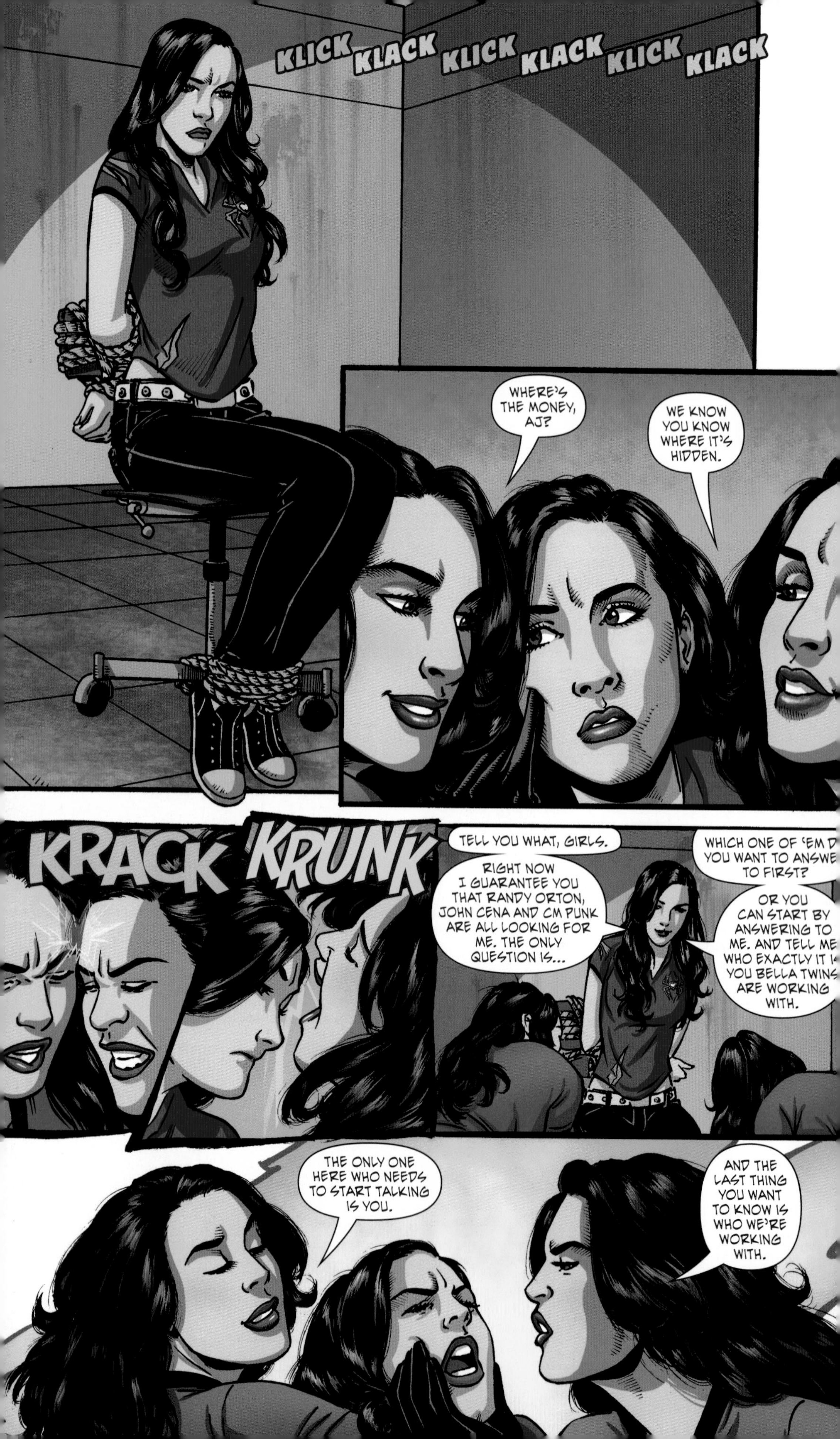
KLICK KLACK KLICK KLACK KLICK KLACK
WHERE'S THE MONEY, AJ?
WE KNOW YOU KNOW WHERE IT'S HIDDEN.
KRACK KRUNK
TELL YOU WHAT, GIRLS.
RIGHT NOW I GUARANTEE YOU THAT RANDY ORTON, JOHN CENA AND CM PUNK ARE ALL LOOKING FOR ME. THE ONLY QUESTION IS...
WHICH ONE OF 'EM D YOU WANT TO ANSWE TO FIRST?
OR YOU CAN START BY ANSWERING TO ME. AND TELL ME WHO EXACTLY IT I YOU BELLA TWINS ARE WORKING WITH.
THE ONLY ONE HERE WHO NEEDS TO START TALKING IS YOU.
AND THE LAST THING YOU WANT TO KNOW IS WHO WE'RE WORKING WITH.

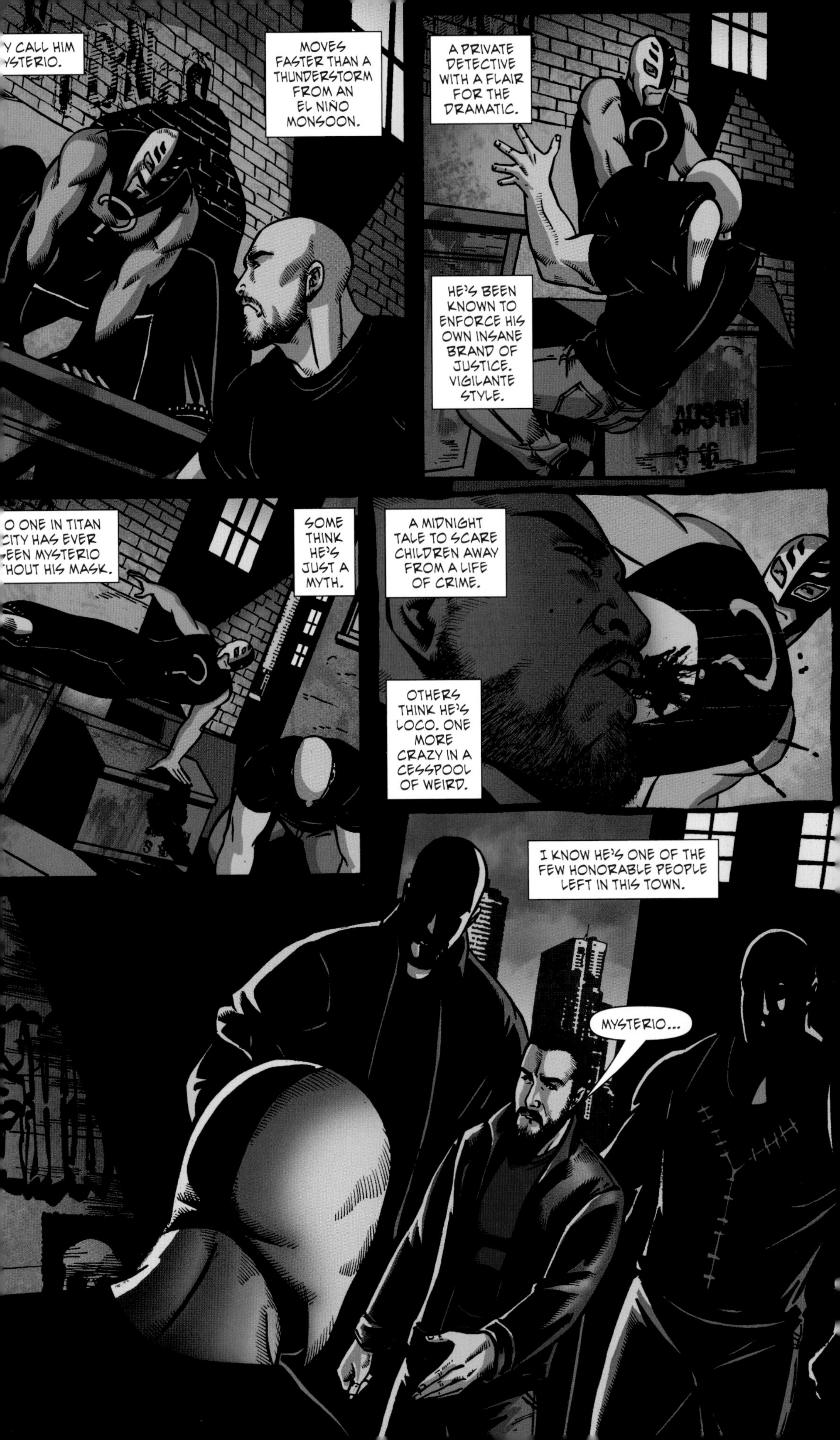
Y CALL HIM
YSTERIO.
MOVES FASTER THAN A THUNDERSTORM FROM AN EL NIÑO MONSOON.
A PRIVATE DETECTIVE WITH A FLAIR FOR THE DRAMATIC.
HE'S BEEN KNOWN TO ENFORCE HIS OWN INSANE BRAND OF JUSTICE. VIGILANTE STYLE.
AUSTIN 3:16
O ONE IN TITAN CITY HAS EVER EEN MYSTERIO THOUT HIS MASK.
SOME THINK HE'S JUST A MYTH.
A MIDNIGHT TALE TO SCARE CHILDREN AWAY FROM A LIFE OF CRIME.
OTHERS THINK HE'S LOCO. ONE MORE CRAZY IN A CESSPOOL OF WEIRD.
I KNOW HE'S ONE OF THE FEW HONORABLE PEOPLE LEFT IN THIS TOWN.
MYSTERIO...

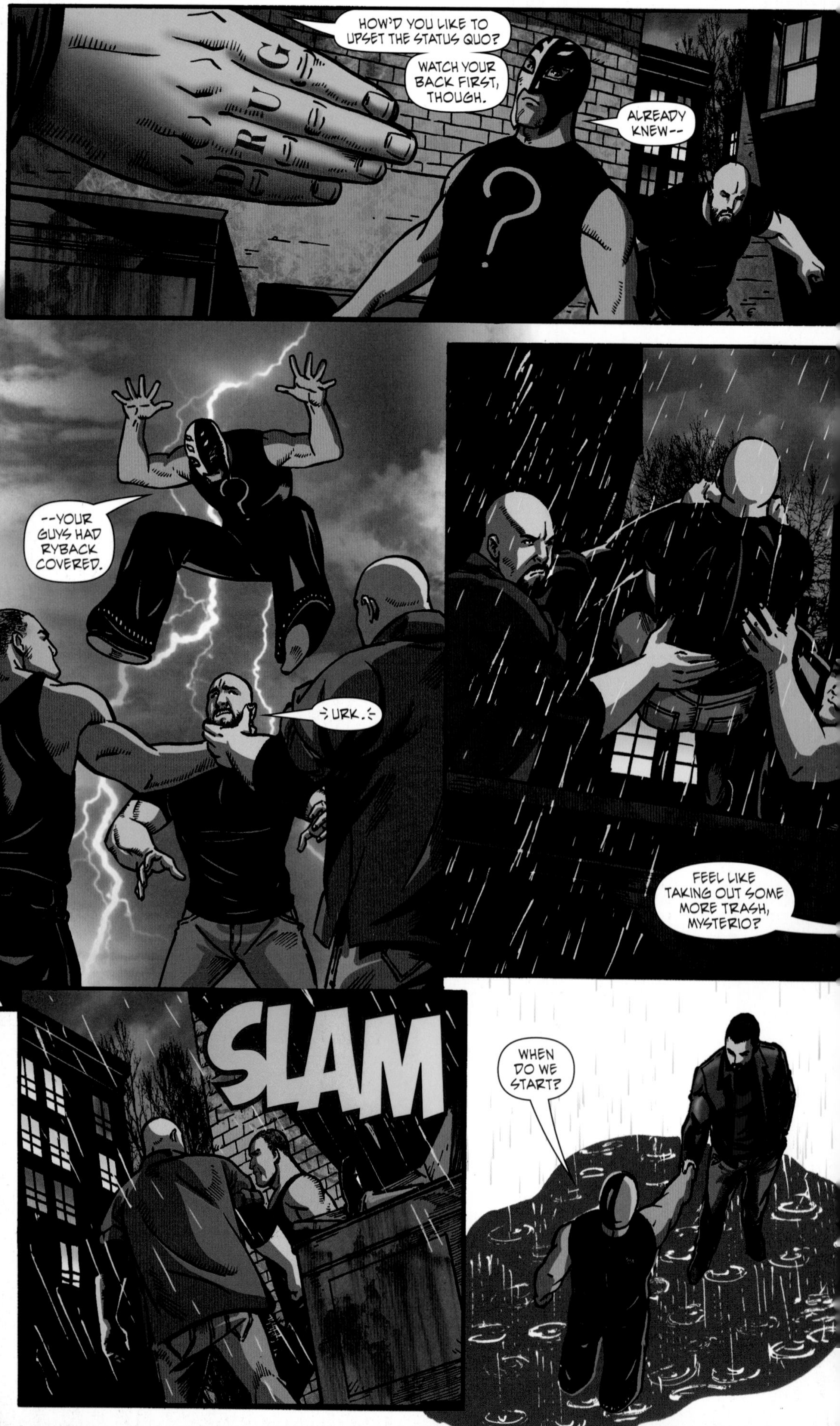
HOW'D YOU LIKE TO UPSET THE STATUS QUO?
WATCH YOUR BACK FIRST, THOUGH.
ALREADY KNEW--
--YOUR GUYS HAD RYBACK COVERED.
URK.
FEEL LIKE TAKING OUT SOME MORE TRASH, MYSTERIO?
SLAM
WHEN DO WE START?

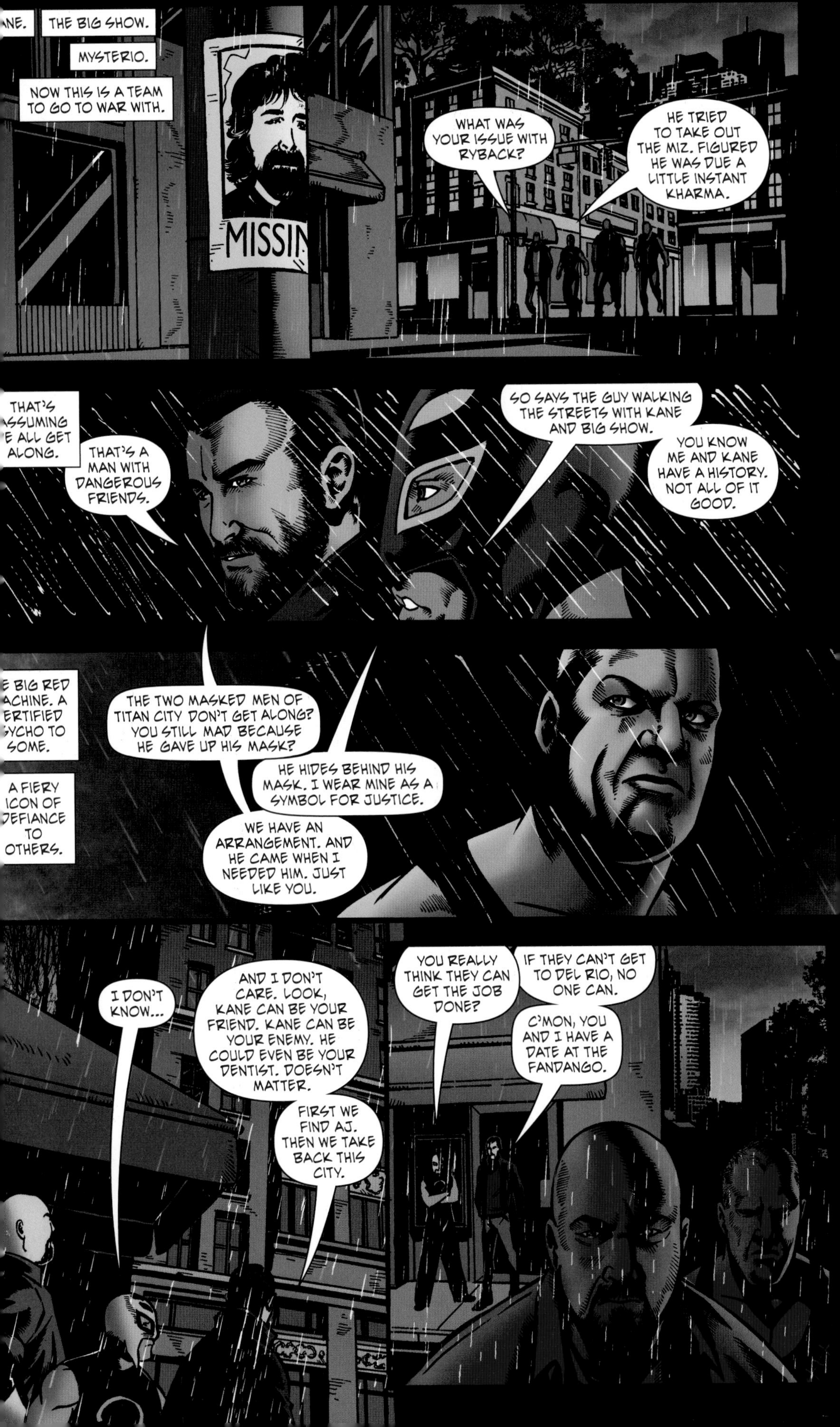
ANE.
THE BIG SHOW.
MYSTERIO.
NOW THIS IS A TEAM TO GO TO WAR WITH.
MISSIN
WHAT WAS YOUR ISSUE WITH RYBACK?
HE TRIED TO TAKE OUT THE MIZ. FIGURED HE WAS DUE A LITTLE INSTANT KHARMA.
THAT'S ASSUMING E ALL GET ALONG.
THAT'S A MAN WITH DANGEROUS FRIENDS.
SO SAYS THE GUY WALKING THE STREETS WITH KANE AND BIG SHOW.
YOU KNOW ME AND KANE HAVE A HISTORY. NOT ALL OF IT GOOD.
E BIG RED ACHINE. A ERTIFIED YCHO TO SOME.
A FIERY ICON OF EFIANCE TO OTHERS.
THE TWO MASKED MEN OF TITAN CITY DON'T GET ALONG? YOU STILL MAD BECAUSE HE GAVE UP HIS MASK?
HE HIDES BEHIND HIS MASK. I WEAR MINE AS A SYMBOL FOR JUSTICE.
WE HAVE AN ARRANGEMENT. AND HE CAME WHEN I NEEDED HIM. JUST LIKE YOU.
I DON'T KNOW...
AND I DON'T CARE. LOOK, KANE CAN BE YOUR FRIEND. KANE CAN BE YOUR ENEMY. HE COULD EVEN BE YOUR DENTIST. DOESN'T MATTER.
FIRST WE FIND AJ. THEN WE TAKE BACK THIS CITY.
YOU REALLY THINK THEY CAN GET THE JOB DONE?
IF THEY CAN'T GET TO DEL RIO, NO ONE CAN.
C'MON, YOU AND I HAVE A DATE AT THE FANDANGO.

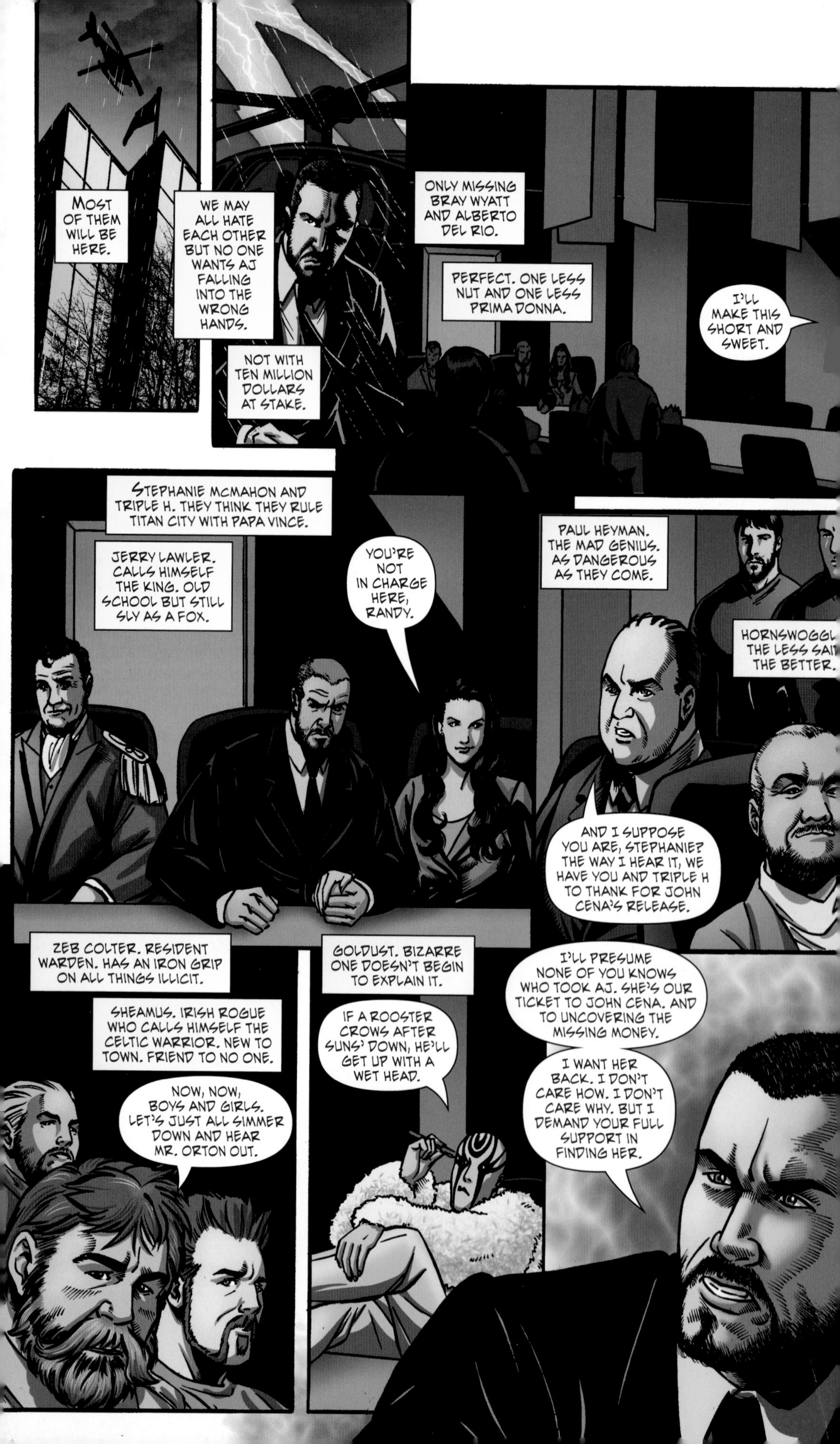
MOST OF THEM WILL BE HERE.
WE MAY ALL HATE EACH OTHER BUT NO ONE WANTS AJ FALLING INTO THE WRONG HANDS.
NOT WITH TEN MILLION DOLLARS AT STAKE.
ONLY MISSING BRAY WYATT AND ALBERTO DEL RIO.
PERFECT. ONE LESS NUT AND ONE LESS PRIMA DONNA.
I'LL MAKE THIS SHORT AND SWEET.
STEPHANIE MCMAHON AND TRIPLE H. THEY THINK THEY RULE TITAN CITY WITH PAPA VINCE.
JERRY LAWLER. CALLS HIMSELF THE KING. OLD SCHOOL BUT STILL SLY AS A FOX.
YOU'RE NOT IN CHARGE HERE, RANDY.
PAUL HEYMAN. THE MAD GENIUS. AS DANGEROUS AS THEY COME.
HORNSWOGGL THE LESS SAI THE BETTER.
AND I SUPPOSE YOU ARE, STEPHANIE? THE WAY I HEAR IT, WE HAVE YOU AND TRIPLE H TO THANK FOR JOHN CENA'S RELEASE.
ZEB COLTER. RESIDENT WARDEN. HAS AN IRON GRIP ON ALL THINGS ILLICIT.
SHEAMUS. IRISH ROGUE WHO CALLS HIMSELF THE CELTIC WARRIOR. NEW TO TOWN. FRIEND TO NO ONE.
NOW, NOW, BOYS AND GIRLS. LET'S JUST ALL SIMMER DOWN AND HEAR MR. ORTON OUT.
GOLDUST. BIZARRE ONE DOESN'T BEGIN TO EXPLAIN IT.
IF A ROOSTER CROWS AFTER SUNS' DOWN, HE'LL GET UP WITH A WET HEAD.
I'LL PRESUME NONE OF YOU KNOWS WHO TOOK AJ. SHE'S OUR TICKET TO JOHN CENA. AND TO UNCOVERING THE MISSING MONEY.
I WANT HER BACK. I DON'T CARE HOW. I DON'T CARE WHY. BUT I DEMAND YOUR FULL SUPPORT IN FINDING HER.

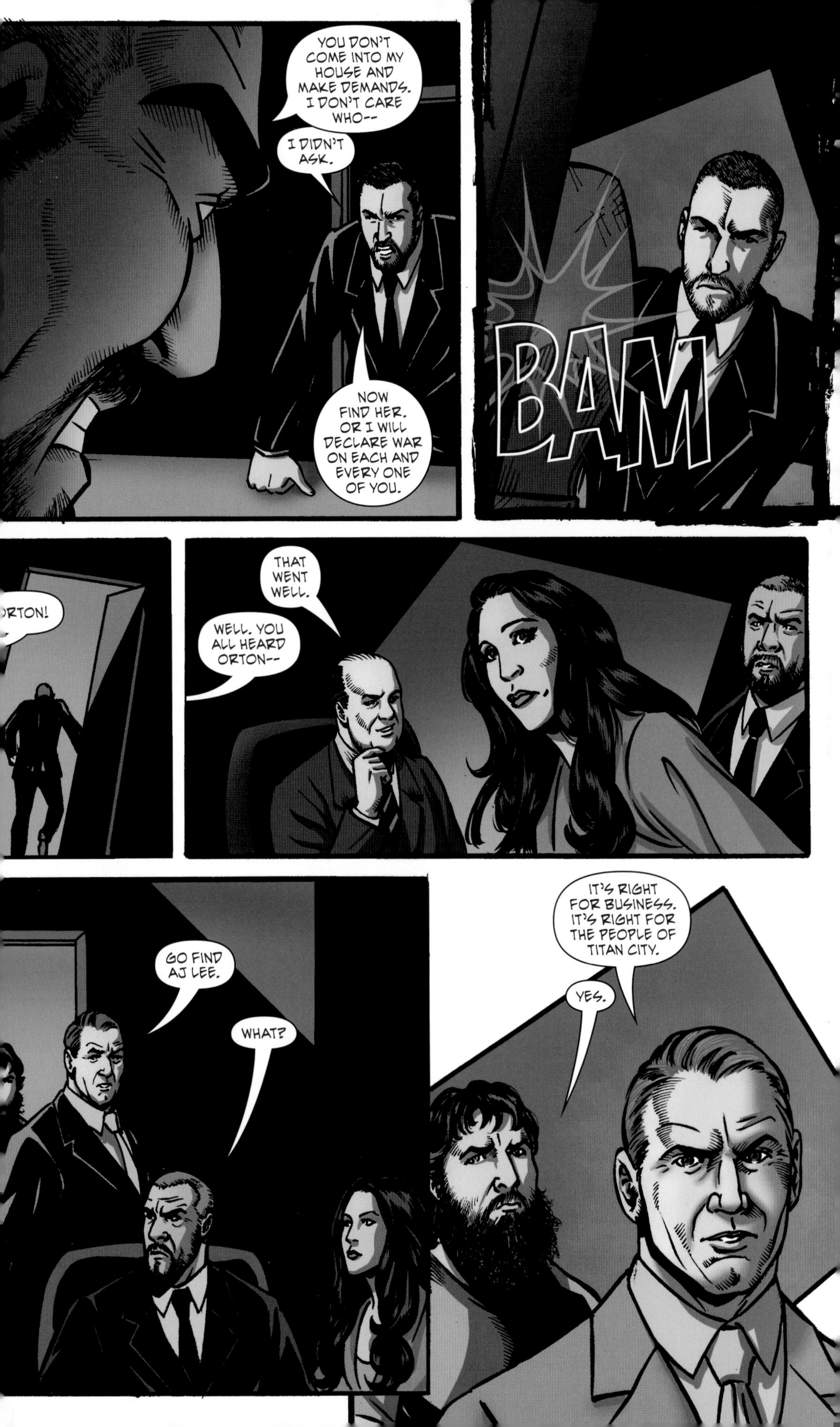
YOU DON'T COME INTO MY HOUSE AND MAKE DEMANDS. I DON'T CARE WHO--
I DIDN'T ASK.
NOW FIND HER. OR I WILL DECLARE WAR ON EACH AND EVERY ONE OF YOU.
BAM
RTON!
THAT WENT WELL.
WELL. YOU ALL HEARD ORTON--
GO FIND AJ LEE.
WHAT?
IT'S RIGHT FOR BUSINESS. IT'S RIGHT FOR THE PEOPLE OF TITAN CITY.
YES.

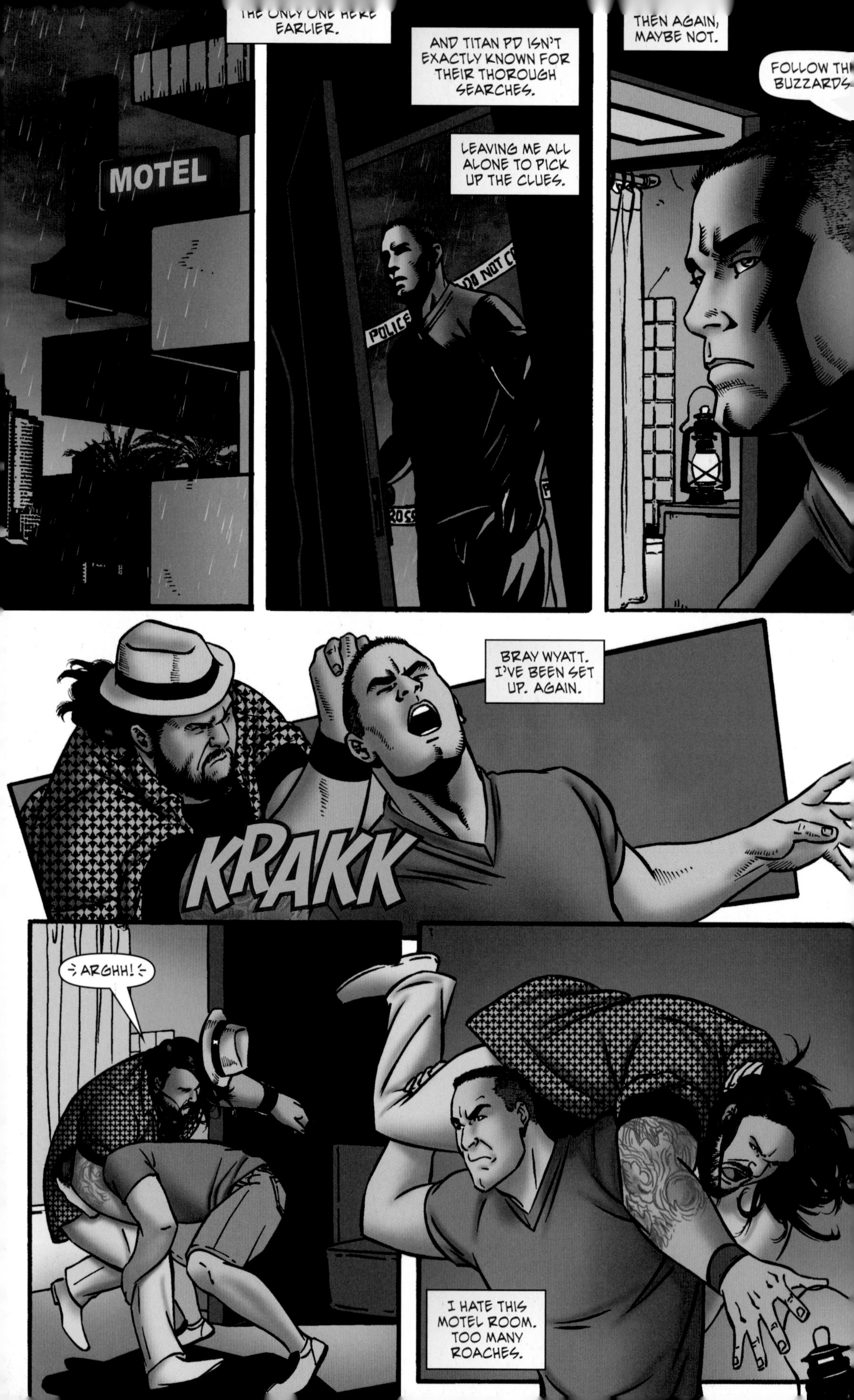
EARLIER.
AND TITAN PD ISN'T EXACTLY KNOWN FOR THEIR THOROUGH SEARCHES.
LEAVING ME ALL ALONE TO PICK UP THE CLUES.
MOTEL
POLICE
DO NOT C
THEN AGAIN, MAYBE NOT.
FOLLOW TH BUZZARDS
BRAY WYATT. I'VE BEEN SET UP. AGAIN.
KRAKK
ARGHH!
I HATE THIS MOTEL ROOM. TOO MANY ROACHES.

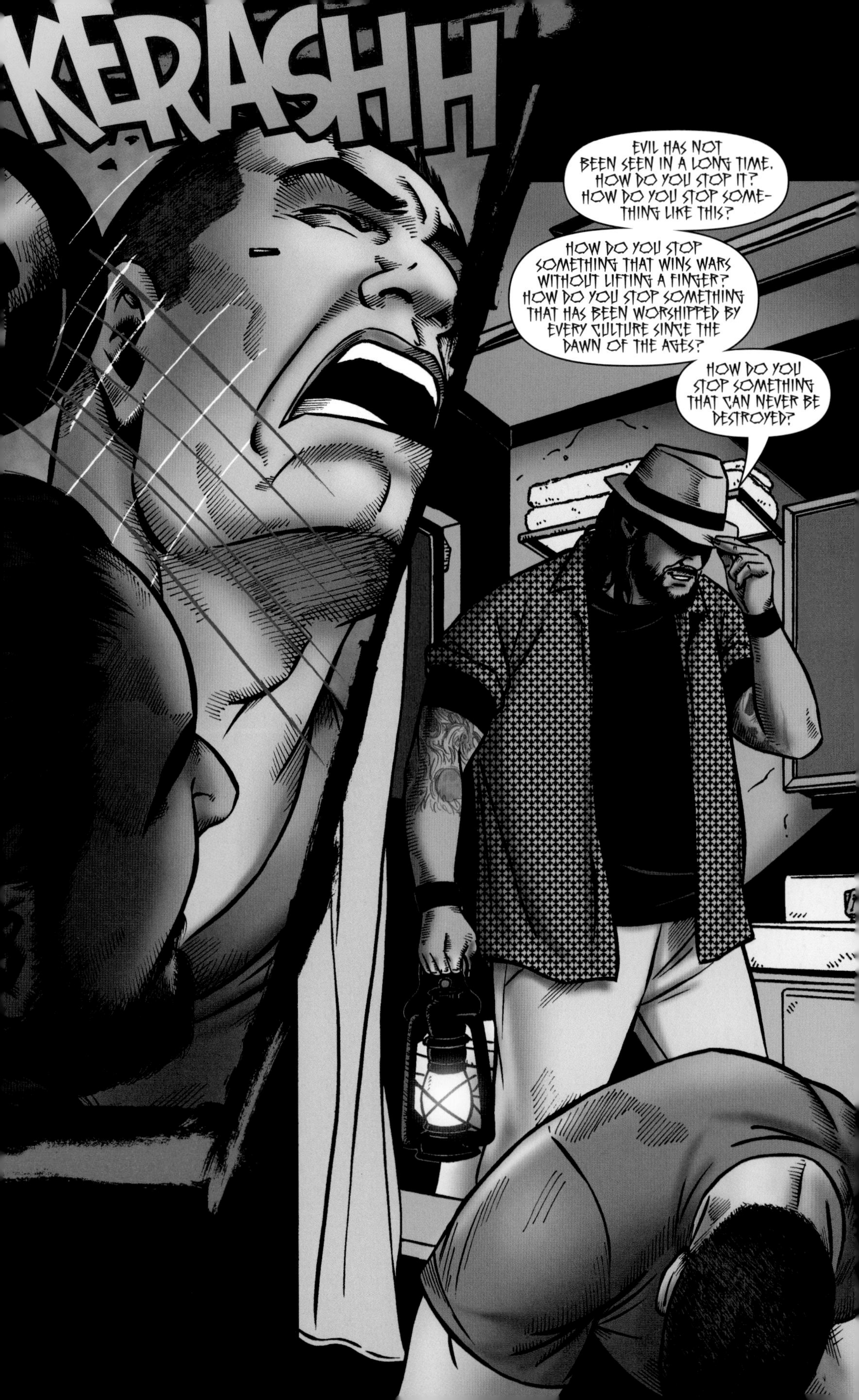
KERASHH
EVIL HAS NOT BEEN SEEN IN A LONG TIME. HOW DO YOU STOP IT? HOW DO YOU STOP SOME-THING LIKE THIS?
HOW DO YOU STOP SOMETHING THAT WINS WARS WITHOUT LIFTING A FINGER? HOW DO YOU STOP SOMETHING THAT HAS BEEN WORSHIPPED BY EVERY CULTURE SINCE THE DAWN OF THE AGES?
HOW DO YOU STOP SOMETHING THAT CAN NEVER BE DESTROYED?

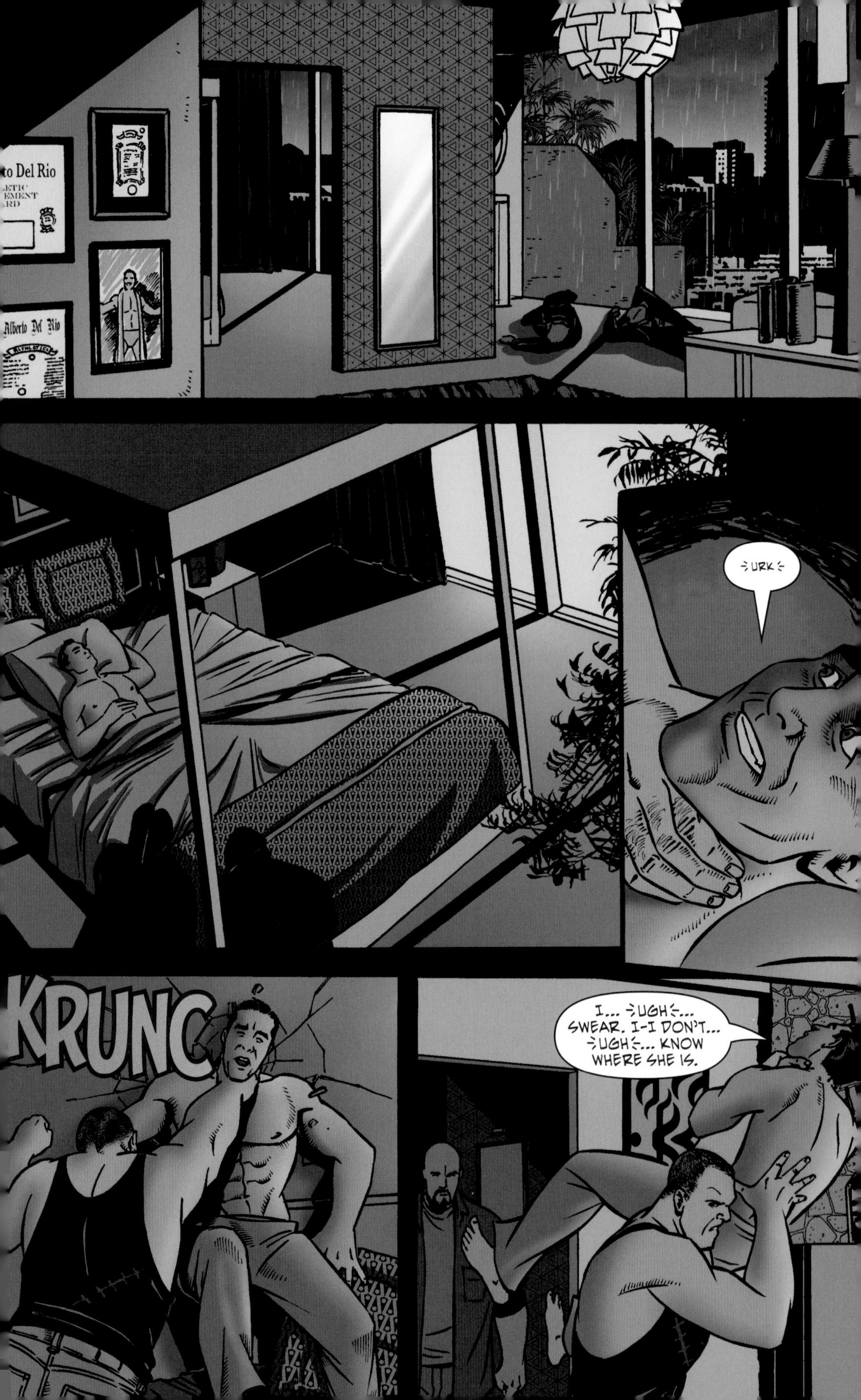
Alberto Del Rio
URK
KRUNC
I... UGH... SWEAR. I-I DON'T... UGH... KNOW WHERE SHE IS.

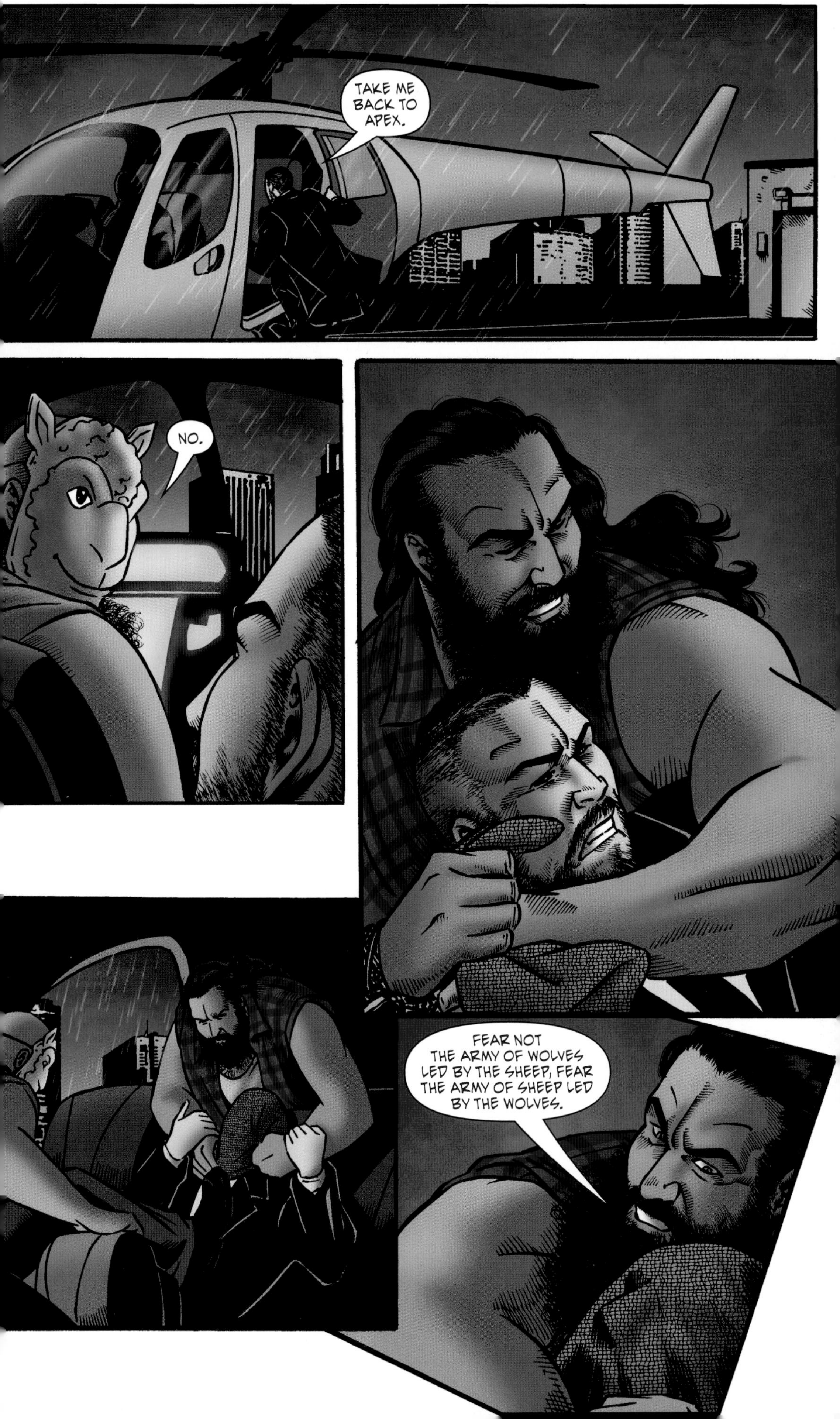
TAKE ME BACK TO APEX.
NO.
FEAR NOT THE ARMY OF WOLVES LED BY THE SHEEP, FEAR THE ARMY OF SHEEP LED BY THE WOLVES.

IS HE HERE?

IN THE BACK ROOM.

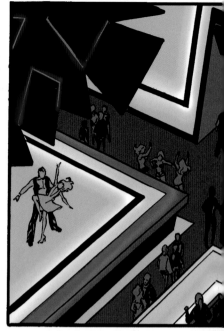

ONLY YOU, PUNK.

NO WAY. I'M GOING--

IT'LL BE FINE.

CM PUNK. YOU WANT AJ. BUT EVERYONE WANTS AJ.

WHY ON EARTH WOULD I HELP YOU?

BECAUSE I KNOW EXACTLY WHERE THE MONEY IS.

THEN SOUN LIKE AND I A DE

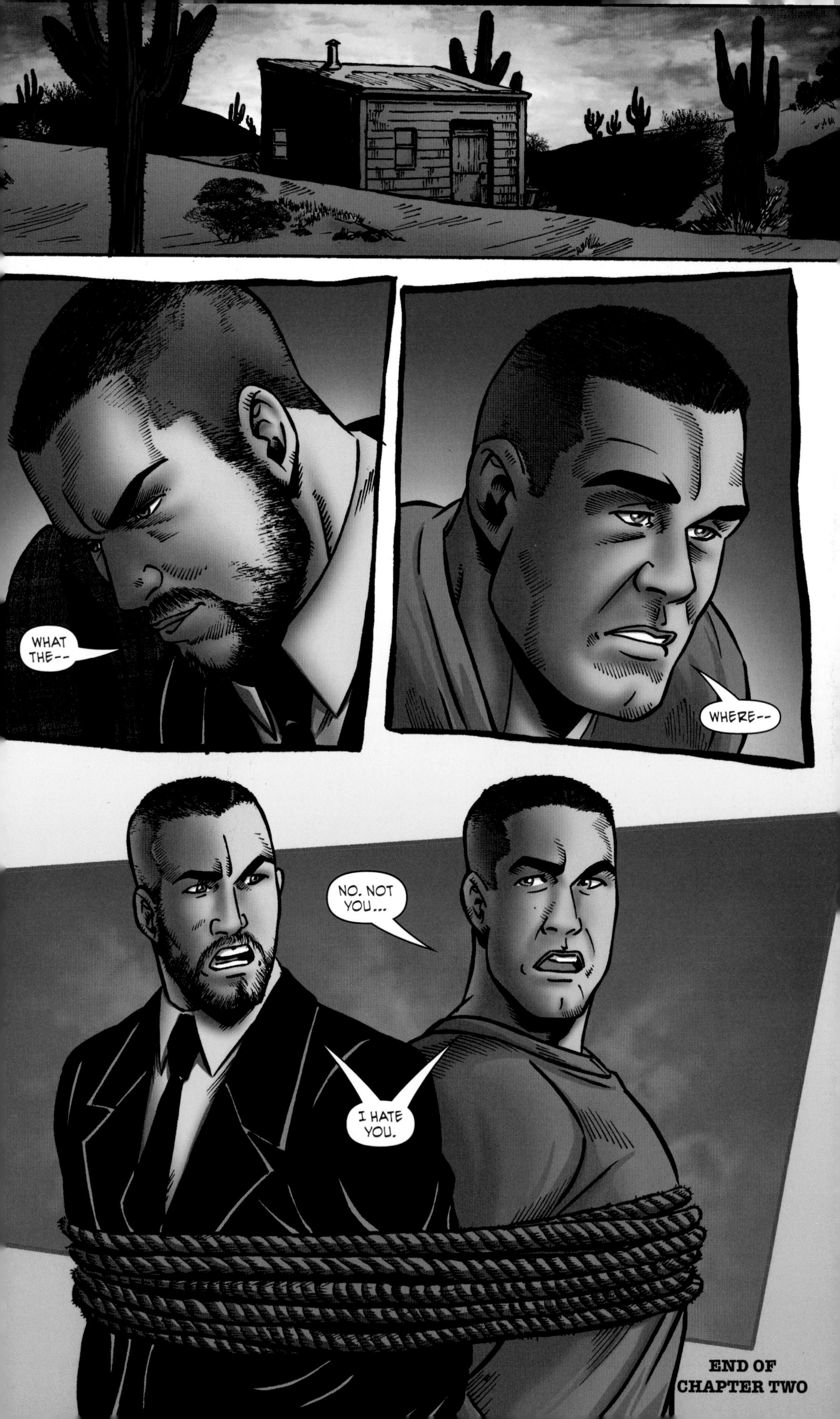
WHAT THE--
WHERE--
NO. NOT YOU...
I HATE YOU.
END OF CHAPTER TWO

CHAPTER THREE:
THE BARRENS

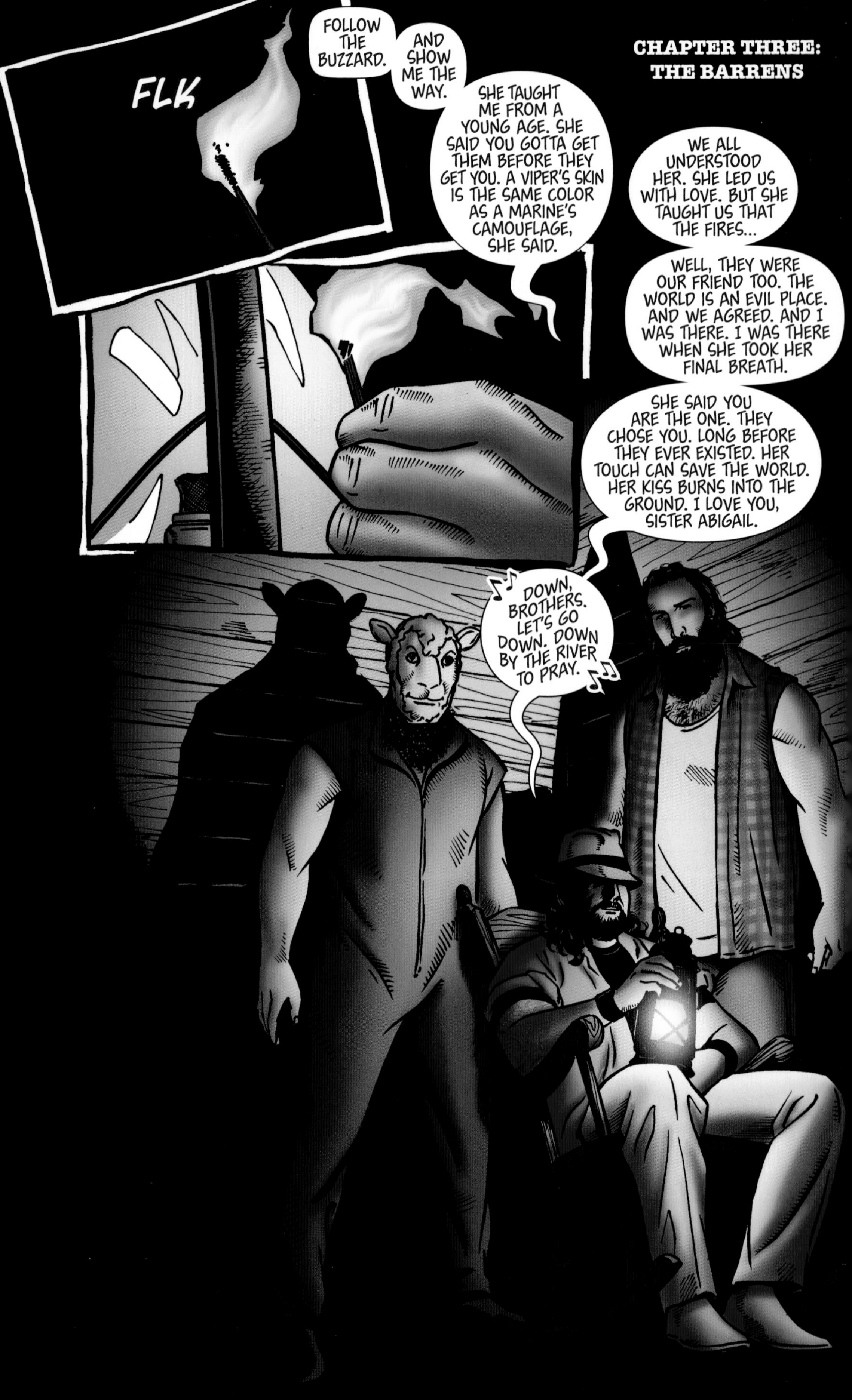
FLK
FOLLOW THE BUZZARD.
AND SHOW ME THE WAY.
SHE TAUGHT ME FROM A YOUNG AGE. SHE SAID YOU GOTTA GET THEM BEFORE THEY GET YOU. A VIPER'S SKIN IS THE SAME COLOR AS A MARINE'S CAMOUFLAGE, SHE SAID.
WE ALL UNDERSTOOD HER. SHE LED US WITH LOVE. BUT SHE TAUGHT US THAT THE FIRES...
WELL, THEY WERE OUR FRIEND TOO. THE WORLD IS AN EVIL PLACE. AND WE AGREED. AND I WAS THERE. I WAS THERE WHEN SHE TOOK HER FINAL BREATH.
SHE SAID YOU ARE THE ONE. THEY CHOSE YOU. LONG BEFORE THEY EVER EXISTED. HER TOUCH CAN SAVE THE WORLD. HER KISS BURNS INTO THE GROUND. I LOVE YOU, SISTER ABIGAIL.
DOWN, BROTHERS. LET'S GO DOWN. DOWN BY THE RIVER TO PRAY.

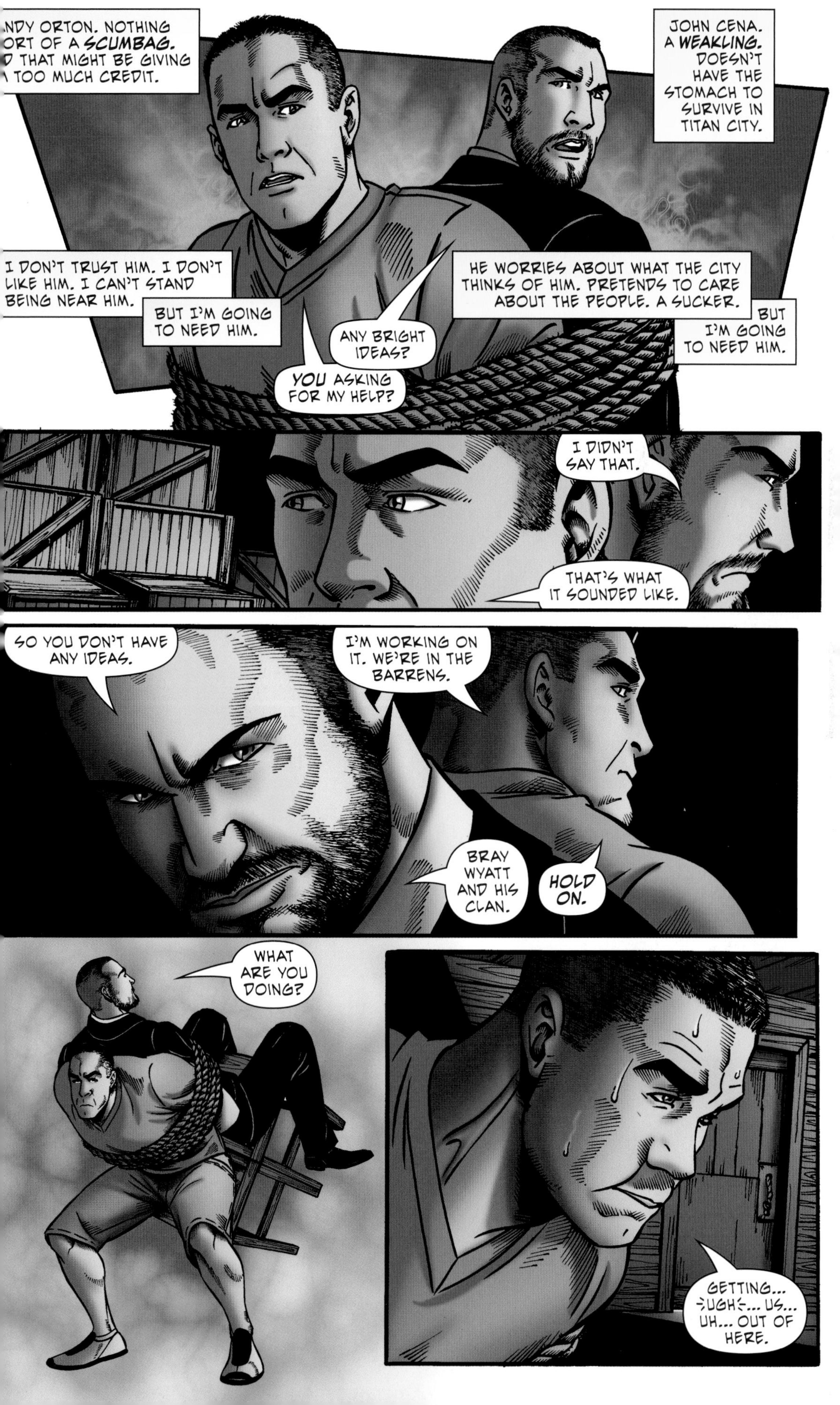

NDY ORTON. NOTHING
ORT OF A SCUMBAG.
D THAT MIGHT BE GIVING
TOO MUCH CREDIT.
JOHN CENA. A WEAKLING. DOESN'T HAVE THE STOMACH TO SURVIVE IN TITAN CITY.
I DON'T TRUST HIM. I DON'T LIKE HIM. I CAN'T STAND BEING NEAR HIM.
BUT I'M GOING TO NEED HIM.
HE WORRIES ABOUT WHAT THE CITY THINKS OF HIM. PRETENDS TO CARE ABOUT THE PEOPLE. A SUCKER.
BUT I'M GOING TO NEED HIM.
ANY BRIGHT IDEAS?
YOU ASKING FOR MY HELP?
I DIDN'T SAY THAT.
THAT'S WHAT IT SOUNDED LIKE.
SO YOU DON'T HAVE ANY IDEAS.
I'M WORKING ON IT. WE'RE IN THE BARRENS.
BRAY WYATT AND HIS CLAN.
HOLD ON.
WHAT ARE YOU DOING?
GETTING... UGH... US... UH... OUT OF HERE.

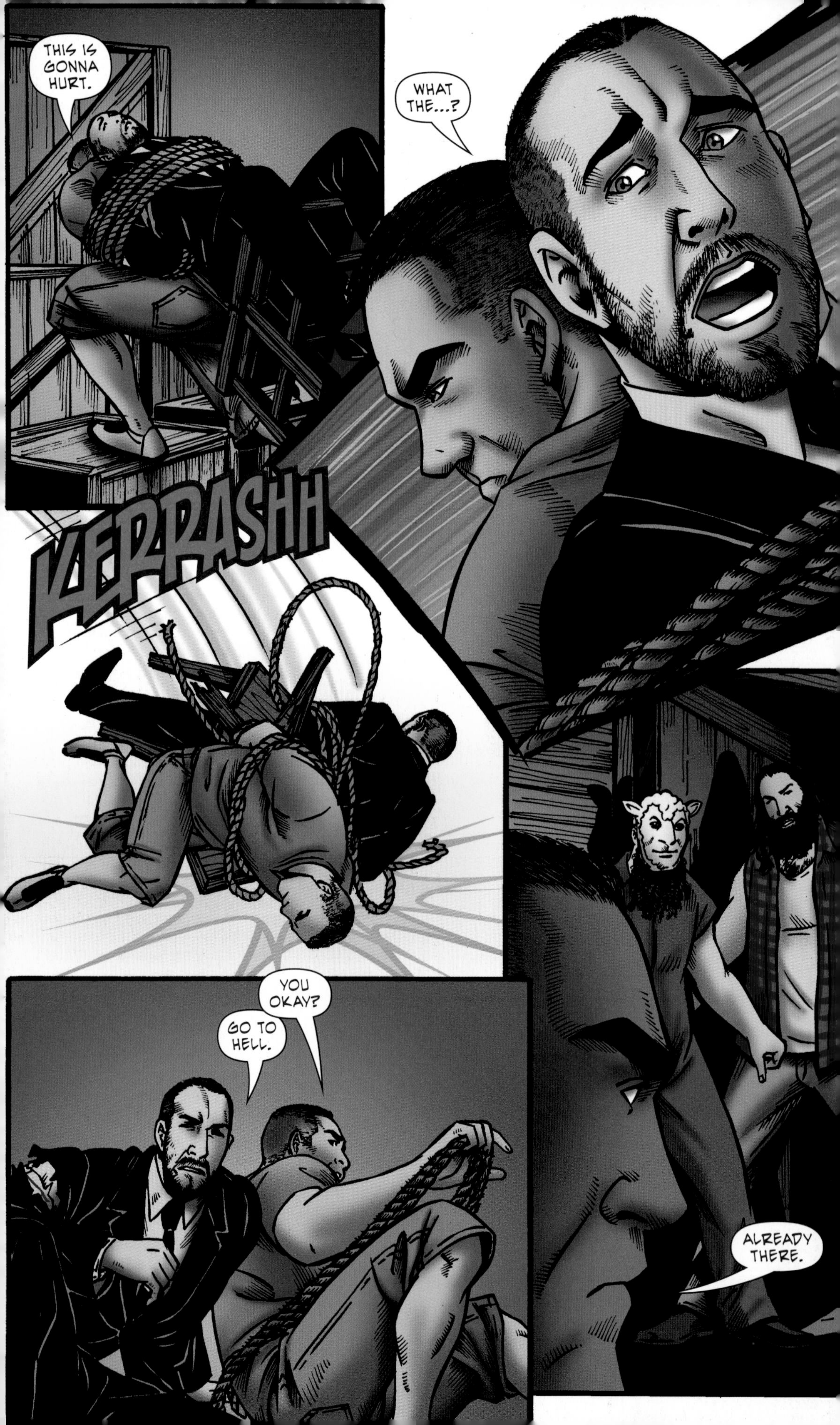
THIS IS GONNA HURT.
WHAT THE...?
KERRASHH
YOU OKAY?
GO TO HELL.
ALREADY THERE.

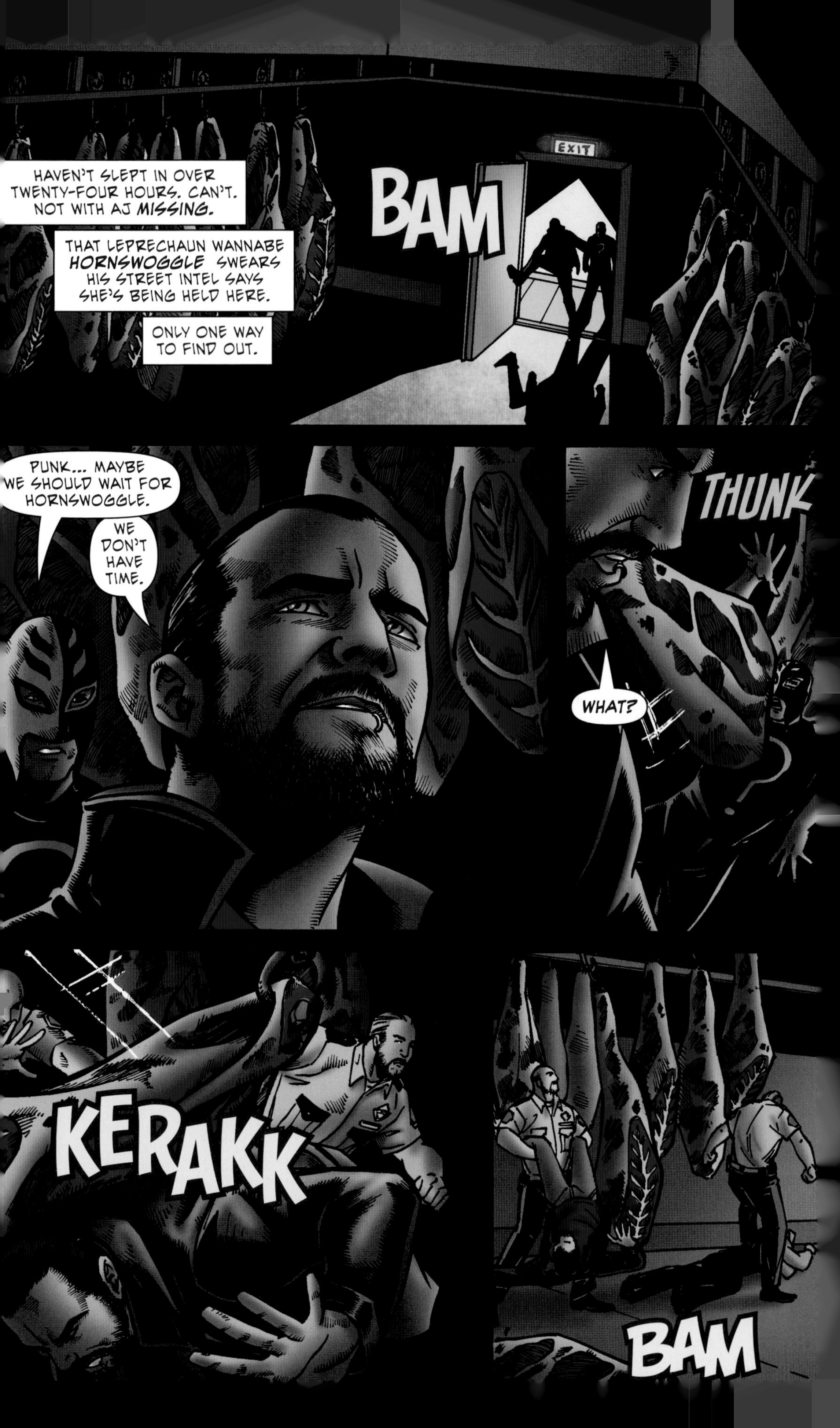
HAVEN'T SLEPT IN OVER TWENTY-FOUR HOURS. CAN'T. NOT WITH AJ *MISSING.*
THAT LEPRECHAUN WANNABE ***HORNSWOGGLE*** SWEARS HIS STREET INTEL SAYS SHE'S BEING HELD HERE.
ONLY ONE WAY TO FIND OUT.
EXIT
BAM
PUNK... MAYBE WE SHOULD WAIT FOR HORNSWOGGLE.
WE DON'T HAVE TIME.
THUNK
WHAT?
KERAKK
BAM

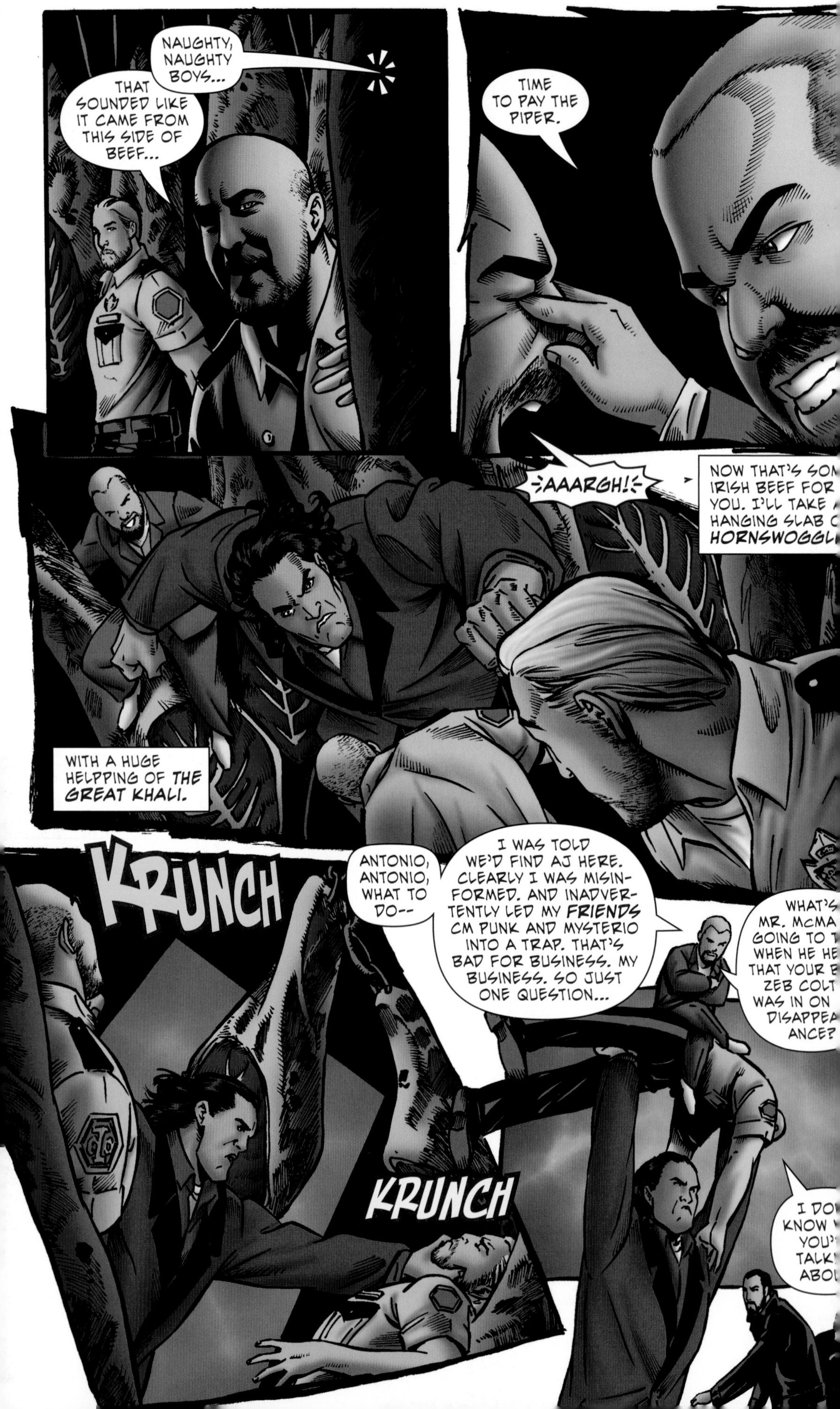
NAUGHTY, NAUGHTY BOYS...
THAT SOUNDED LIKE IT CAME FROM THIS SIDE OF BEEF...
TIME TO PAY THE PIPER.
AAARGH!
NOW THAT'S SOM
IRISH BEEF FOR
YOU. I'LL TAKE A
HANGING SLAB O
HORNSWOGGL
WITH A HUGE HELPING OF THE GREAT KHALI.
KRUNCH
ANTONIO, ANTONIO, WHAT TO DO--
I WAS TOLD WE'D FIND AJ HERE. CLEARLY I WAS MISIN-FORMED. AND INADVER-TENTLY LED MY FRIENDS CM PUNK AND MYSTERIO INTO A TRAP. THAT'S BAD FOR BUSINESS. MY BUSINESS. SO JUST ONE QUESTION...
WHAT'S
MR. MCMA
GOING TO
WHEN HE HE
THAT YOUR
ZEB COLT
WAS IN ON
DISAPPEA
ANCE?
KRUNCH
I DO
KNOW
YOU'
TALK
ABO

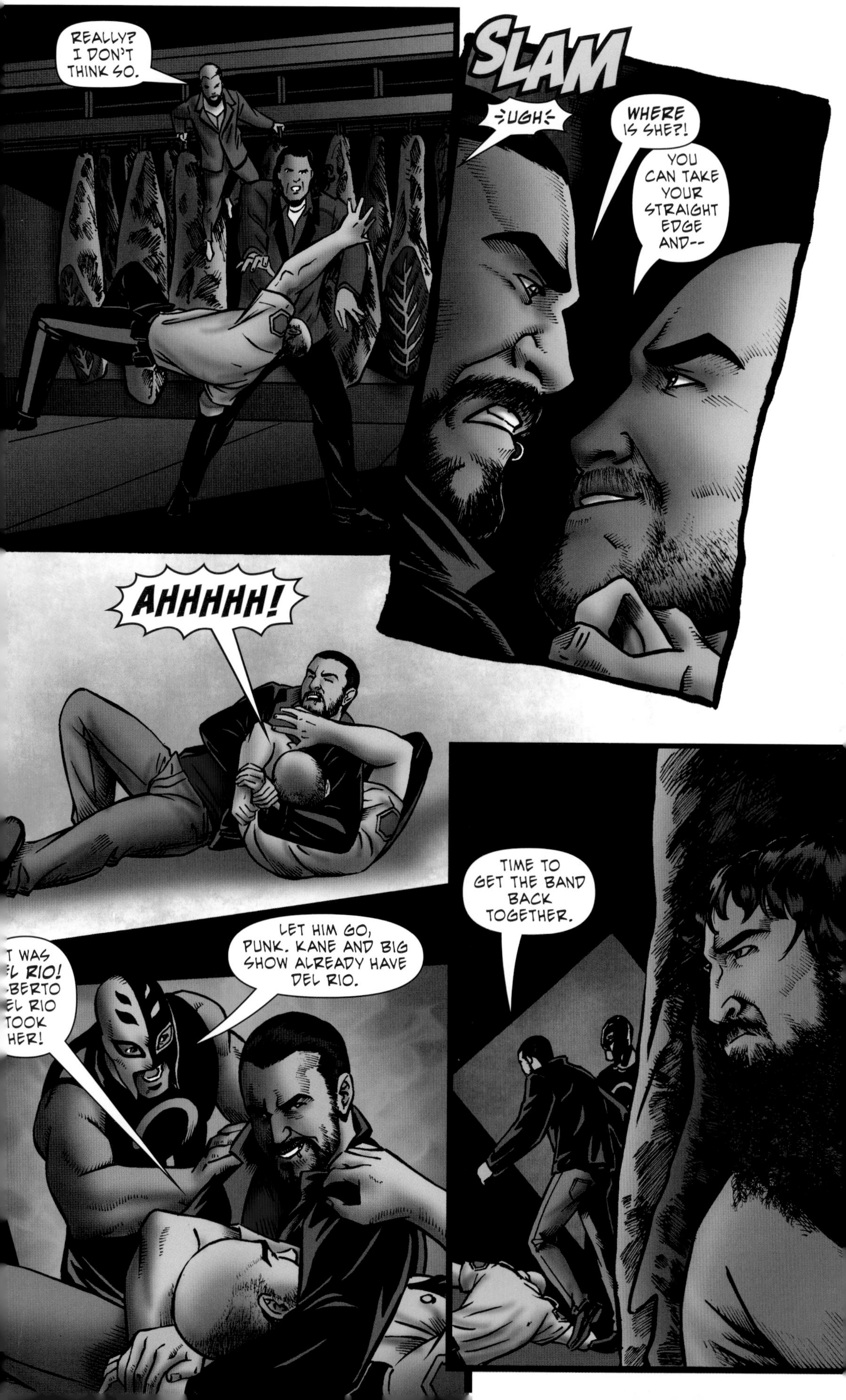
REALLY? I DON'T THINK SO.
SLAM
UGH
WHERE IS SHE?!
YOU CAN TAKE YOUR STRAIGHT EDGE AND--
AHHHHH!
T WAS
L RIO!
BERTO
EL RIO
TOOK
HER!
LET HIM GO, PUNK. KANE AND BIG SHOW ALREADY HAVE DEL RIO.
TIME TO GET THE BAND BACK TOGETHER.

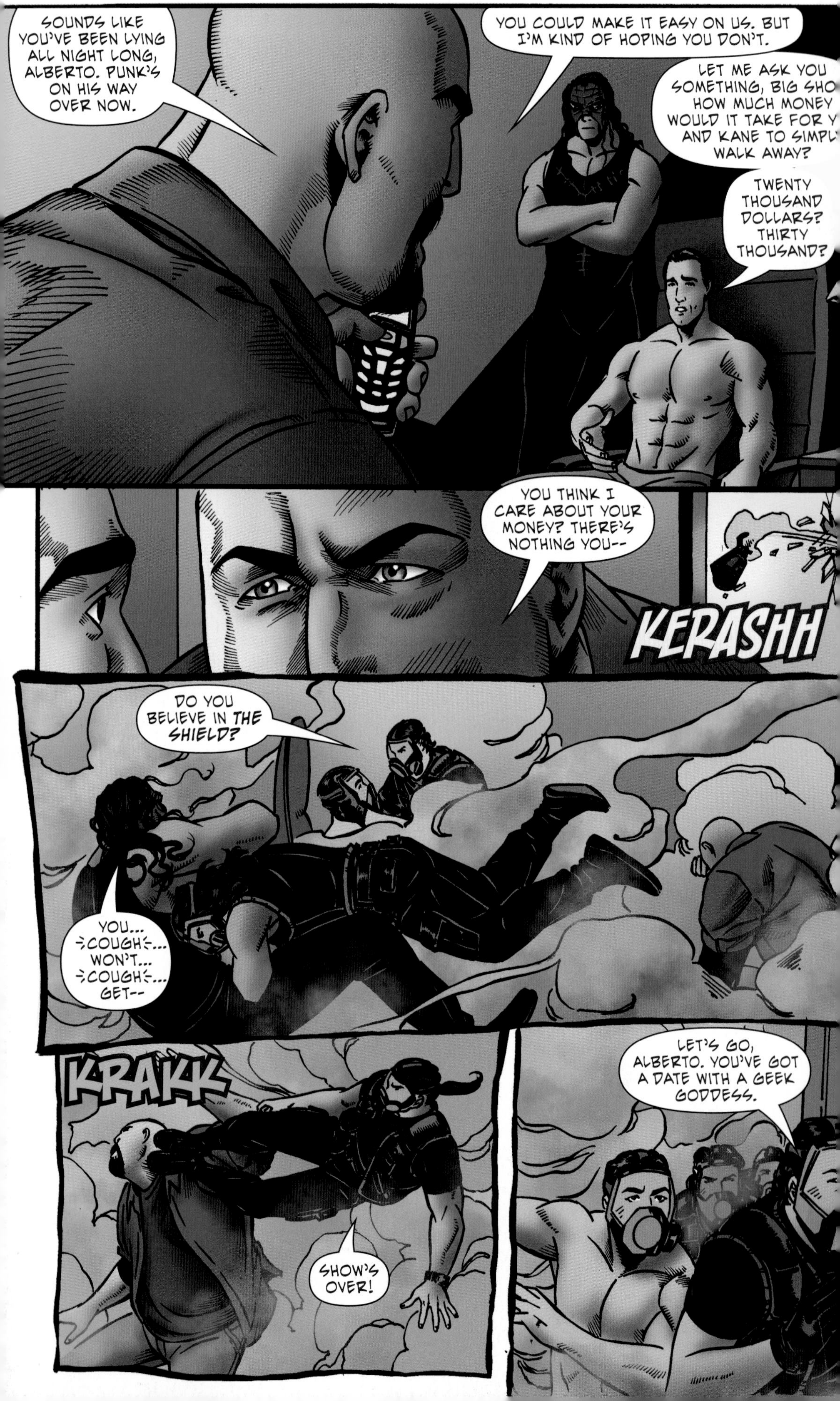
SOUNDS LIKE YOU'VE BEEN LYING ALL NIGHT LONG, ALBERTO. PUNK'S ON HIS WAY OVER NOW.
YOU COULD MAKE IT EASY ON US. BUT I'M KIND OF HOPING YOU DON'T.
LET ME ASK YOU SOMETHING, BIG SHO HOW MUCH MONEY WOULD IT TAKE FOR Y AND KANE TO SIMPL WALK AWAY?
TWENTY THOUSAND DOLLARS? THIRTY THOUSAND?
YOU THINK I CARE ABOUT YOUR MONEY? THERE'S NOTHING YOU--
KERASHH
DO YOU BELIEVE IN THE SHIELD?
YOU... COUGH... WON'T... COUGH... GET--
KRAKK
SHOW'S OVER!
LET'S GO, ALBERTO. YOU'VE GOT A DATE WITH A GEEK GODDESS.

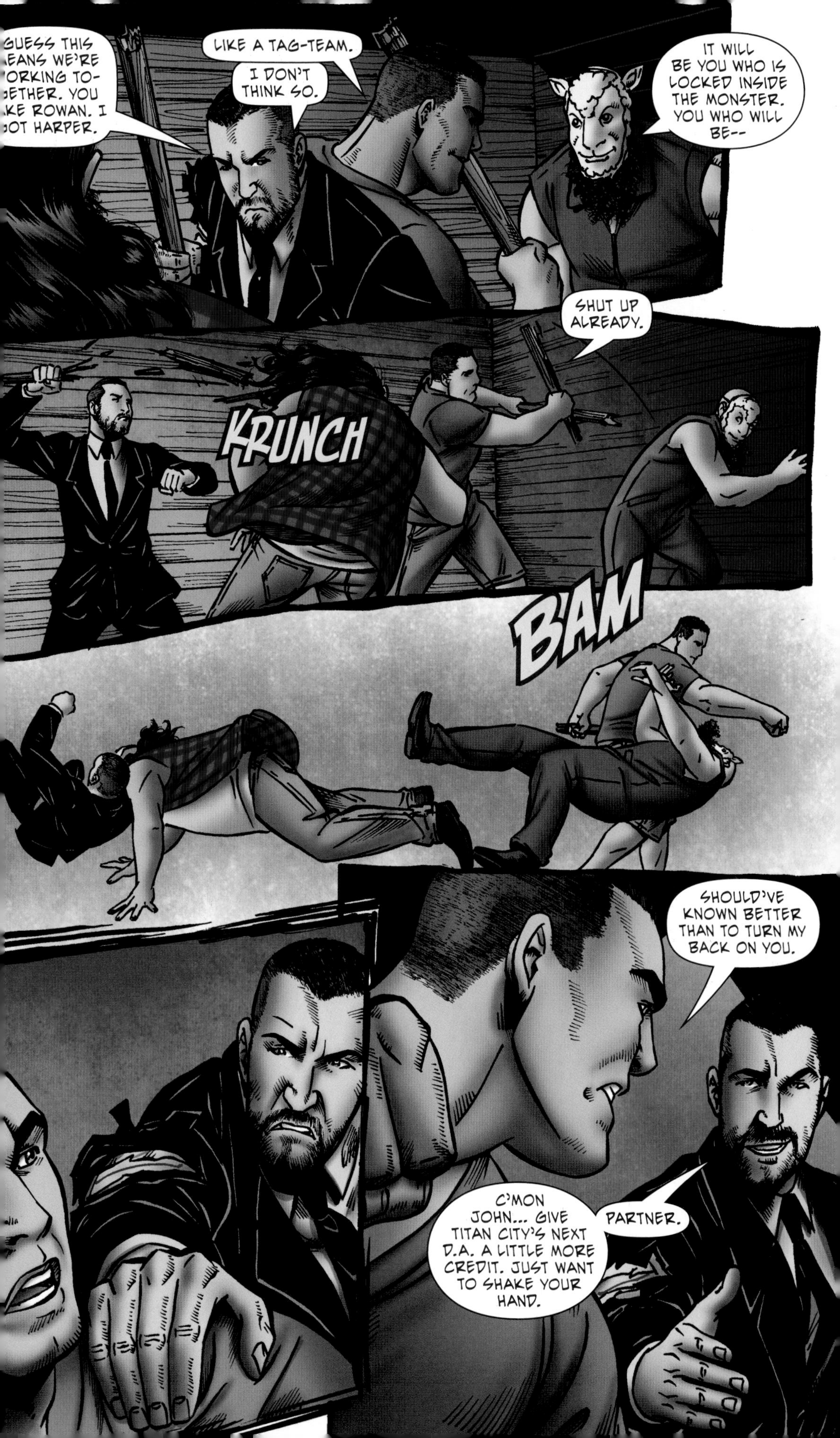

GUESS THIS
EANS WE'RE
ORKING TO-
GETHER. YOU
KE ROWAN. I
GOT HARPER.
LIKE A TAG-TEAM.
I DON'T THINK SO.
IT WILL BE YOU WHO IS LOCKED INSIDE THE MONSTER. YOU WHO WILL BE--
SHUT UP ALREADY.
KRUNCH
BAM
SHOULD'VE KNOWN BETTER THAN TO TURN MY BACK ON YOU.
C'MON JOHN... GIVE TITAN CITY'S NEXT D.A. A LITTLE MORE CREDIT. JUST WANT TO SHAKE YOUR HAND.
PARTNER.

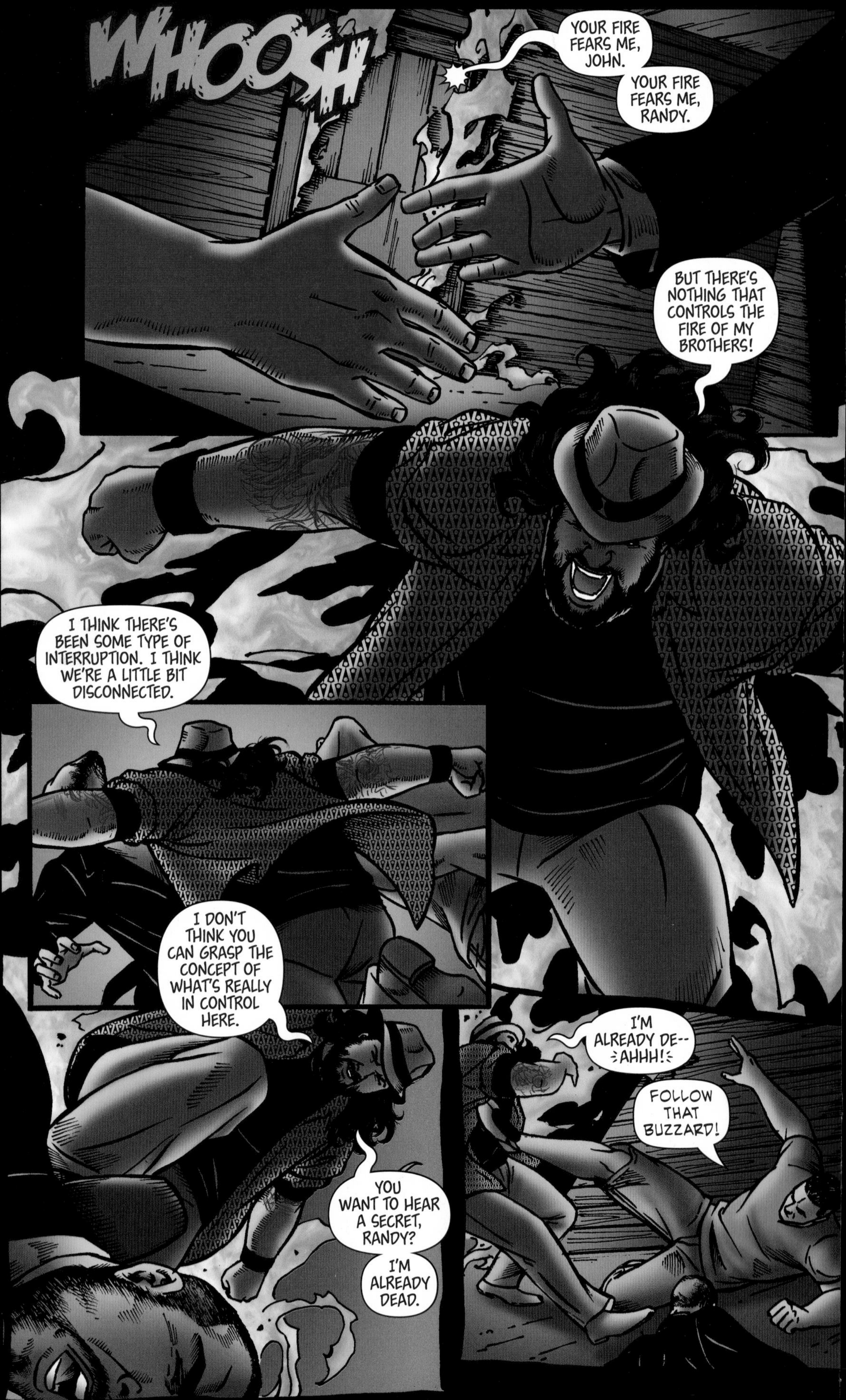
WHOOSH
YOUR FIRE FEARS ME, JOHN.
YOUR FIRE FEARS ME, RANDY.
BUT THERE'S NOTHING THAT CONTROLS THE FIRE OF MY BROTHERS!
I THINK THERE'S BEEN SOME TYPE OF INTERRUPTION. I THINK WE'RE A LITTLE BIT DISCONNECTED.
I DON'T THINK YOU CAN GRASP THE CONCEPT OF WHAT'S REALLY IN CONTROL HERE.
YOU WANT TO HEAR A SECRET, RANDY?
I'M ALREADY DEAD.
I'M ALREADY DE-- AHHH!
FOLLOW THAT BUZZARD!

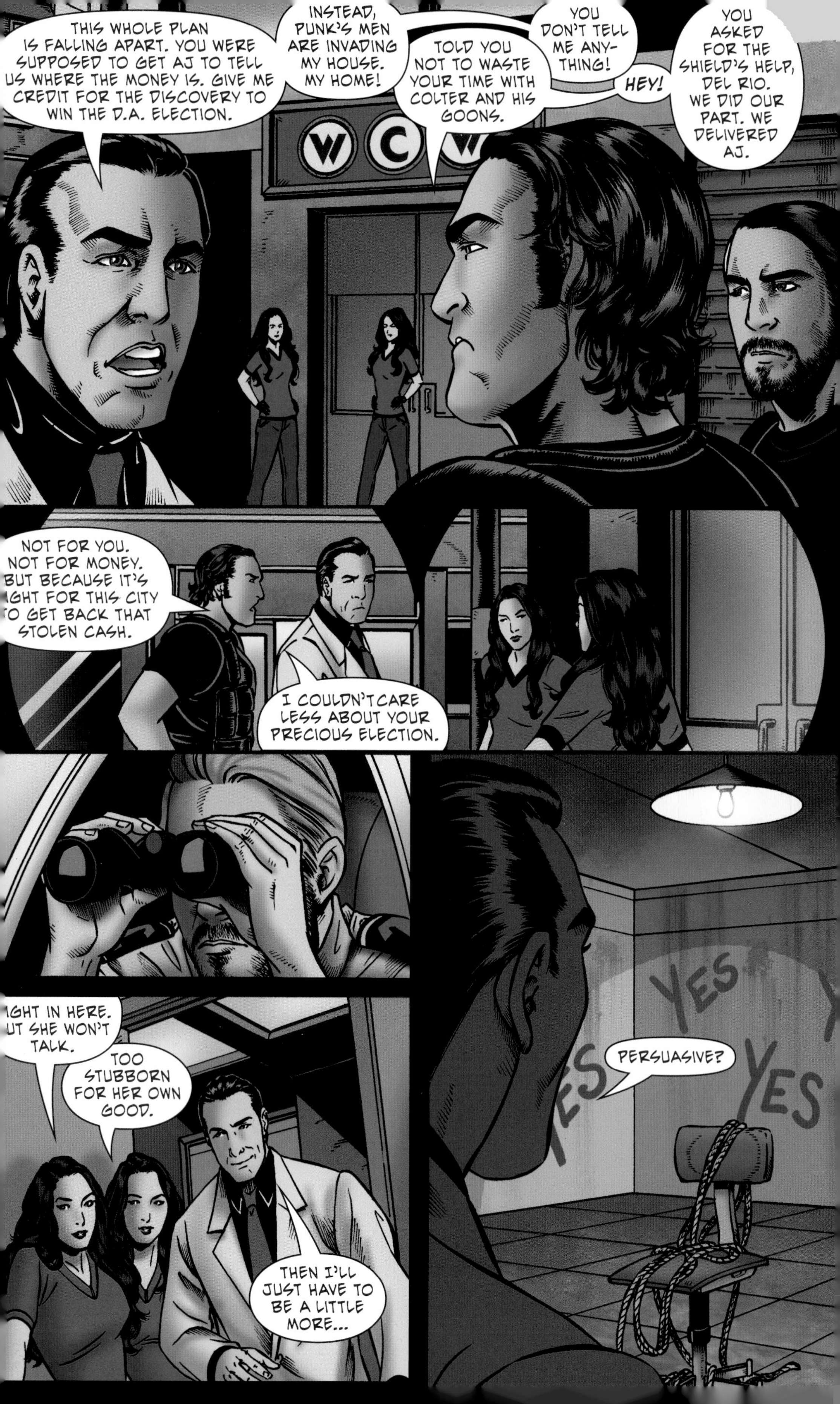
THIS WHOLE PLAN IS FALLING APART. YOU WERE SUPPOSED TO GET AJ TO TELL US WHERE THE MONEY IS. GIVE ME CREDIT FOR THE DISCOVERY TO WIN THE D.A. ELECTION.
INSTEAD, PUNK'S MEN ARE INVADING MY HOUSE. MY HOME!
TOLD YOU NOT TO WASTE YOUR TIME WITH COLTER AND HIS GOONS.
YOU DON'T TELL ME ANY-THING!
HEY!
YOU ASKED FOR THE SHIELD'S HELP, DEL RIO. WE DID OUR PART. WE DELIVERED AJ.
WCW
NOT FOR YOU. NOT FOR MONEY. BUT BECAUSE IT'S IGHT FOR THIS CITY O GET BACK THAT STOLEN CASH.
I COULDN'T CARE LESS ABOUT YOUR PRECIOUS ELECTION.
IGHT IN HERE. UT SHE WON'T TALK.
TOO STUBBORN FOR HER OWN GOOD.
THEN I'LL JUST HAVE TO BE A LITTLE MORE...
PERSUASIVE?
YES YES YES YES

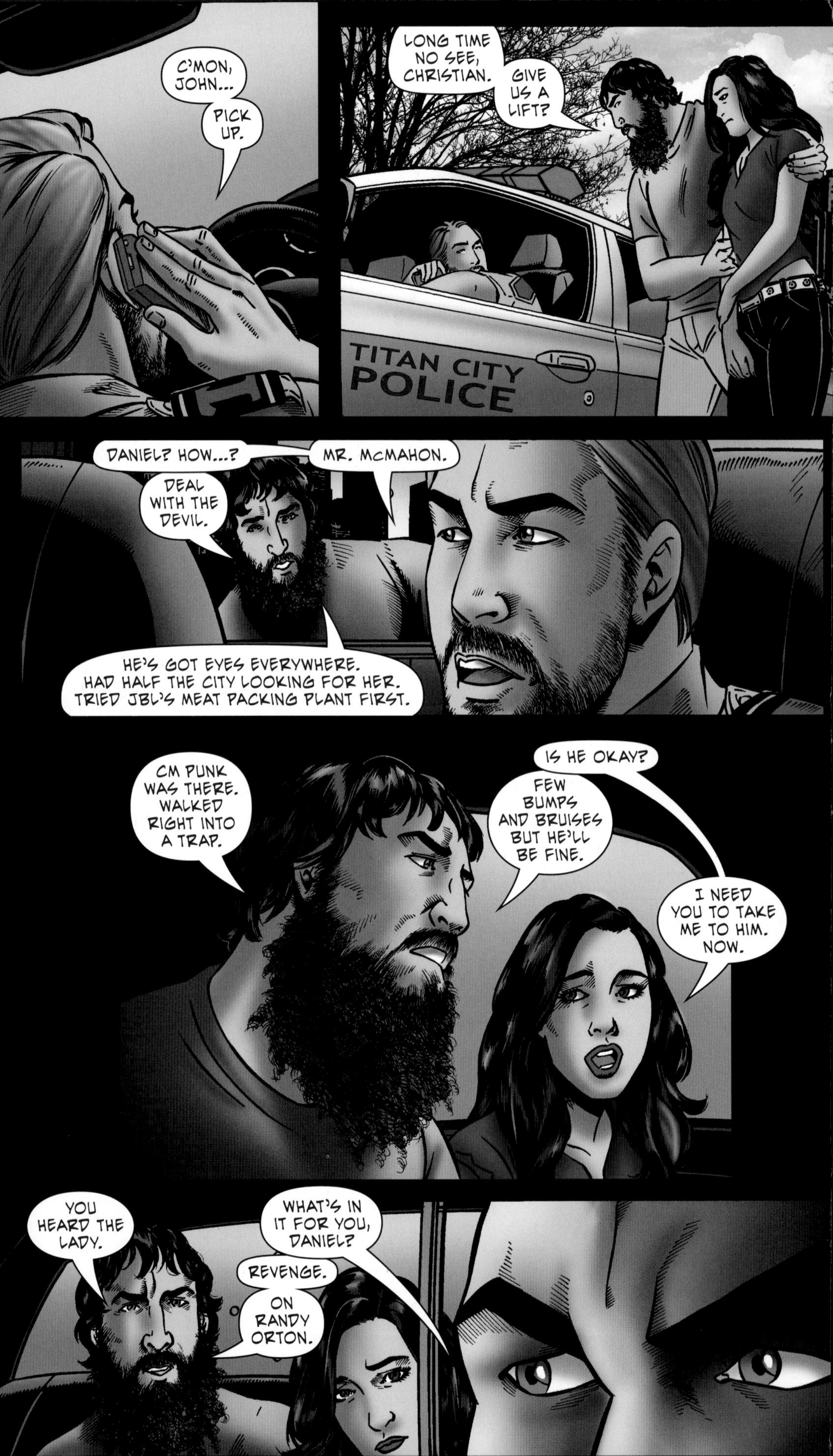
C'MON, JOHN...
PICK UP.
LONG TIME NO SEE, CHRISTIAN.
GIVE US A LIFT?
TITAN CITY POLICE
DANIEL? HOW...?
MR. MCMAHON.
DEAL WITH THE DEVIL.
HE'S GOT EYES EVERYWHERE. HAD HALF THE CITY LOOKING FOR HER. TRIED JBL'S MEAT PACKING PLANT FIRST.
CM PUNK WAS THERE. WALKED RIGHT INTO A TRAP.
IS HE OKAY?
FEW BUMPS AND BRUISES BUT HE'LL BE FINE.
I NEED YOU TO TAKE ME TO HIM. NOW.
YOU HEARD THE LADY.
WHAT'S IN IT FOR YOU, DANIEL?
REVENGE.
ON RANDY ORTON.

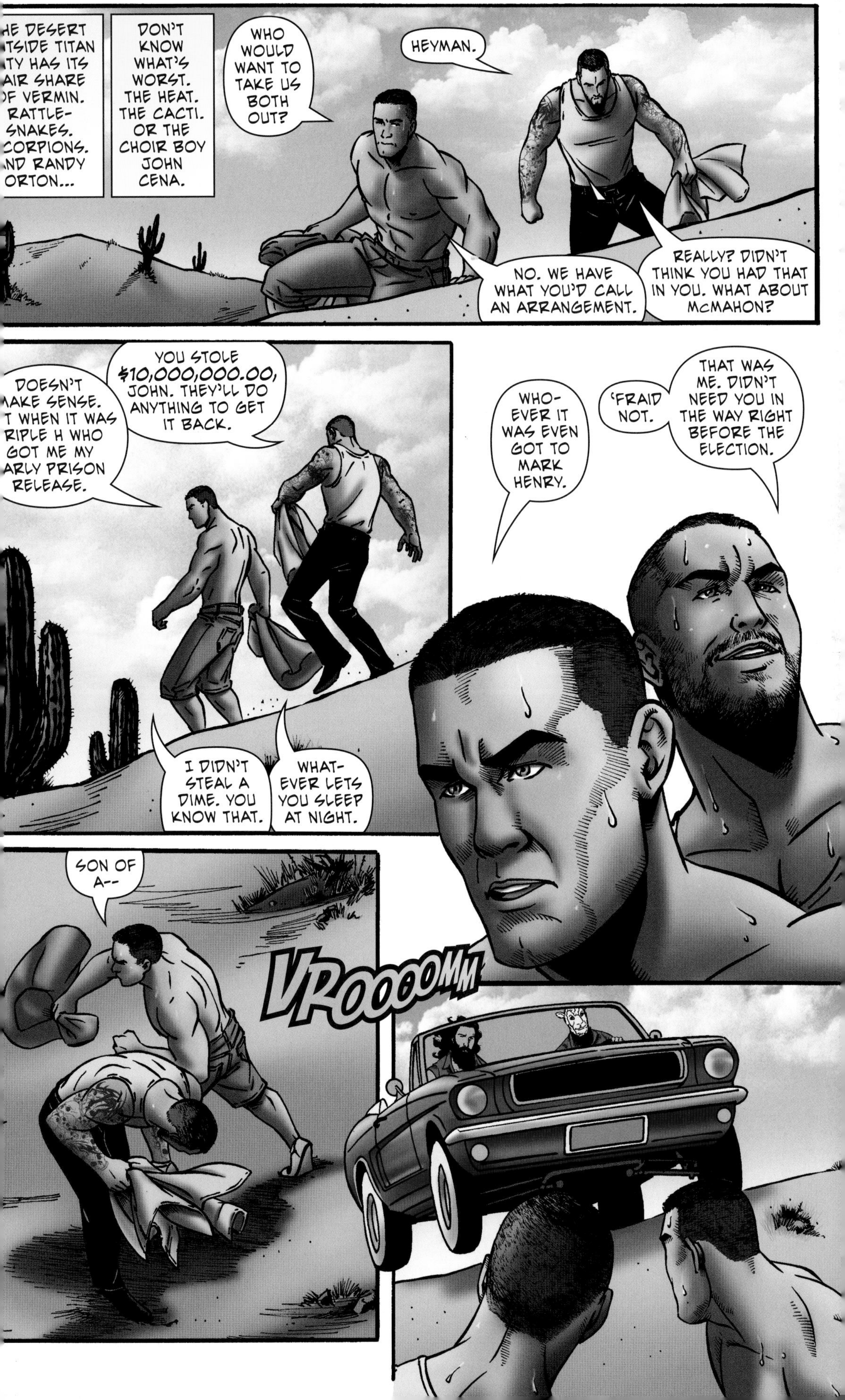
HE DESERT TSIDE TITAN TY HAS ITS AIR SHARE F VERMIN. RATTLE-SNAKES. CORPIONS. ND RANDY ORTON...
DON'T KNOW WHAT'S WORST. THE HEAT. THE CACTI. OR THE CHOIR BOY JOHN CENA.
WHO WOULD WANT TO TAKE US BOTH OUT?
HEYMAN.
NO. WE HAVE WHAT YOU'D CALL AN ARRANGEMENT.
REALLY? DIDN'T THINK YOU HAD THAT IN YOU. WHAT ABOUT McMAHON?
DOESN'T AKE SENSE. T WHEN IT WAS RIPLE H WHO GOT ME MY ARLY PRISON RELEASE.
YOU STOLE $10,000,000.00, JOHN. THEY'LL DO ANYTHING TO GET IT BACK.
I DIDN'T STEAL A DIME. YOU KNOW THAT.
WHAT-EVER LETS YOU SLEEP AT NIGHT.
WHO-EVER IT WAS EVEN GOT TO MARK HENRY.
'FRAID NOT.
THAT WAS ME. DIDN'T NEED YOU IN THE WAY RIGHT BEFORE THE ELECTION.
SON OF A--
VROOOOOMM

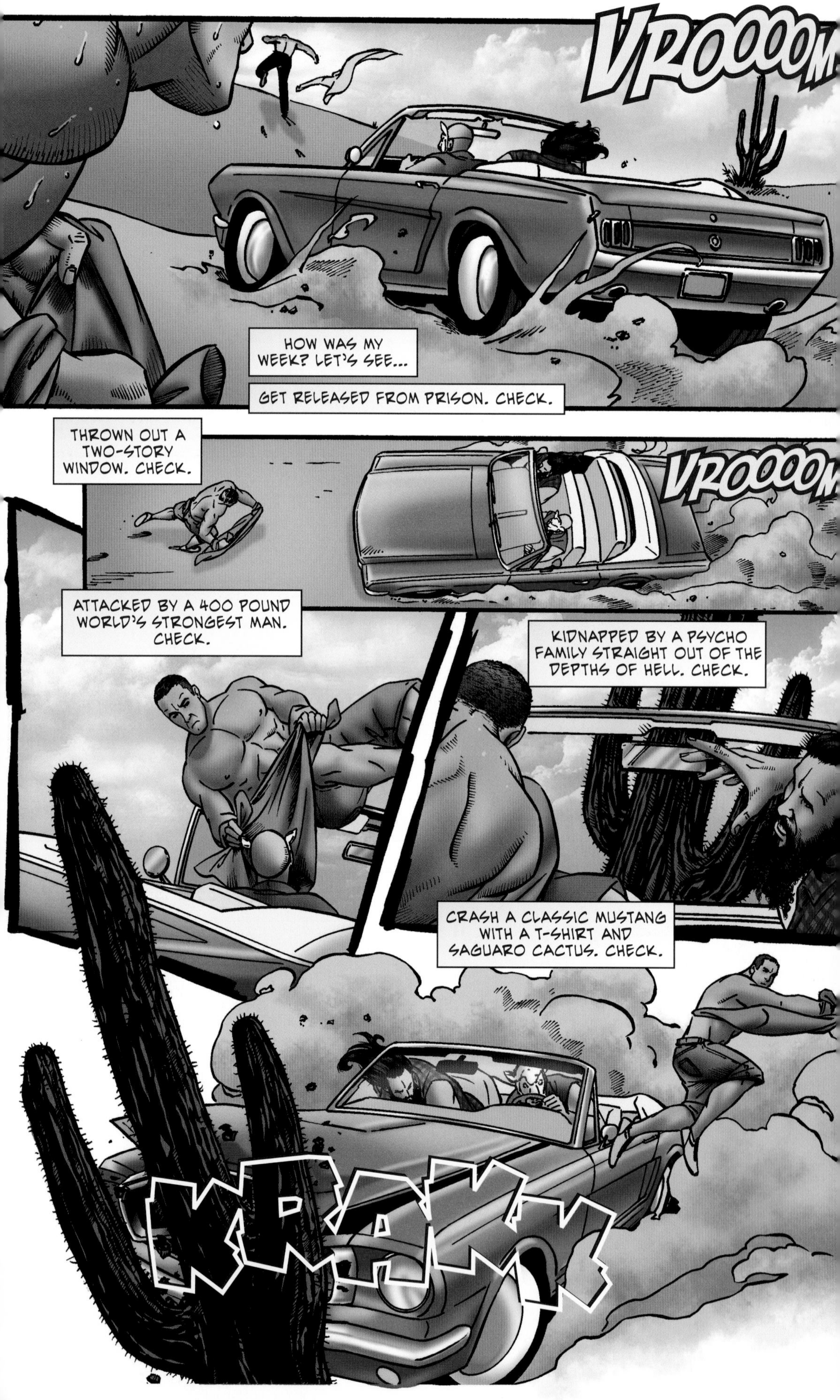
VROOOOM
HOW WAS MY WEEK? LET'S SEE...
GET RELEASED FROM PRISON. CHECK.
THROWN OUT A TWO-STORY WINDOW. CHECK.
VROOOOM
ATTACKED BY A 400 POUND WORLD'S STRONGEST MAN. CHECK.
KIDNAPPED BY A PSYCHO FAMILY STRAIGHT OUT OF THE DEPTHS OF HELL. CHECK.
CRASH A CLASSIC MUSTANG WITH A T-SHIRT AND SAGUARO CACTUS. CHECK.
KRAKK

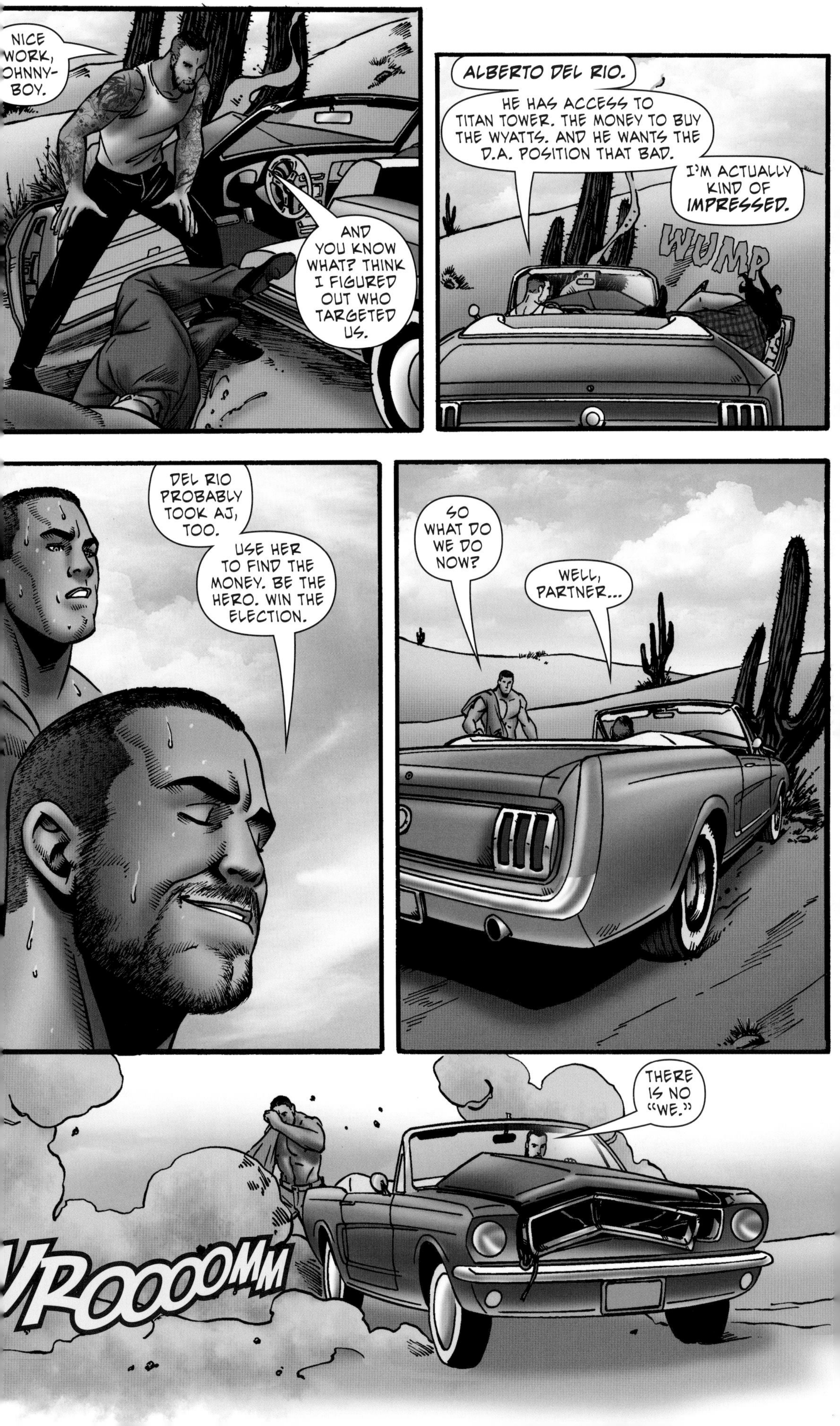
NICE WORK, JOHNNY-BOY.
AND YOU KNOW WHAT? THINK I FIGURED OUT WHO TARGETED US.
ALBERTO DEL RIO.
HE HAS ACCESS TO TITAN TOWER. THE MONEY TO BUY THE WYATTS. AND HE WANTS THE D.A. POSITION THAT BAD.
I'M ACTUALLY KIND OF IMPRESSED.
WUMP
DEL RIO PROBABLY TOOK AJ, TOO.
USE HER TO FIND THE MONEY. BE THE HERO. WIN THE ELECTION.
SO WHAT DO WE DO NOW?
WELL, PARTNER...
THERE IS NO "WE."
VROOOOMM

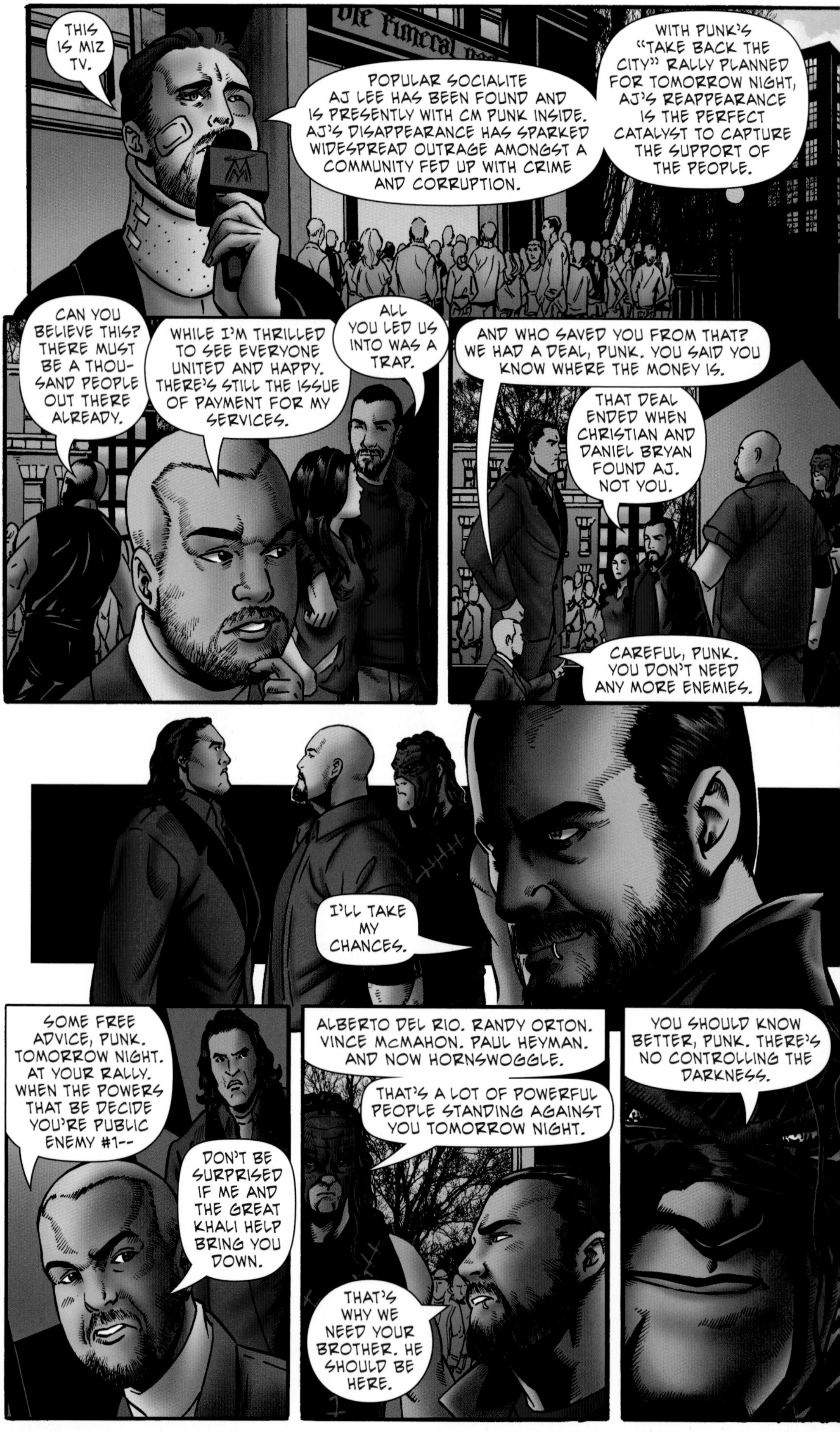

THIS IS MIZ TV.
POPULAR SOCIALITE AJ LEE HAS BEEN FOUND AND IS PRESENTLY WITH CM PUNK INSIDE. AJ'S DISAPPEARANCE HAS SPARKED WIDESPREAD OUTRAGE AMONGST A COMMUNITY FED UP WITH CRIME AND CORRUPTION.
WITH PUNK'S "TAKE BACK THE CITY" RALLY PLANNED FOR TOMORROW NIGHT, AJ'S REAPPEARANCE IS THE PERFECT CATALYST TO CAPTURE THE SUPPORT OF THE PEOPLE.
CAN YOU BELIEVE THIS? THERE MUST BE A THOU-SAND PEOPLE OUT THERE ALREADY.
WHILE I'M THRILLED TO SEE EVERYONE UNITED AND HAPPY. THERE'S STILL THE ISSUE OF PAYMENT FOR MY SERVICES.
ALL YOU LED US INTO WAS A TRAP.
AND WHO SAVED YOU FROM THAT? WE HAD A DEAL, PUNK. YOU SAID YOU KNOW WHERE THE MONEY IS.
THAT DEAL ENDED WHEN CHRISTIAN AND DANIEL BRYAN FOUND AJ. NOT YOU.
CAREFUL, PUNK. YOU DON'T NEED ANY MORE ENEMIES.
I'LL TAKE MY CHANCES.
SOME FREE ADVICE, PUNK. TOMORROW NIGHT. AT YOUR RALLY. WHEN THE POWERS THAT BE DECIDE YOU'RE PUBLIC ENEMY #1--
DON'T BE SURPRISED IF ME AND THE GREAT KHALI HELP BRING YOU DOWN.
ALBERTO DEL RIO. RANDY ORTON. VINCE McMAHON. PAUL HEYMAN. AND NOW HORNSWOGGLE.
THAT'S A LOT OF POWERFUL PEOPLE STANDING AGAINST YOU TOMORROW NIGHT.
THAT'S WHY WE NEED YOUR BROTHER. HE SHOULD BE HERE.
YOU SHOULD KNOW BETTER, PUNK. THERE'S NO CONTROLLING THE DARKNESS.

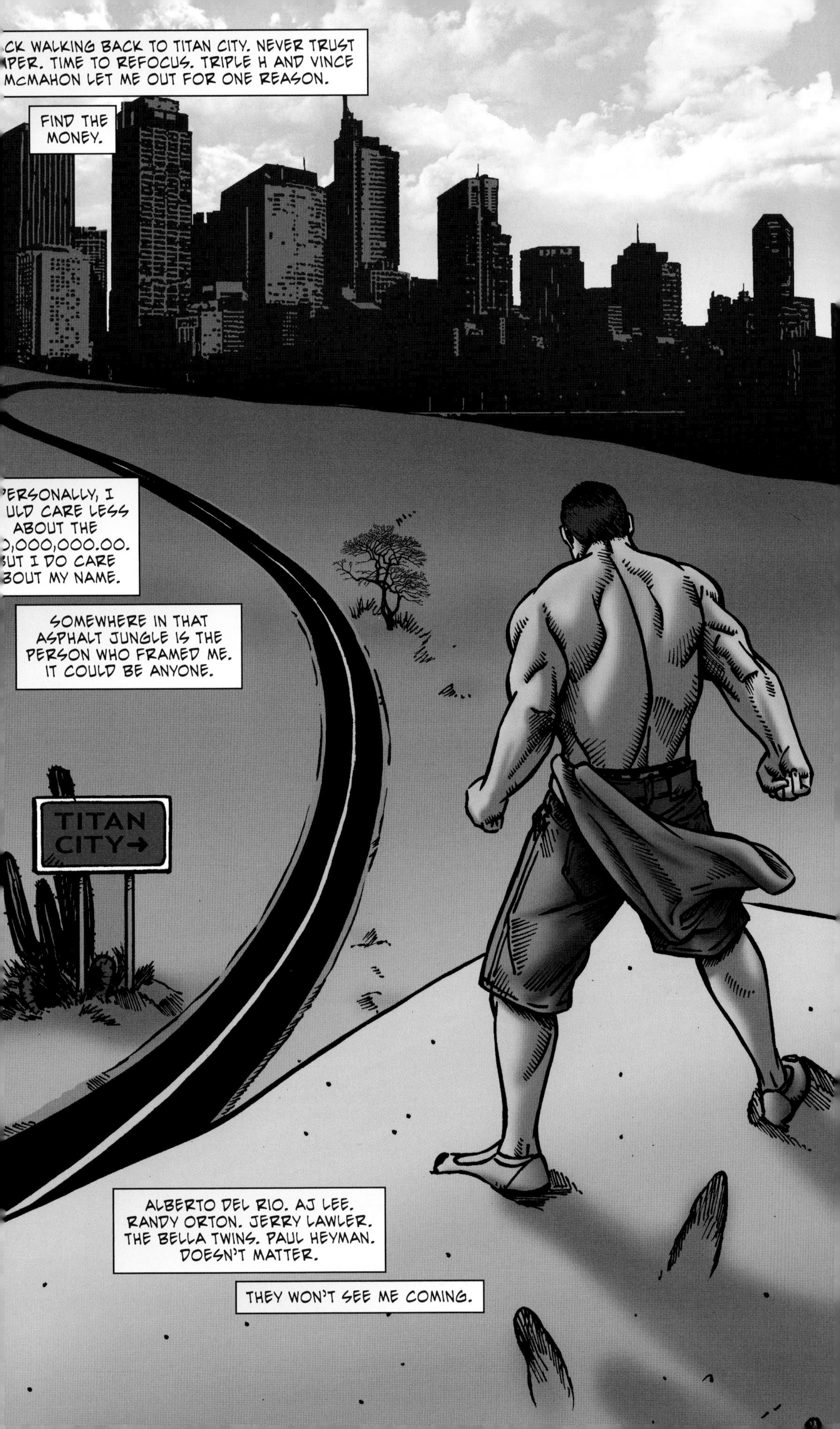
CK WALKING BACK TO TITAN CITY. NEVER TRUST
PER. TIME TO REFOCUS. TRIPLE H AND VINCE
McMAHON LET ME OUT FOR ONE REASON.
FIND THE MONEY.
ERSONALLY, I
ULD CARE LESS
ABOUT THE
,000,000.00.
UT I DO CARE
BOUT MY NAME.
SOMEWHERE IN THAT ASPHALT JUNGLE IS THE PERSON WHO FRAMED ME. IT COULD BE ANYONE.
TITAN CITY→
ALBERTO DEL RIO. AJ LEE. RANDY ORTON. JERRY LAWLER. THE BELLA TWINS. PAUL HEYMAN. DOESN'T MATTER.
THEY WON'T SEE ME COMING.

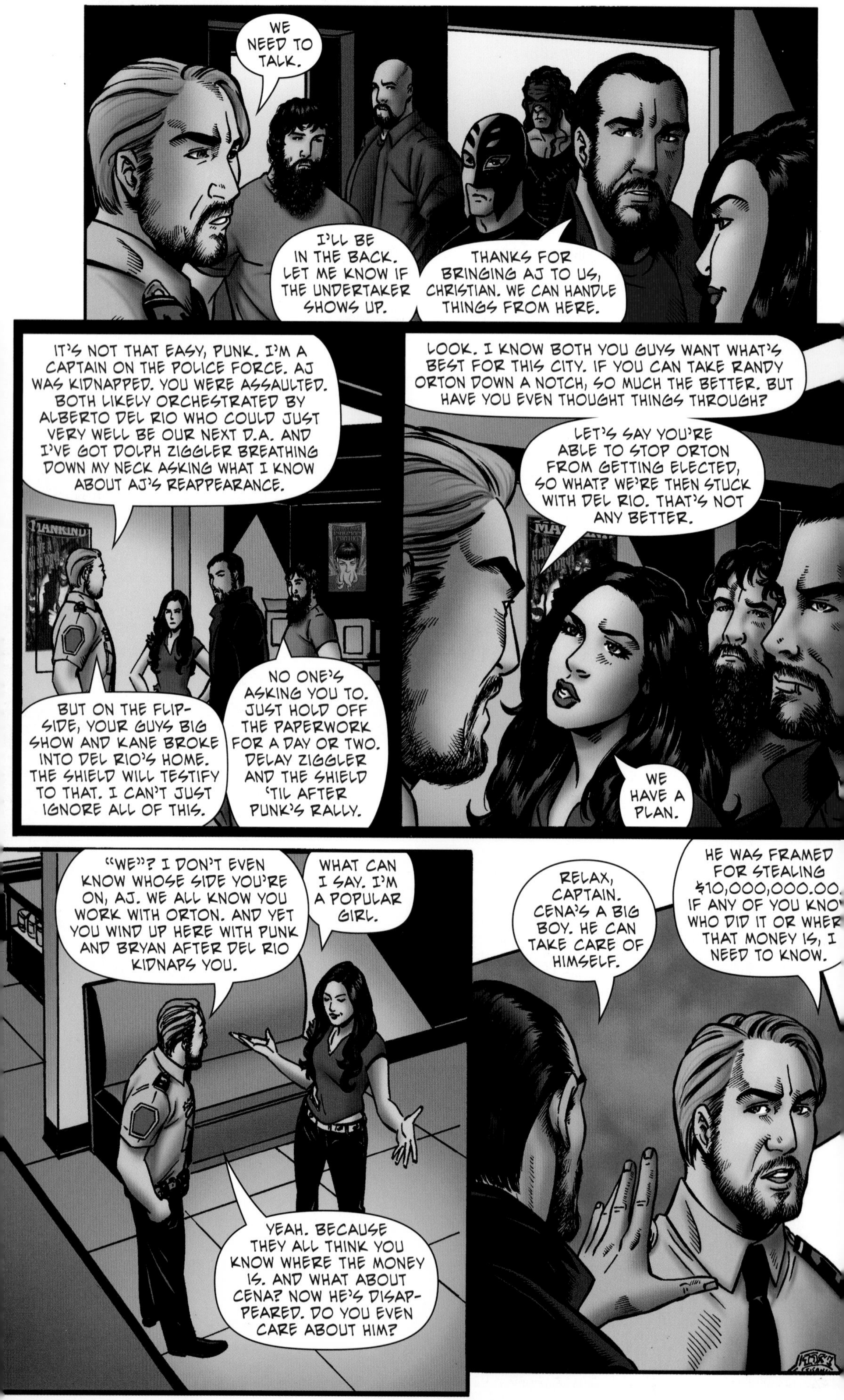
WE NEED TO TALK.
I'LL BE IN THE BACK. LET ME KNOW IF THE UNDERTAKER SHOWS UP.
THANKS FOR BRINGING AJ TO US, CHRISTIAN. WE CAN HANDLE THINGS FROM HERE.
IT'S NOT THAT EASY, PUNK. I'M A CAPTAIN ON THE POLICE FORCE. AJ WAS KIDNAPPED. YOU WERE ASSAULTED. BOTH LIKELY ORCHESTRATED BY ALBERTO DEL RIO WHO COULD JUST VERY WELL BE OUR NEXT D.A. AND I'VE GOT DOLPH ZIGGLER BREATHING DOWN MY NECK ASKING WHAT I KNOW ABOUT AJ'S REAPPEARANCE.
BUT ON THE FLIP-SIDE, YOUR GUYS BIG SHOW AND KANE BROKE INTO DEL RIO'S HOME. THE SHIELD WILL TESTIFY TO THAT. I CAN'T JUST IGNORE ALL OF THIS.
NO ONE'S ASKING YOU TO. JUST HOLD OFF THE PAPERWORK FOR A DAY OR TWO. DELAY ZIGGLER AND THE SHIELD 'TIL AFTER PUNK'S RALLY.
LOOK. I KNOW BOTH YOU GUYS WANT WHAT'S BEST FOR THIS CITY. IF YOU CAN TAKE RANDY ORTON DOWN A NOTCH, SO MUCH THE BETTER. BUT HAVE YOU EVEN THOUGHT THINGS THROUGH?
LET'S SAY YOU'RE ABLE TO STOP ORTON FROM GETTING ELECTED, SO WHAT? WE'RE THEN STUCK WITH DEL RIO. THAT'S NOT ANY BETTER.
WE HAVE A PLAN.
"WE"? I DON'T EVEN KNOW WHOSE SIDE YOU'RE ON, AJ. WE ALL KNOW YOU WORK WITH ORTON. AND YET YOU WIND UP HERE WITH PUNK AND BRYAN AFTER DEL RIO KIDNAPS YOU.
WHAT CAN I SAY. I'M A POPULAR GIRL.
YEAH. BECAUSE THEY ALL THINK YOU KNOW WHERE THE MONEY IS. AND WHAT ABOUT CENA? NOW HE'S DISAP-PEARED. DO YOU EVEN CARE ABOUT HIM?
RELAX, CAPTAIN. CENA'S A BIG BOY. HE CAN TAKE CARE OF HIMSELF.
HE WAS FRAMED FOR STEALING $10,000,000.00 IF ANY OF YOU KNO WHO DID IT OR WHER THAT MONEY IS, I NEED TO KNOW.

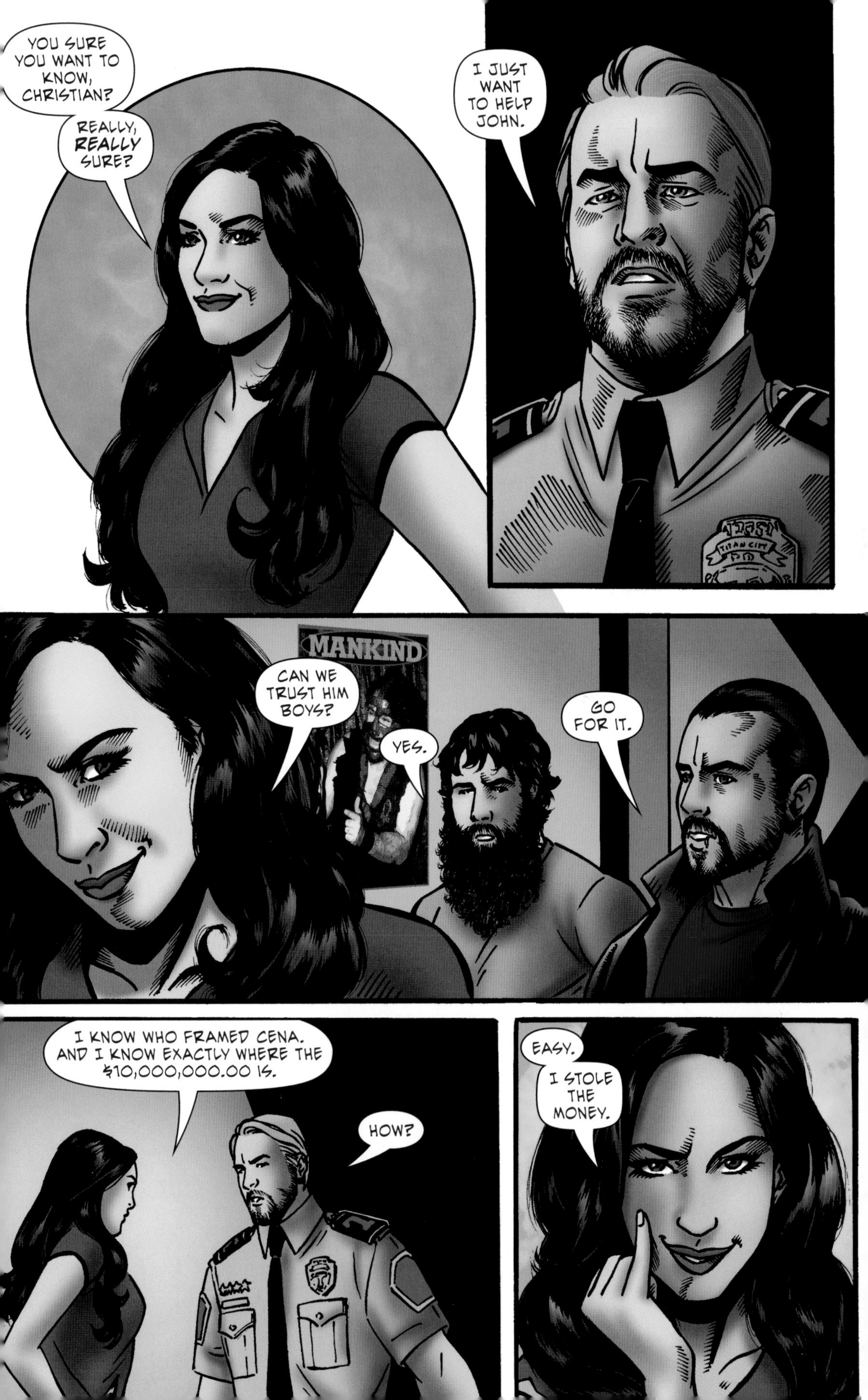

YOU SURE YOU WANT TO KNOW, CHRISTIAN?
REALLY, **REALLY** SURE?
I JUST WANT TO HELP JOHN.
MANKIND
CAN WE TRUST HIM BOYS?
YES.
GO FOR IT.
I KNOW WHO FRAMED CENA. AND I KNOW EXACTLY WHERE THE $10,000,000.00 IS.
HOW?
EASY.
I STOLE THE MONEY.

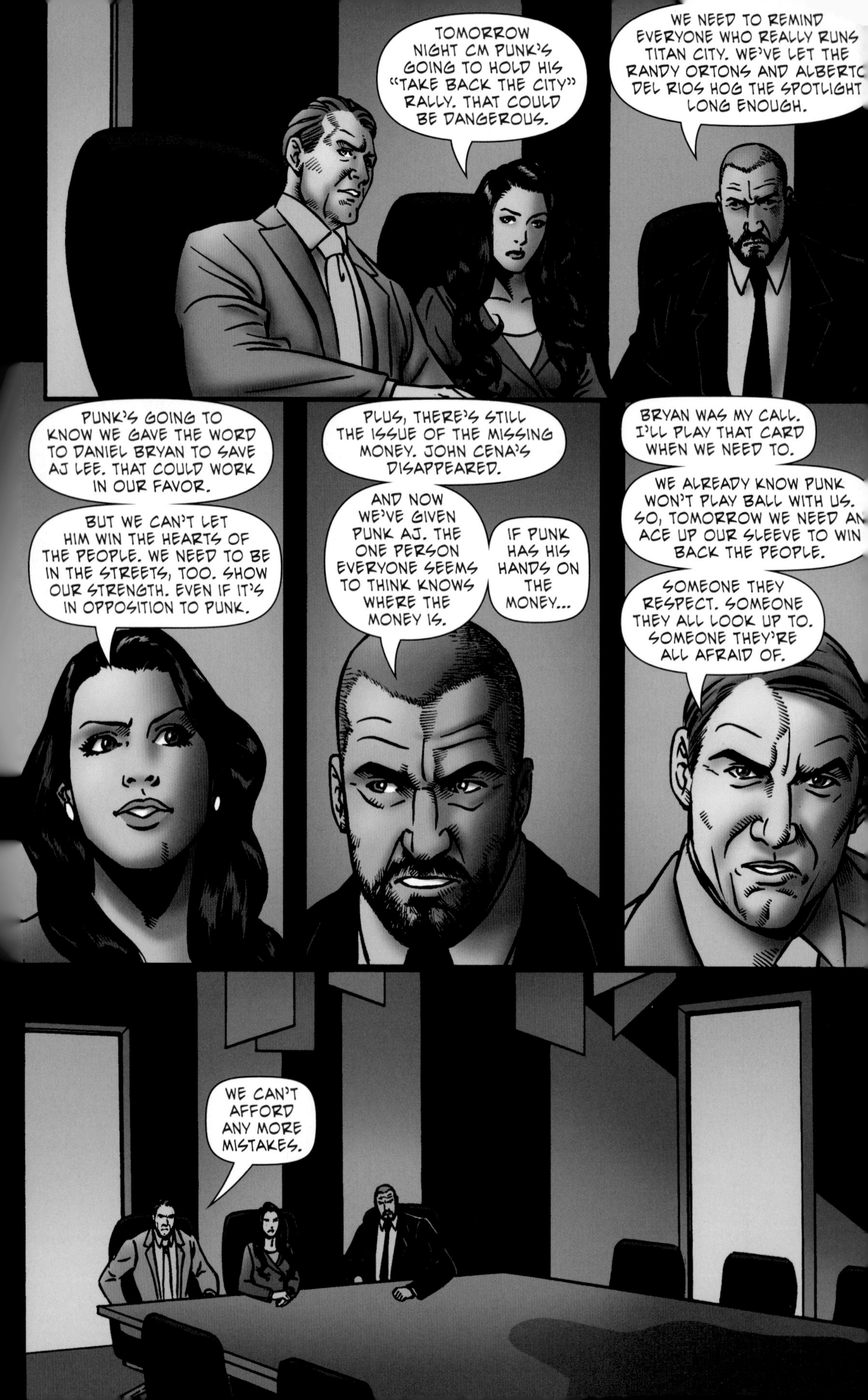
TOMORROW NIGHT CM PUNK'S GOING TO HOLD HIS "TAKE BACK THE CITY" RALLY. THAT COULD BE DANGEROUS.
WE NEED TO REMIND EVERYONE WHO REALLY RUNS TITAN CITY. WE'VE LET THE RANDY ORTONS AND ALBERTO DEL RIOS HOG THE SPOTLIGHT LONG ENOUGH.
PUNK'S GOING TO KNOW WE GAVE THE WORD TO DANIEL BRYAN TO SAVE AJ LEE. THAT COULD WORK IN OUR FAVOR.
BUT WE CAN'T LET HIM WIN THE HEARTS OF THE PEOPLE. WE NEED TO BE IN THE STREETS, TOO. SHOW OUR STRENGTH. EVEN IF IT'S IN OPPOSITION TO PUNK.
PLUS, THERE'S STILL THE ISSUE OF THE MISSING MONEY. JOHN CENA'S DISAPPEARED.
AND NOW WE'VE GIVEN PUNK AJ. THE ONE PERSON EVERYONE SEEMS TO THINK KNOWS WHERE THE MONEY IS.
IF PUNK HAS HIS HANDS ON THE MONEY...
BRYAN WAS MY CALL. I'LL PLAY THAT CARD WHEN WE NEED TO.
WE ALREADY KNOW PUNK WON'T PLAY BALL WITH US. SO, TOMORROW WE NEED AN ACE UP OUR SLEEVE TO WIN BACK THE PEOPLE.
SOMEONE THEY RESPECT. SOMEONE THEY ALL LOOK UP TO. SOMEONE THEY'RE ALL AFRAID OF.
WE CAN'T AFFORD ANY MORE MISTAKES.

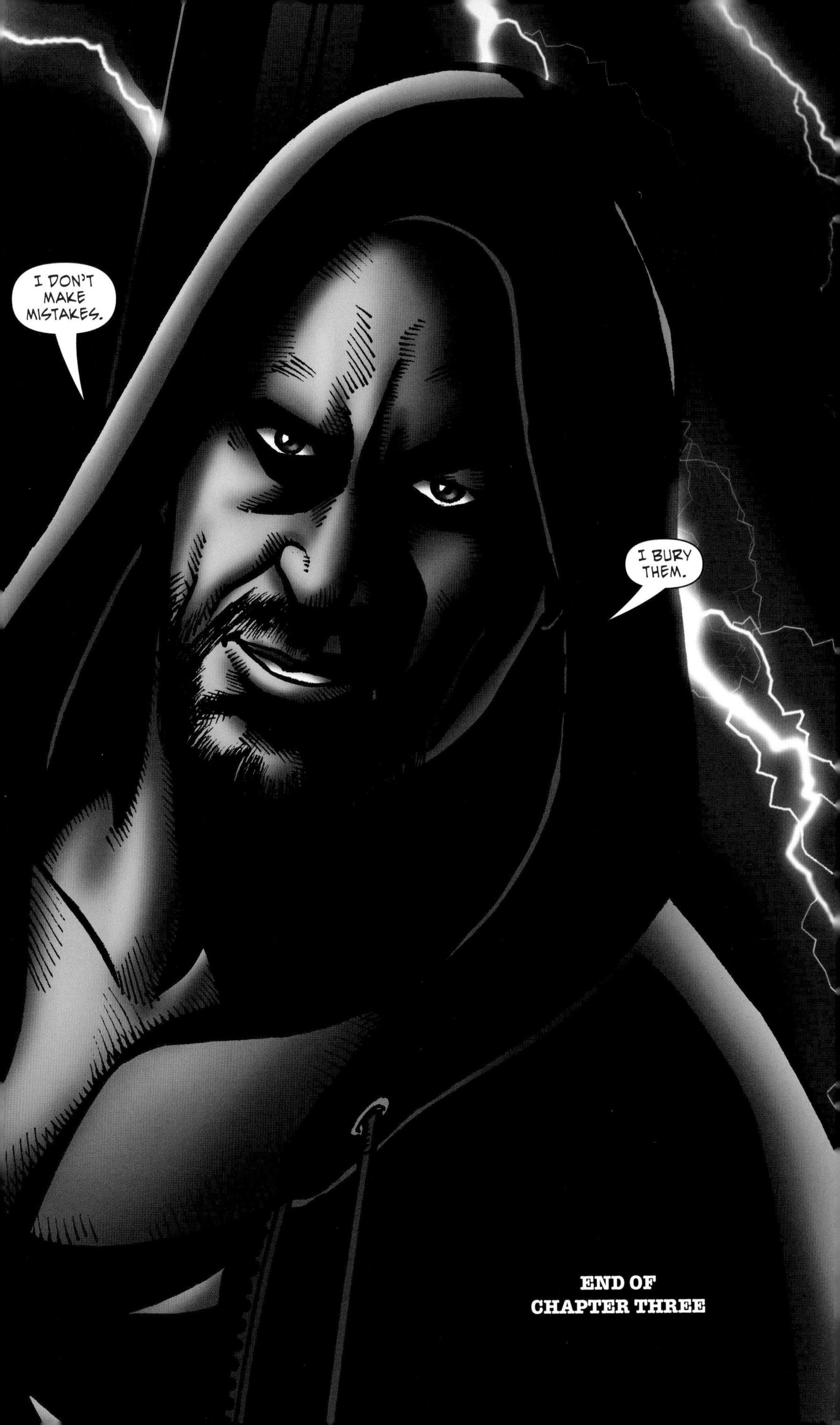
I DON'T MAKE MISTAKES.
I BURY THEM.
END OF CHAPTER THREE

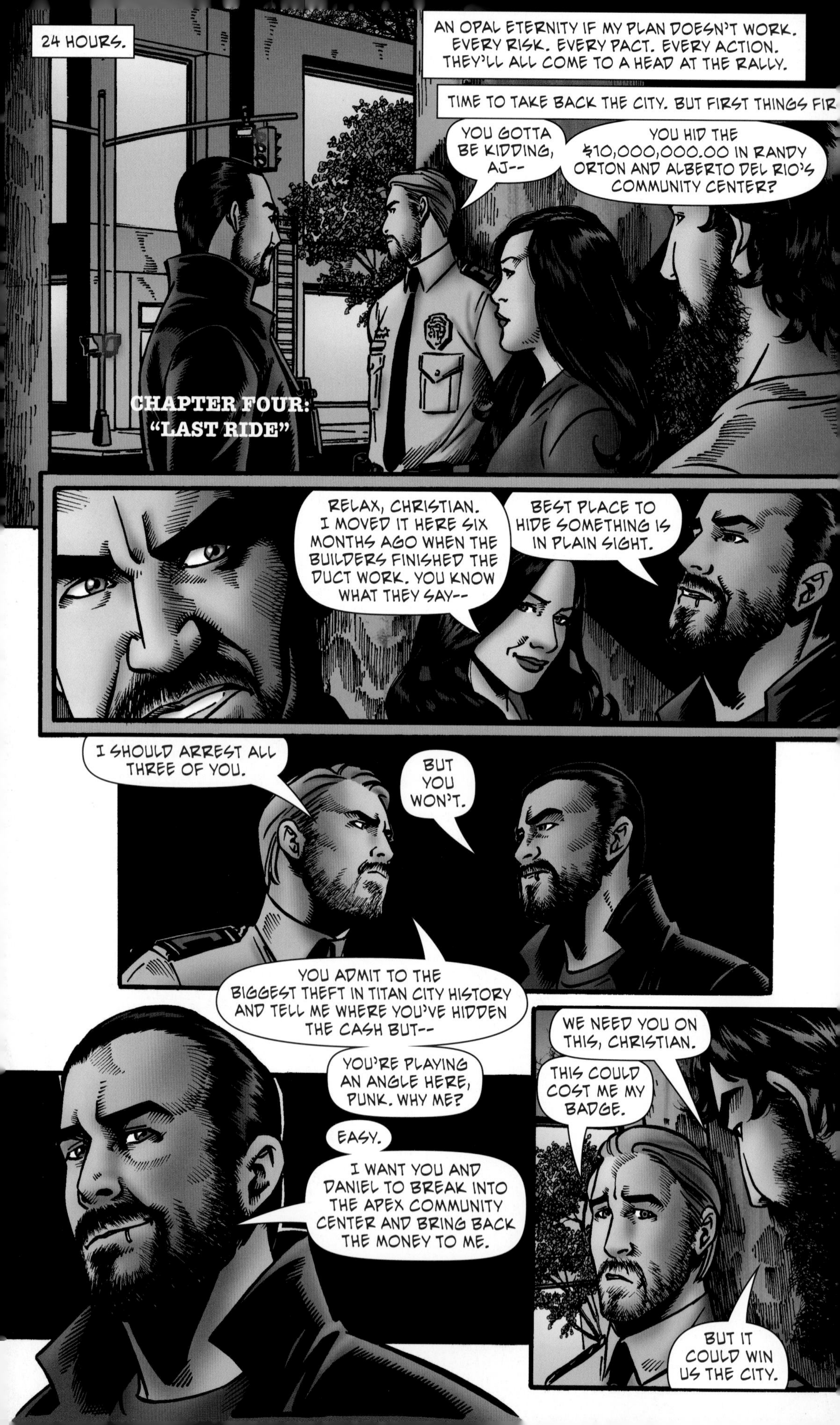
24 HOURS.
AN OPAL ETERNITY IF MY PLAN DOESN'T WORK. EVERY RISK. EVERY PACT. EVERY ACTION. THEY'LL ALL COME TO A HEAD AT THE RALLY.
TIME TO TAKE BACK THE CITY. BUT FIRST THINGS FIR
YOU GOTTA BE KIDDING, AJ--
YOU HID THE $10,000,000.00 IN RANDY ORTON AND ALBERTO DEL RIO'S COMMUNITY CENTER?
CHAPTER FOUR: "LAST RIDE"
RELAX, CHRISTIAN. I MOVED IT HERE SIX MONTHS AGO WHEN THE BUILDERS FINISHED THE DUCT WORK. YOU KNOW WHAT THEY SAY--
BEST PLACE TO HIDE SOMETHING IS IN PLAIN SIGHT.
I SHOULD ARREST ALL THREE OF YOU.
BUT YOU WON'T.
YOU ADMIT TO THE BIGGEST THEFT IN TITAN CITY HISTORY AND TELL ME WHERE YOU'VE HIDDEN THE CASH BUT--
YOU'RE PLAYING AN ANGLE HERE, PUNK. WHY ME?
EASY.
I WANT YOU AND DANIEL TO BREAK INTO THE APEX COMMUNITY CENTER AND BRING BACK THE MONEY TO ME.
WE NEED YOU ON THIS, CHRISTIAN.
THIS COULD COST ME MY BADGE.
BUT IT COULD WIN US THE CITY.

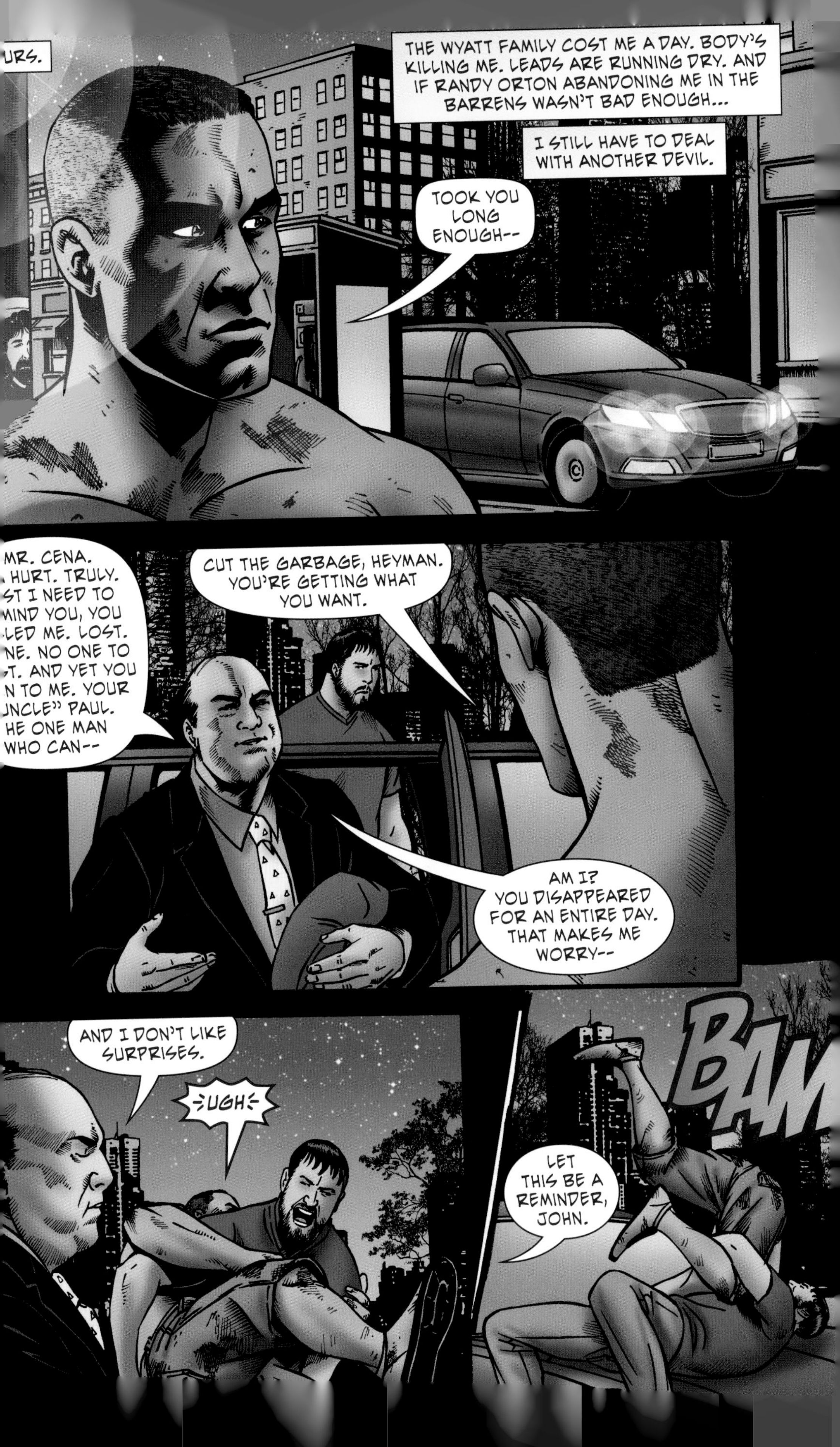
URS.
THE WYATT FAMILY COST ME A DAY. BODY'S KILLING ME. LEADS ARE RUNNING DRY. AND IF RANDY ORTON ABANDONING ME IN THE BARRENS WASN'T BAD ENOUGH...
I STILL HAVE TO DEAL WITH ANOTHER DEVIL.
TOOK YOU LONG ENOUGH--
MR. CENA.
HURT. TRULY.
ST I NEED TO
MIND YOU, YOU
LED ME. LOST.
NE. NO ONE TO
T. AND YET YOU
N TO ME. YOUR
JNCLE" PAUL.
HE ONE MAN
WHO CAN--
CUT THE GARBAGE, HEYMAN. YOU'RE GETTING WHAT YOU WANT.
AM I? YOU DISAPPEARED FOR AN ENTIRE DAY. THAT MAKES ME WORRY--
AND I DON'T LIKE SURPRISES.
UGH
LET THIS BE A REMINDER, JOHN.
BAM

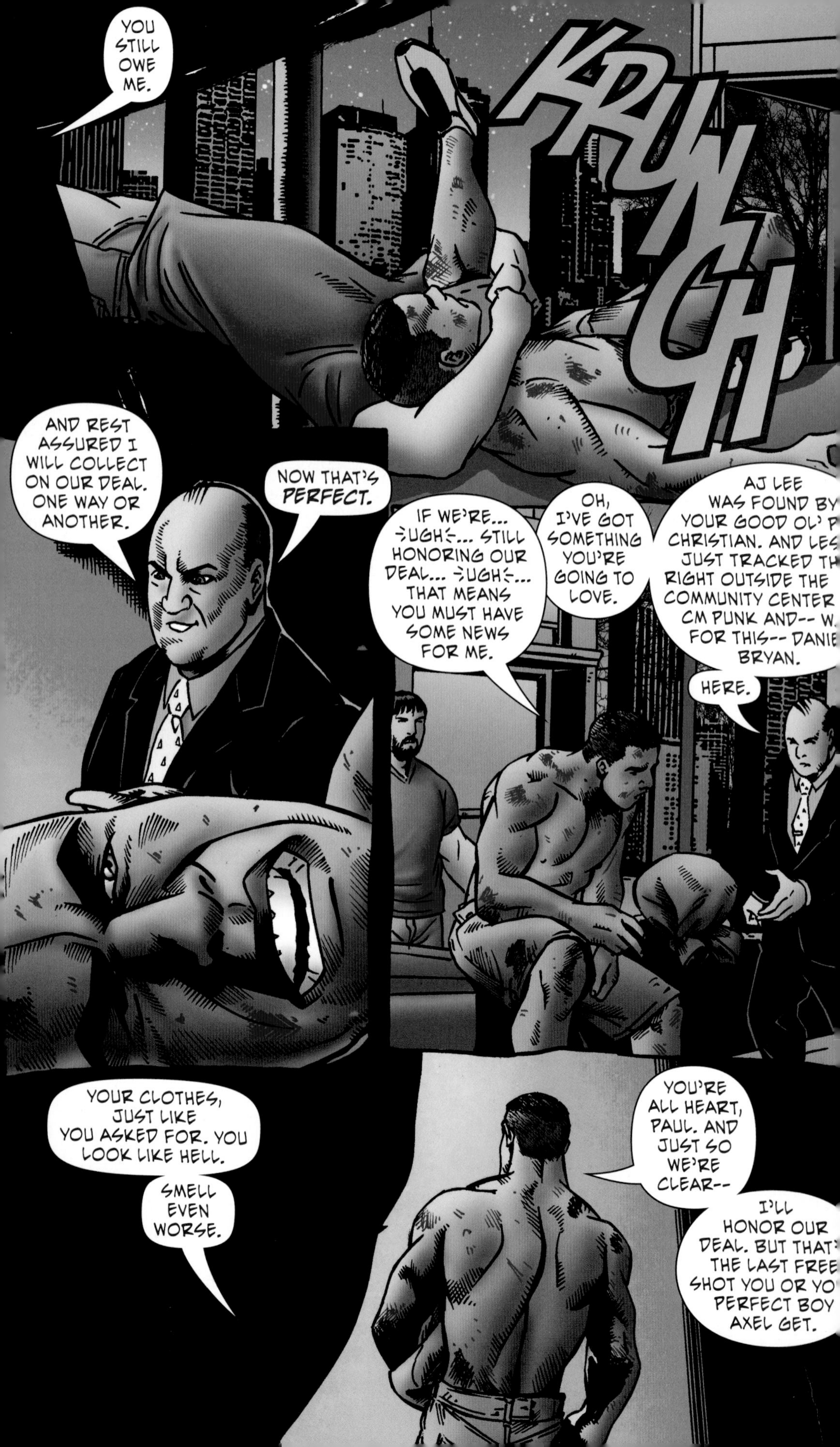
YOU STILL OWE ME.
KRUNCH
AND REST ASSURED I WILL COLLECT ON OUR DEAL. ONE WAY OR ANOTHER.
NOW THAT'S PERFECT.
IF WE'RE... ≥UGH≤... STILL HONORING OUR DEAL... ≥UGH≤... THAT MEANS YOU MUST HAVE SOME NEWS FOR ME.
OH, I'VE GOT SOMETHING YOU'RE GOING TO LOVE.
AJ LEE WAS FOUND BY YOUR GOOD OL' P CHRISTIAN. AND LES JUST TRACKED TH RIGHT OUTSIDE THE COMMUNITY CENTER CM PUNK AND-- W. FOR THIS-- DANIE BRYAN.
HERE.
YOUR CLOTHES, JUST LIKE YOU ASKED FOR. YOU LOOK LIKE HELL.
SMELL EVEN WORSE.
YOU'RE ALL HEART, PAUL. AND JUST SO WE'RE CLEAR--
I'LL HONOR OUR DEAL. BUT THAT' THE LAST FREE SHOT YOU OR YO PERFECT BOY AXEL GET.

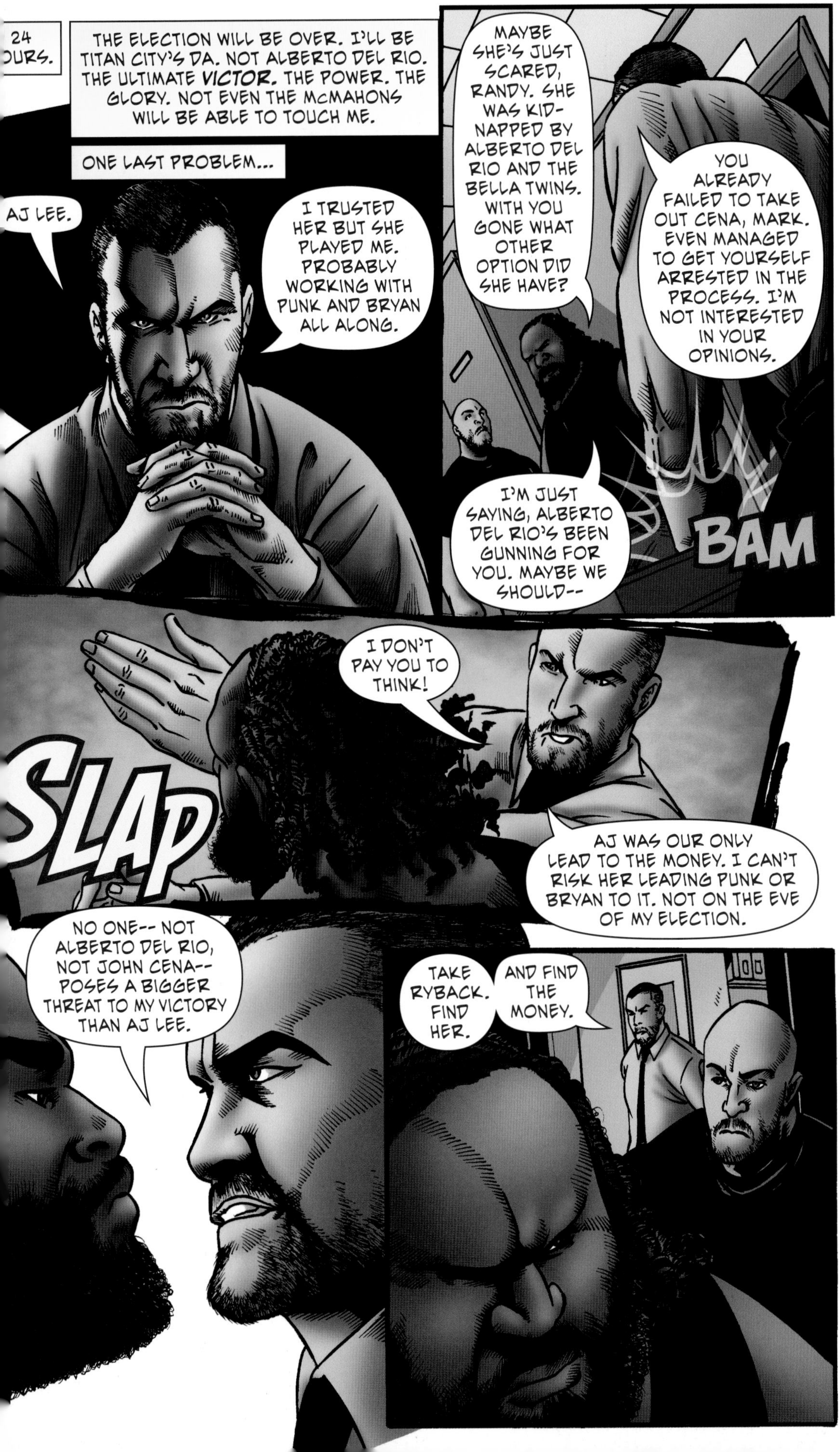
24 ...OURS.
THE ELECTION WILL BE OVER. I'LL BE TITAN CITY'S DA. NOT ALBERTO DEL RIO. THE ULTIMATE VICTOR. THE POWER. THE GLORY. NOT EVEN THE McMAHONS WILL BE ABLE TO TOUCH ME.
ONE LAST PROBLEM...
AJ LEE.
I TRUSTED HER BUT SHE PLAYED ME. PROBABLY WORKING WITH PUNK AND BRYAN ALL ALONG.
MAYBE SHE'S JUST SCARED, RANDY. SHE WAS KID-NAPPED BY ALBERTO DEL RIO AND THE BELLA TWINS. WITH YOU GONE WHAT OTHER OPTION DID SHE HAVE?
YOU ALREADY FAILED TO TAKE OUT CENA, MARK. EVEN MANAGED TO GET YOURSELF ARRESTED IN THE PROCESS. I'M NOT INTERESTED IN YOUR OPINIONS.
I'M JUST SAYING, ALBERTO DEL RIO'S BEEN GUNNING FOR YOU. MAYBE WE SHOULD--
BAM
SLAP
I DON'T PAY YOU TO THINK!
AJ WAS OUR ONLY LEAD TO THE MONEY. I CAN'T RISK HER LEADING PUNK OR BRYAN TO IT. NOT ON THE EVE OF MY ELECTION.
NO ONE-- NOT ALBERTO DEL RIO, NOT JOHN CENA-- POSES A BIGGER THREAT TO MY VICTORY THAN AJ LEE.
TAKE RYBACK. FIND HER.
AND FIND THE MONEY.

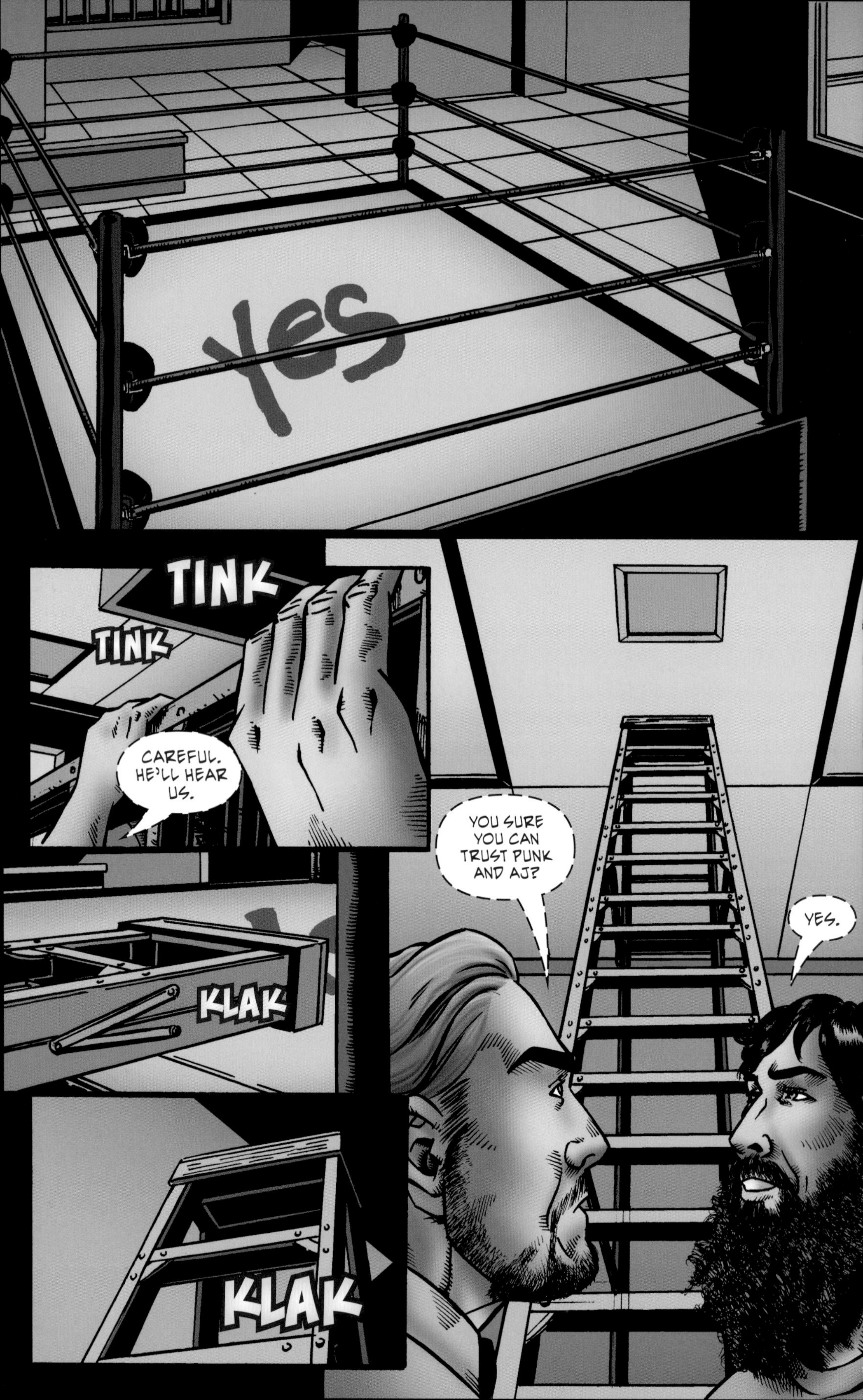
YES
TINK
TINK
CAREFUL. HE'LL HEAR US.
YOU SURE YOU CAN TRUST PUNK AND AJ?
YES.
KLAK
KLAK

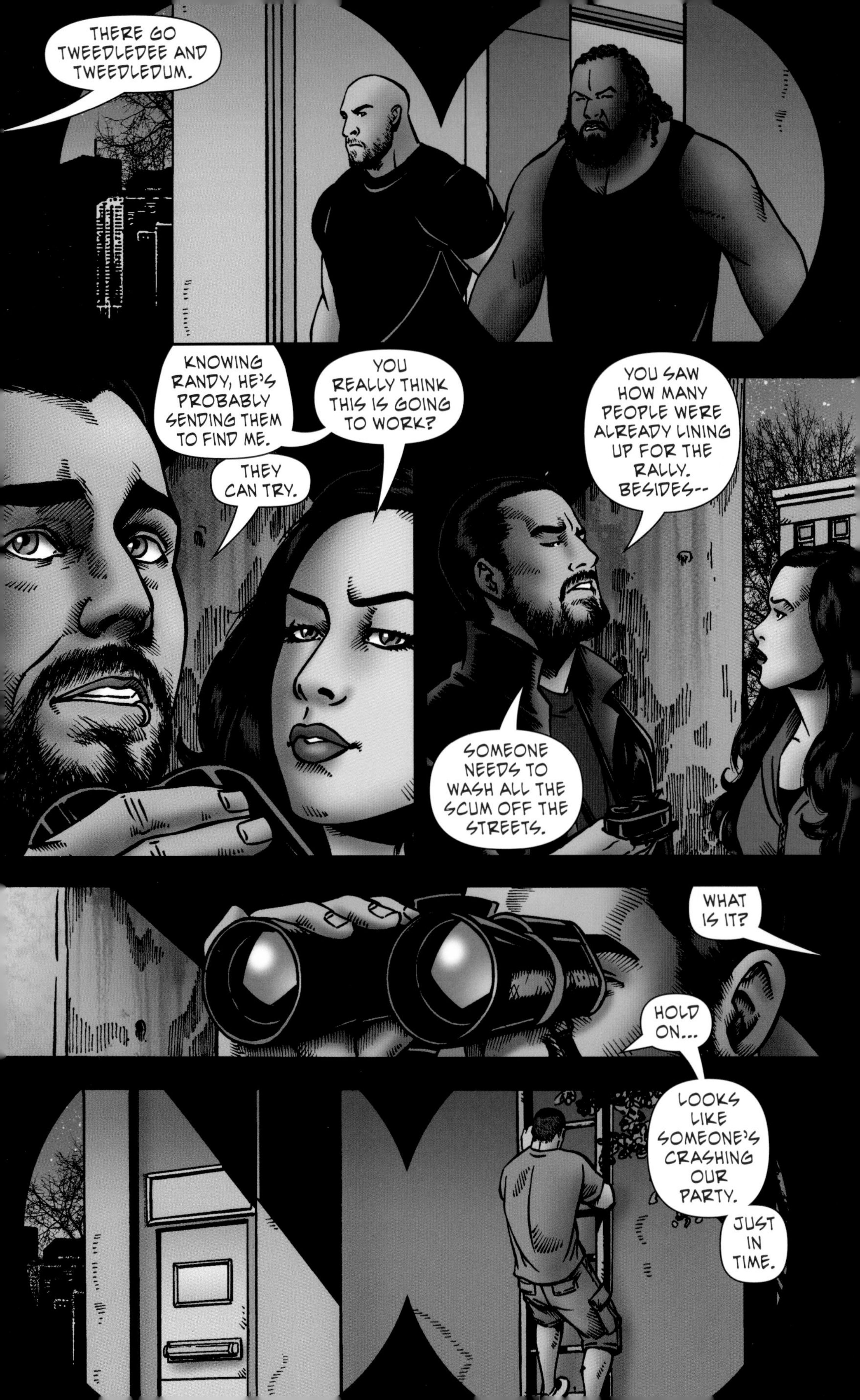
THERE GO TWEEDLEDEE AND TWEEDLEDUM.
KNOWING RANDY, HE'S PROBABLY SENDING THEM TO FIND ME.
YOU REALLY THINK THIS IS GOING TO WORK?
THEY CAN TRY.
YOU SAW HOW MANY PEOPLE WERE ALREADY LINING UP FOR THE RALLY. BESIDES--
SOMEONE NEEDS TO WASH ALL THE SCUM OFF THE STREETS.
WHAT IS IT?
HOLD ON...
LOOKS LIKE SOMEONE'S CRASHING OUR PARTY.
JUST IN TIME.

WELL, WELL, WELL LOOK WHAT CAT DRAGG OUT.

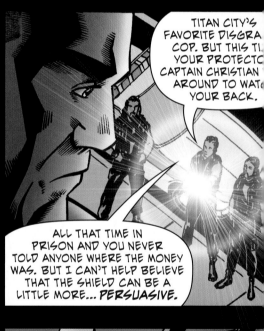

TITAN CITY'S FAVORITE DISGRA COP. BUT THIS TI YOUR PROTECTO CAPTAIN CHRISTIAN AROUND TO WAT YOUR BACK.

ALL THAT TIME IN PRISON AND YOU NEVER TOLD ANYONE WHERE THE MONEY WAS. BUT I CAN'T HELP BELIEVE THAT THE SHIELD CAN BE A LITTLE MORE... *PERSUASIVE.*

≈URK!≈

BELIEVE IN THIS!

LAST THING I NE IS A FIGHT WITH T COPS. AMBROS REIGNS AND ROLL ARE A DISGRAC TO THE BLUE.

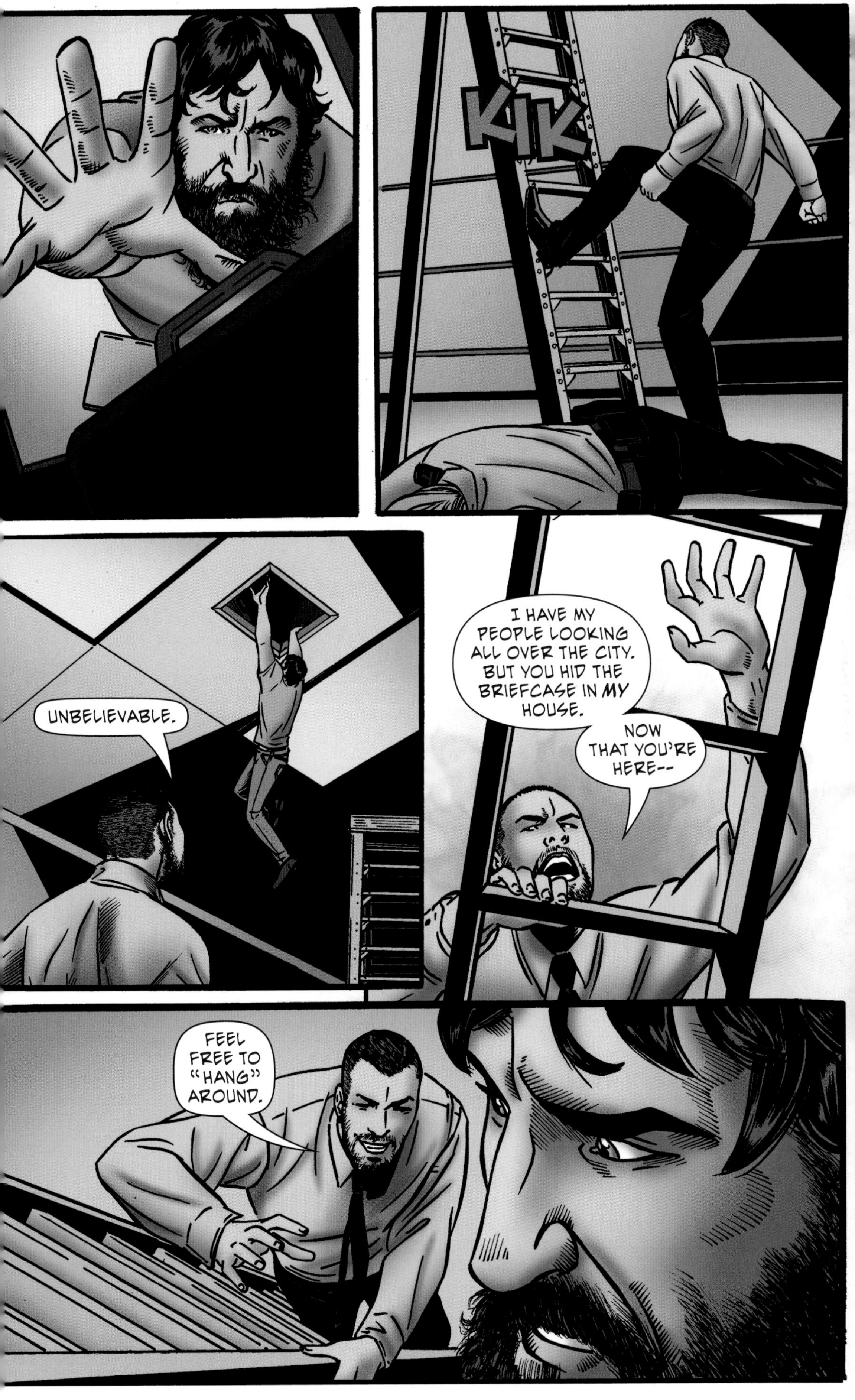
KIK
UNBELIEVABLE.
I HAVE MY PEOPLE LOOKING ALL OVER THE CITY. BUT YOU HID THE BRIEFCASE IN MY HOUSE.
NOW THAT YOU'RE HERE--
FEEL FREE TO "HANG" AROUND.

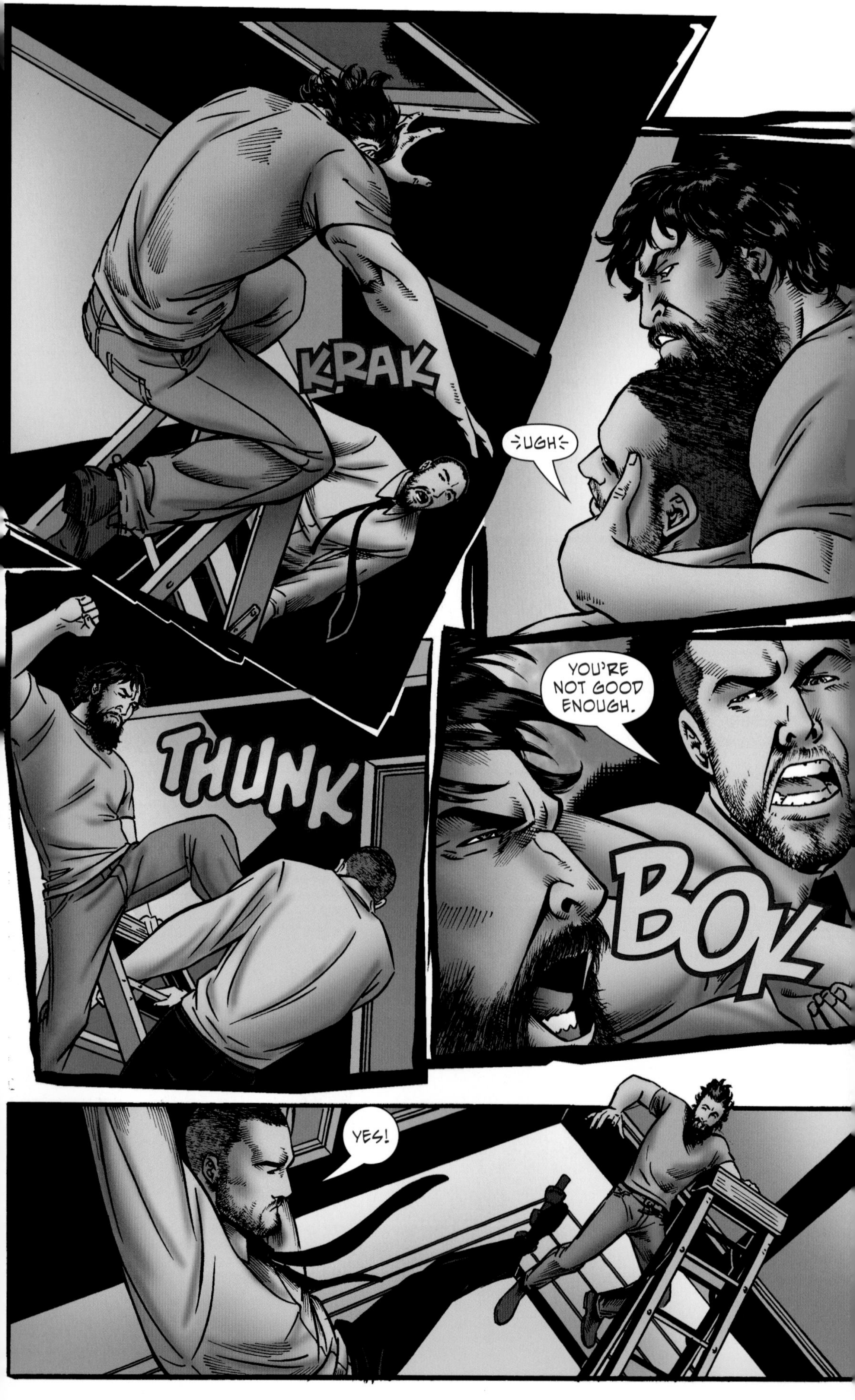
KRAK
UGH
THUNK
YOU'RE NOT GOOD ENOUGH.
BOK
YES!

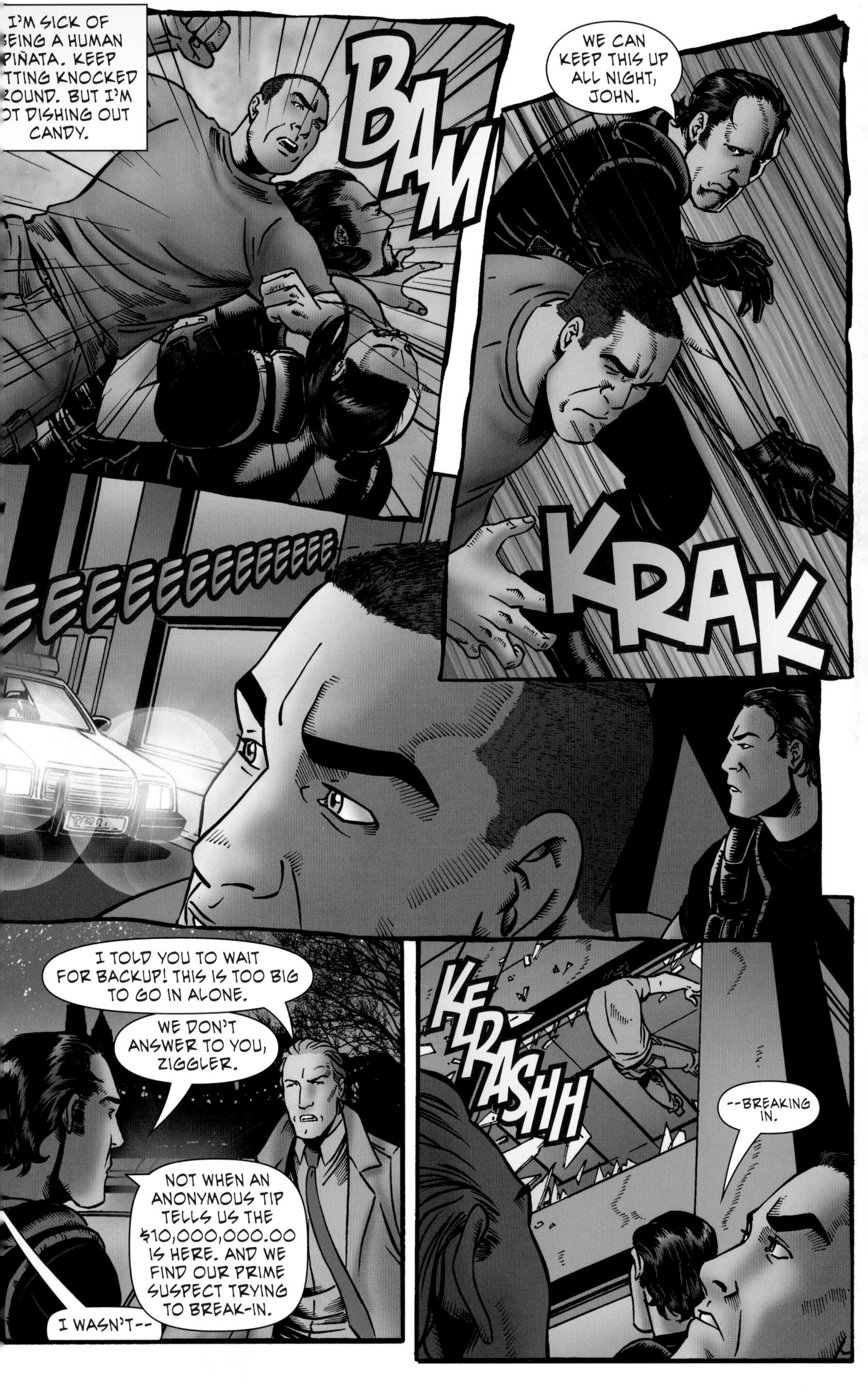
I'M SICK OF
EING A HUMAN
PIÑATA. KEEP
TTING KNOCKED
ROUND. BUT I'M
T DISHING OUT
CANDY.
BAM
WE CAN KEEP THIS UP ALL NIGHT, JOHN.
KRAK
EEEEEEEEEEEEEEEEE
I TOLD YOU TO WAIT FOR BACKUP! THIS IS TOO BIG TO GO IN ALONE.
WE DON'T ANSWER TO YOU, ZIGGLER.
NOT WHEN AN ANONYMOUS TIP TELLS US THE $10,000,000.00 IS HERE. AND WE FIND OUR PRIME SUSPECT TRYING TO BREAK-IN.
I WASN'T--
KERASHH
--BREAKING IN.

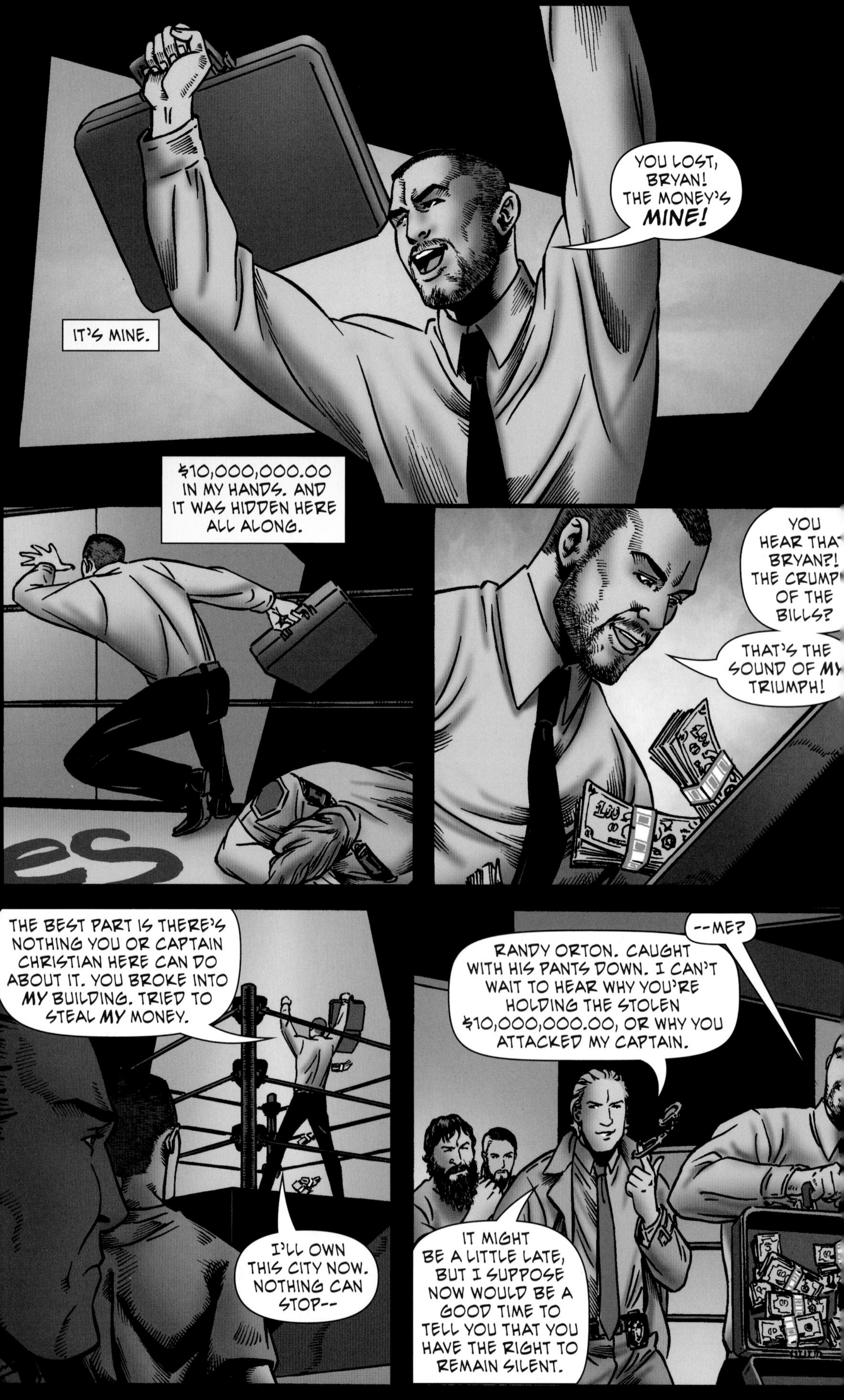
YOU LOST, BRYAN! THE MONEY'S MINE!
IT'S MINE.
$10,000,000.00 IN MY HANDS. AND IT WAS HIDDEN HERE ALL ALONG.
YOU HEAR THAT BRYAN?! THE CRUMP OF THE BILLS?
THAT'S THE SOUND OF MY TRIUMPH!
THE BEST PART IS THERE'S NOTHING YOU OR CAPTAIN CHRISTIAN HERE CAN DO ABOUT IT. YOU BROKE INTO MY BUILDING. TRIED TO STEAL MY MONEY.
I'LL OWN THIS CITY NOW. NOTHING CAN STOP--
--ME?
RANDY ORTON. CAUGHT WITH HIS PANTS DOWN. I CAN'T WAIT TO HEAR WHY YOU'RE HOLDING THE STOLEN $10,000,000.00, OR WHY YOU ATTACKED MY CAPTAIN.
IT MIGHT BE A LITTLE LATE, BUT I SUPPOSE NOW WOULD BE A GOOD TIME TO TELL YOU THAT YOU HAVE THE RIGHT TO REMAIN SILENT.

OUBT. THE PERFECT WEAPON. SPRINKLE A LITTLE ON EVEN THE STRONGEST FOUNDATION AND--

STAND BACK AND WATCH EVERY-THING COME TUMBLING DOWN.

AL SNOW SH

YOU SET ME UP!

ND I'D DO IT AGAIN.

ORTON'S IN JAIL.

FOR A CRIME WE ALL KNOW HE DIDN'T COMMIT!

DOESN'T MATTER. ORTON NOW HAS ZERO CHANCE OF WINNING THE D.A. ELECTION TOMORROW.

HAT'S NOT HOW I ROLL. YOU RAMED ORTON. MADE ME AN COMPLICE. THE TRUTH HAS GOT TO COUNT FOR SOMETHING!

BOO.

HOO.

HOO.

CRY US A RIVER, CHRISTIAN. WE PLANNED THIS FOR A YEAR. STOLE THE MONEY AND HID IT AWAY. WATCHED YOUR BOY SCOUT CENA TAKE THE FALL. ALL IN ANTICIPATION OF CUTTING THE HEAD OFF THE VIPER AT JUST THE RIGHT TIME.

N'T TELL ME YOU BUY THIS, MYSTERIO? ING ORTON. LETTING CENA ROT IN PRISON FOR A YEAR. THIS ALL STINKS.

THEY GOT ORTON OFF THE STREETS.

AND THE CROWDS OUT-SIDE HAVE ONLY GOTTEN BIGGER FOR THE RALLY TODAY.

IT HAD TO BE DONE, CHRISTIAN. IT'S TITAN CITY. FIGHT FIRE WITH FIRE.

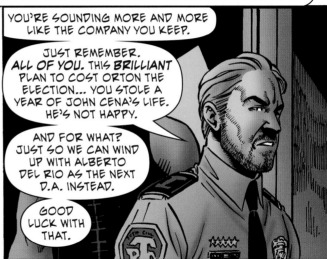

YOU'RE SOUNDING MORE AND MORE LIKE THE COMPANY YOU KEEP.

JUST REMEMBER. ALL OF YOU. THIS BRILLIANT PLAN TO COST ORTON THE ELECTION... YOU STOLE A YEAR OF JOHN CENA'S LIFE. HE'S NOT HAPPY.

AND FOR WHAT? JUST SO WE CAN WIND UP WITH ALBERTO DEL RIO AS THE NEXT D.A. INSTEAD.

GOOD LUCK WITH THAT.

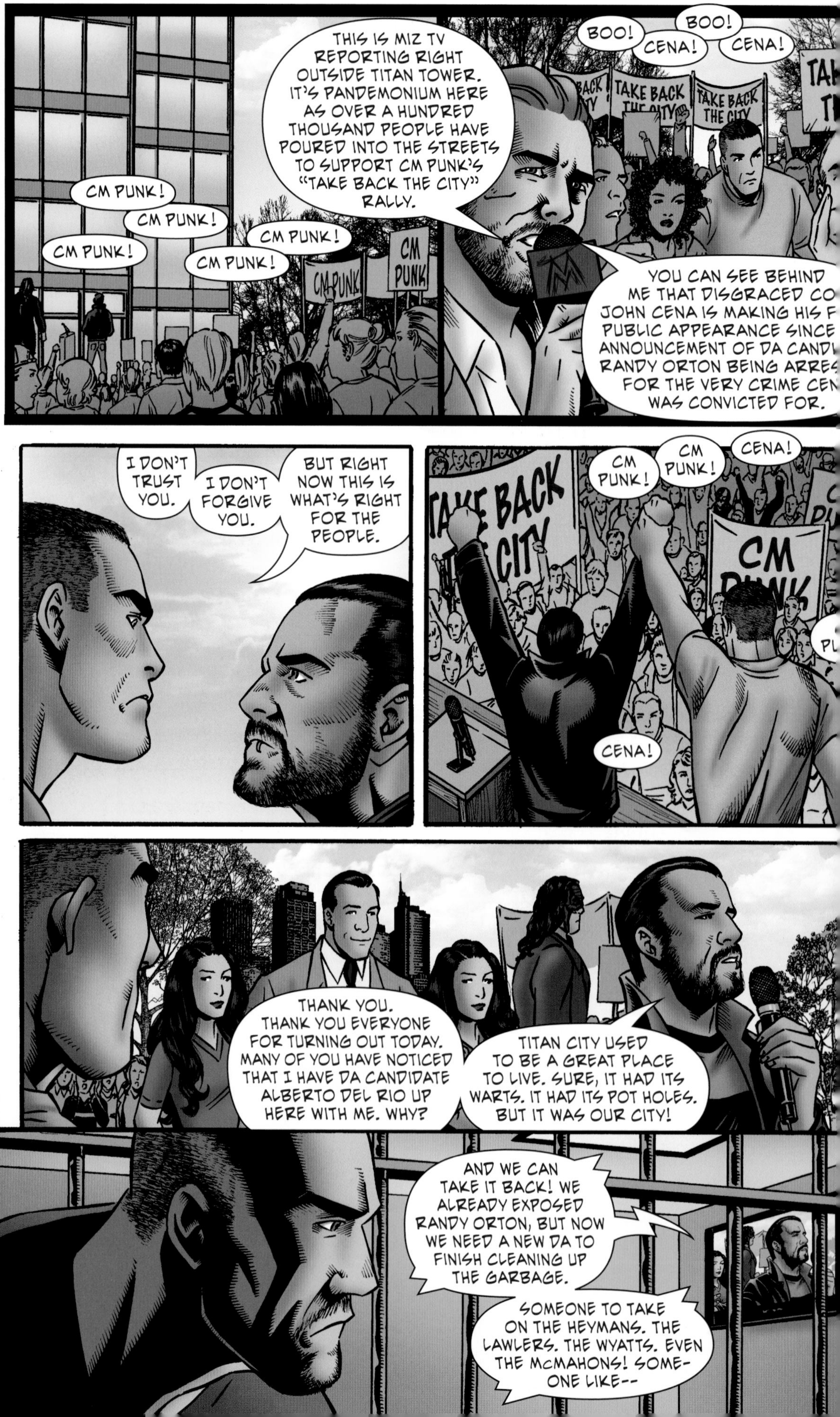
THIS IS MIZ TV REPORTING RIGHT OUTSIDE TITAN TOWER. IT'S PANDEMONIUM HERE AS OVER A HUNDRED THOUSAND PEOPLE HAVE POURED INTO THE STREETS TO SUPPORT CM PUNK'S "TAKE BACK THE CITY" RALLY.
BOO!
CENA!
BOO!
CENA!
CM PUNK!
CM PUNK!
CM PUNK!
CM PUNK!
CM PUNK!
YOU CAN SEE BEHIND ME THAT DISGRACED CO
JOHN CENA IS MAKING HIS F
PUBLIC APPEARANCE SINCE
ANNOUNCEMENT OF DA CANDI
RANDY ORTON BEING ARRES
FOR THE VERY CRIME CEN
WAS CONVICTED FOR.
I DON'T TRUST YOU.
I DON'T FORGIVE YOU.
BUT RIGHT NOW THIS IS WHAT'S RIGHT FOR THE PEOPLE.
CM PUNK!
CM PUNK!
CENA!
CENA!
THANK YOU. THANK YOU EVERYONE FOR TURNING OUT TODAY. MANY OF YOU HAVE NOTICED THAT I HAVE DA CANDIDATE ALBERTO DEL RIO UP HERE WITH ME. WHY?
TITAN CITY USED TO BE A GREAT PLACE TO LIVE. SURE, IT HAD ITS WARTS. IT HAD ITS POT HOLES. BUT IT WAS OUR CITY!
AND WE CAN TAKE IT BACK! WE ALREADY EXPOSED RANDY ORTON, BUT NOW WE NEED A NEW DA TO FINISH CLEANING UP THE GARBAGE.
SOMEONE TO TAKE ON THE HEYMANS. THE LAWLERS. THE WYATTS. EVEN THE McMAHONS! SOME-ONE LIKE--

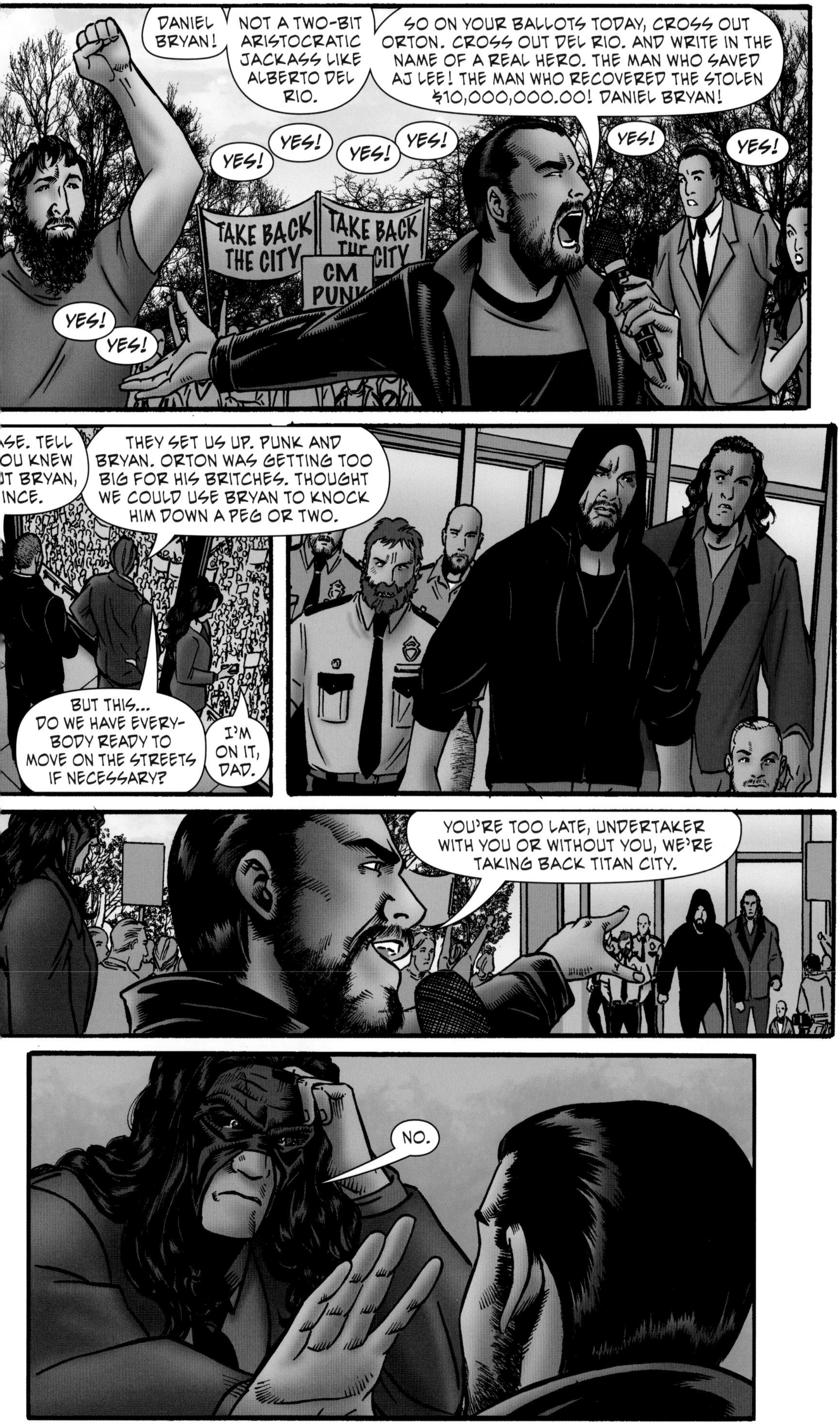
DANIEL BRYAN!
NOT A TWO-BIT ARISTOCRATIC JACKASS LIKE ALBERTO DEL RIO.
SO ON YOUR BALLOTS TODAY, CROSS OUT ORTON. CROSS OUT DEL RIO. AND WRITE IN THE NAME OF A REAL HERO. THE MAN WHO SAVED AJ LEE! THE MAN WHO RECOVERED THE STOLEN $10,000,000.00! DANIEL BRYAN!
YES!
YES!
YES!
YES!
YES!
YES!
TAKE BACK THE CITY
TAKE BACK THE CITY
CM PUNK
YES!
YES!
SE. TELL
OU KNEW
T BRYAN,
INCE.
THEY SET US UP. PUNK AND BRYAN. ORTON WAS GETTING TOO BIG FOR HIS BRITCHES. THOUGHT WE COULD USE BRYAN TO KNOCK HIM DOWN A PEG OR TWO.
BUT THIS... DO WE HAVE EVERY-BODY READY TO MOVE ON THE STREETS IF NECESSARY?
I'M ON IT, DAD.
YOU'RE TOO LATE, UNDERTAKER WITH YOU OR WITHOUT YOU, WE'RE TAKING BACK TITAN CITY.
NO.

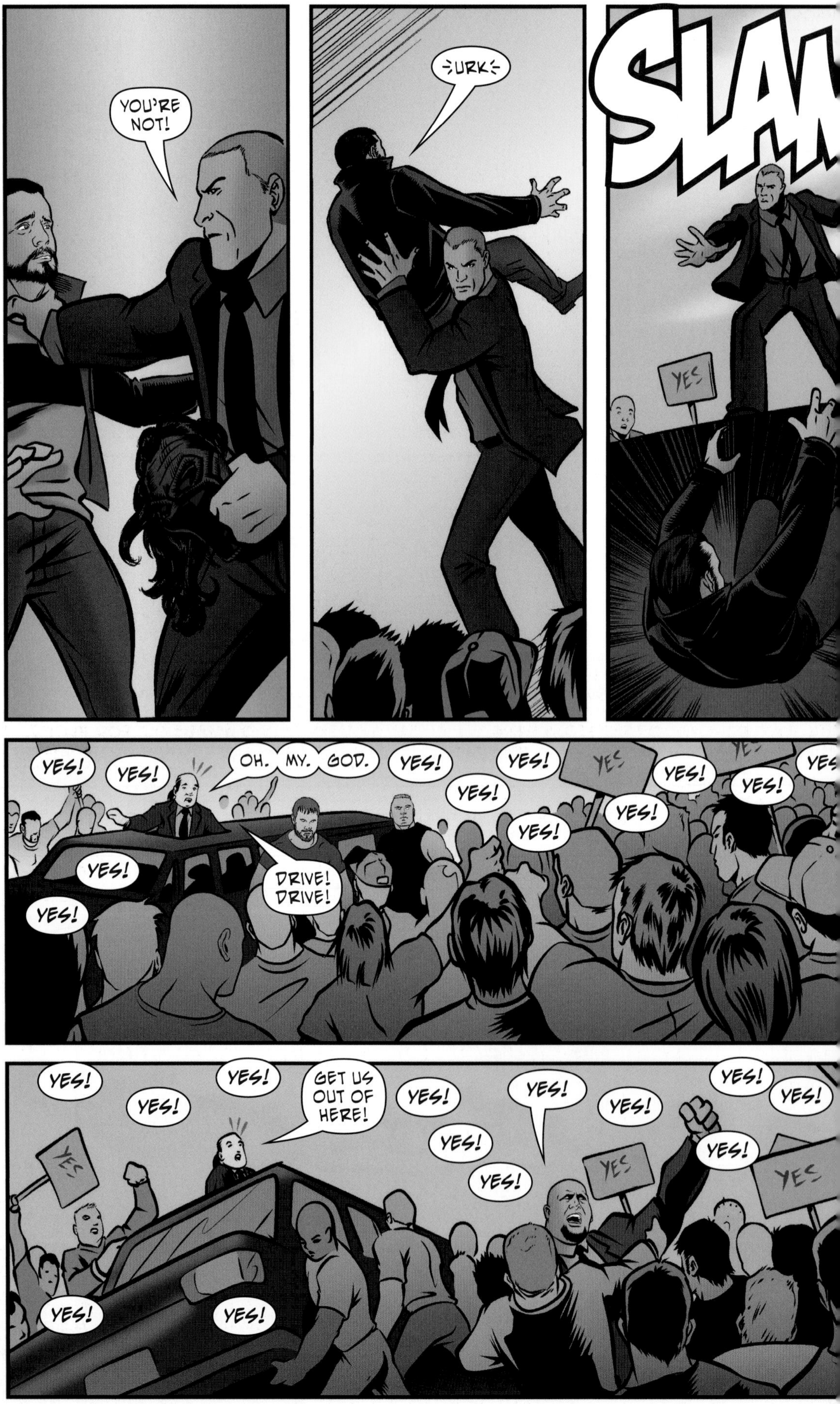
YOU'RE NOT!
URK
SLAM
YES
YES!
YES!
OH. MY. GOD.
YES!
YES!
YES!
YES!
YES!
YES!
YES!
DRIVE! DRIVE!
YES!
YES!
YES!
YES!
GET US OUT OF HERE!
YES!
YES!
YES!
YES!
YES!
YES!
YES!
YES!
YES!
YES!

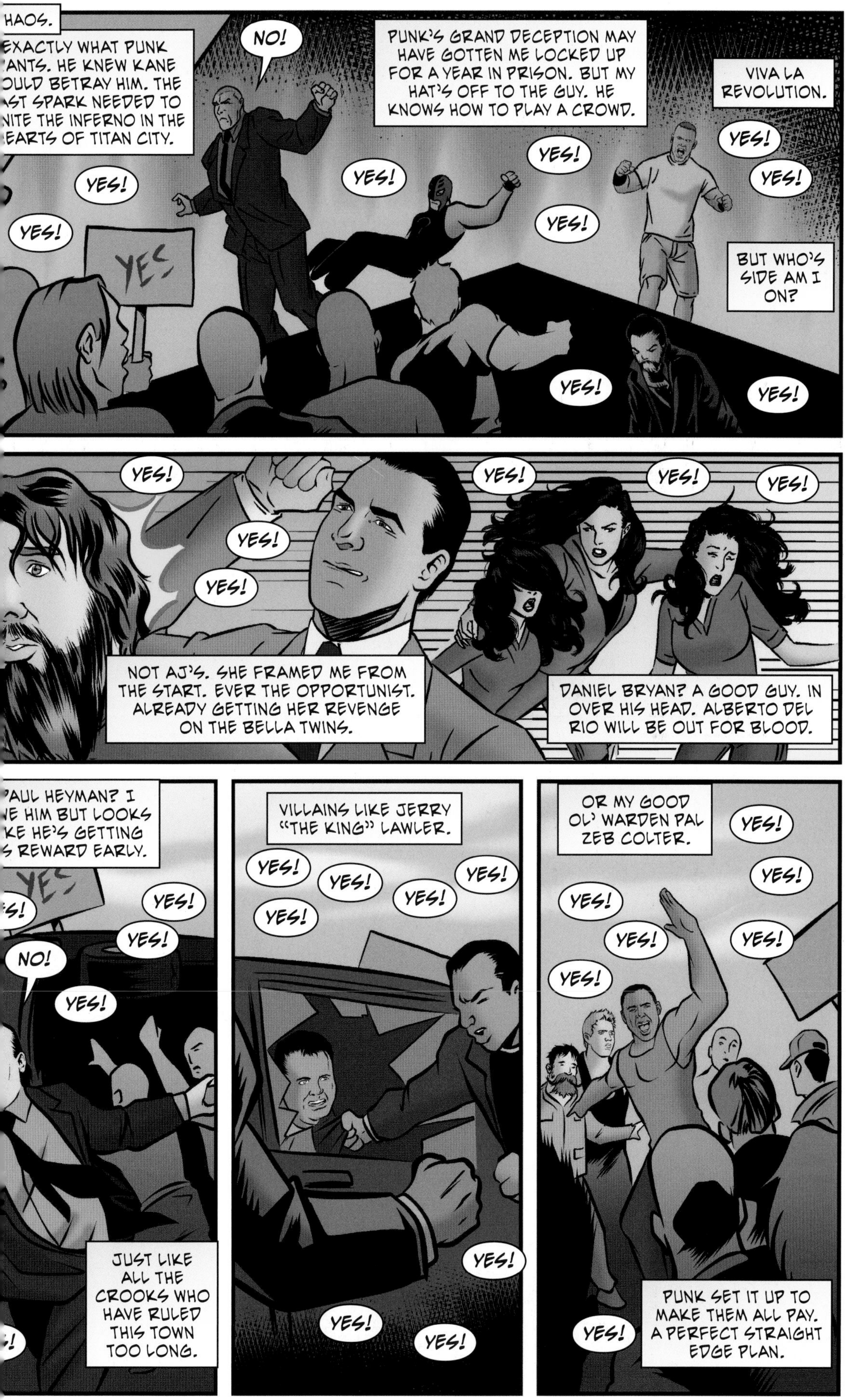
HAOS.
EXACTLY WHAT PUNK ANTS. HE KNEW KANE OULD BETRAY HIM. THE AST SPARK NEEDED TO NITE THE INFERNO IN THE EARTS OF TITAN CITY.
NO!
PUNK'S GRAND DECEPTION MAY HAVE GOTTEN ME LOCKED UP FOR A YEAR IN PRISON. BUT MY HAT'S OFF TO THE GUY. HE KNOWS HOW TO PLAY A CROWD.
VIVA LA REVOLUTION.
YES!
YES!
YES!
YES!
YES!
YES!
YES
YES!
BUT WHO'S SIDE AM I ON?
YES!
YES!
YES!
YES!
YES!
YES!
YES!
YES!
NOT AJ'S. SHE FRAMED ME FROM THE START. EVER THE OPPORTUNIST. ALREADY GETTING HER REVENGE ON THE BELLA TWINS.
DANIEL BRYAN? A GOOD GUY. IN OVER HIS HEAD. ALBERTO DEL RIO WILL BE OUT FOR BLOOD.
PAUL HEYMAN? I VE HIM BUT LOOKS KE HE'S GETTING S REWARD EARLY.
YES!
YES!
NO!
YES!
JUST LIKE ALL THE CROOKS WHO HAVE RULED THIS TOWN TOO LONG.
VILLAINS LIKE JERRY "THE KING" LAWLER.
YES!
YES!
YES!
YES!
YES!
YES!
YES!
YES!
OR MY GOOD OL' WARDEN PAL ZEB COLTER.
YES!
YES!
YES!
YES!
YES!
YES!
YES!
PUNK SET IT UP TO MAKE THEM ALL PAY. A PERFECT STRAIGHT EDGE PLAN.

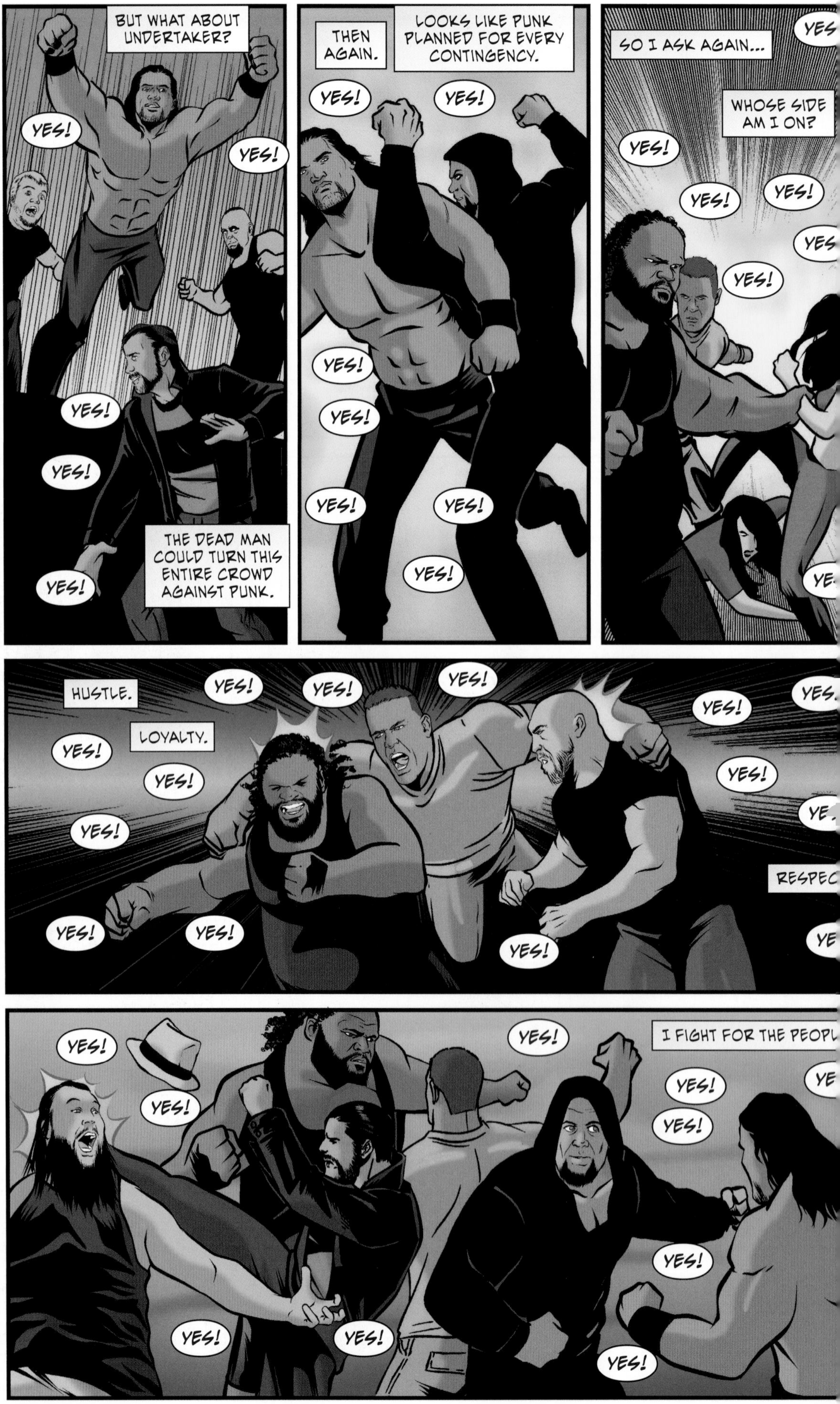
BUT WHAT ABOUT UNDERTAKER?
YES!
YES!
YES!
YES!
THE DEAD MAN COULD TURN THIS ENTIRE CROWD AGAINST PUNK.
YES!
THEN AGAIN.
LOOKS LIKE PUNK PLANNED FOR EVERY CONTINGENCY.
YES!
YES!
YES!
YES!
YES!
YES!
YES!
SO I ASK AGAIN...
WHOSE SIDE AM I ON?
YES!
YES!
YES!
YES!
HUSTLE.
YES!
YES!
YES!
LOYALTY.
YES!
YES!
YES!
YES!
YES!
YES!
YES!
YES!
RESPEC
YES!
YES!
YES!
I FIGHT FOR THE PEOPL
YES!
YES!
YES!
YES!
YES!
YES!

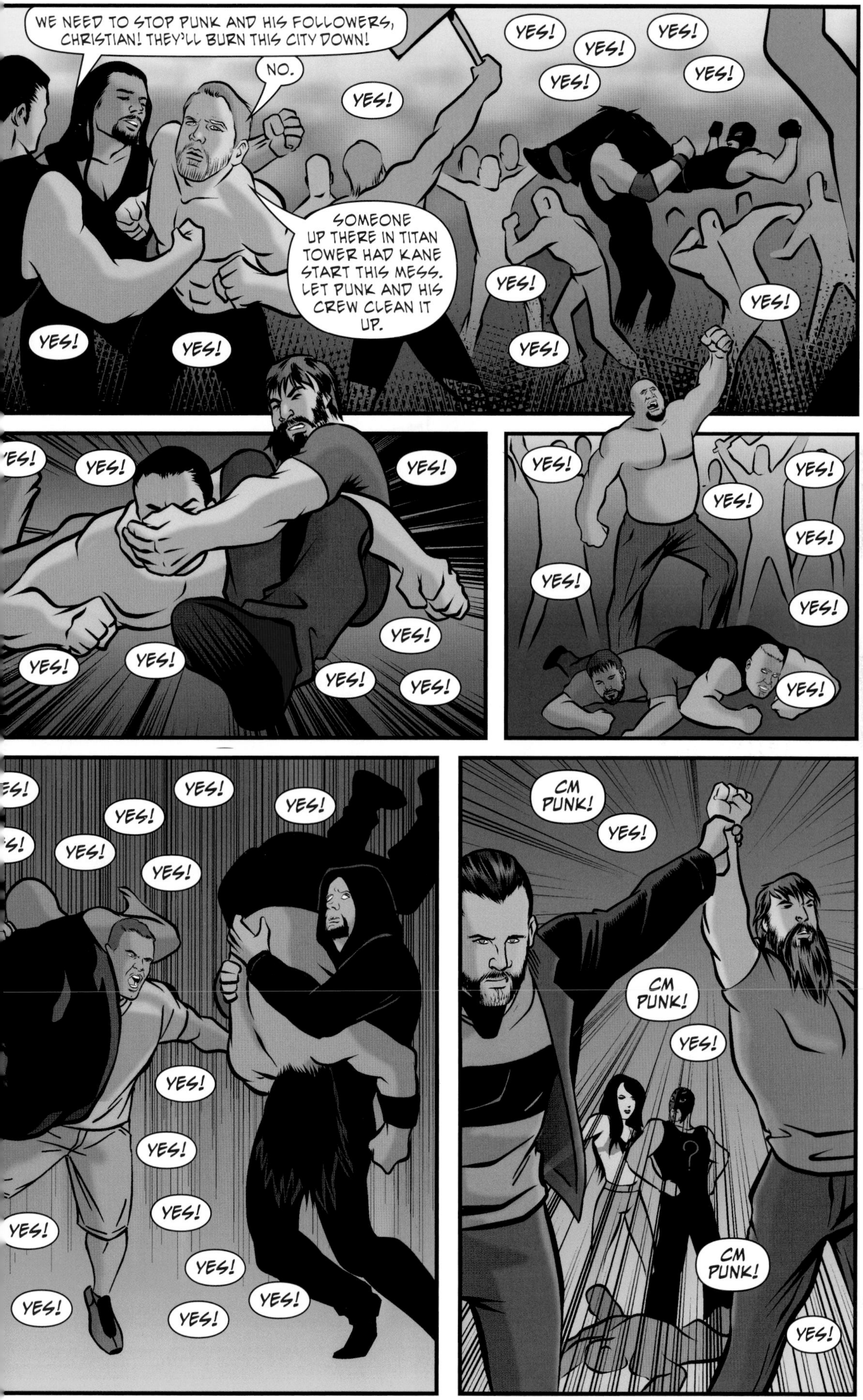
WE NEED TO STOP PUNK AND HIS FOLLOWERS, CHRISTIAN! THEY'LL BURN THIS CITY DOWN!
NO.
YES!
YES!
YES!
YES!
YES!
YES!
SOMEONE UP THERE IN TITAN TOWER HAD KANE START THIS MESS. LET PUNK AND HIS CREW CLEAN IT UP.
YES!
YES!
YES!
YES!
YES!
YES!
YES!
YES!
YES!
YES!
YES!
YES!
YES!
YES!
YES!
YES!
YES!
YES!
YES!
YES!
YES!
YES!
YES!
YES!
YES!
YES!
YES!
YES!
YES!
YES!
YES!
YES!
CM PUNK!
YES!
CM PUNK!
YES!
CM PUNK!
YES!

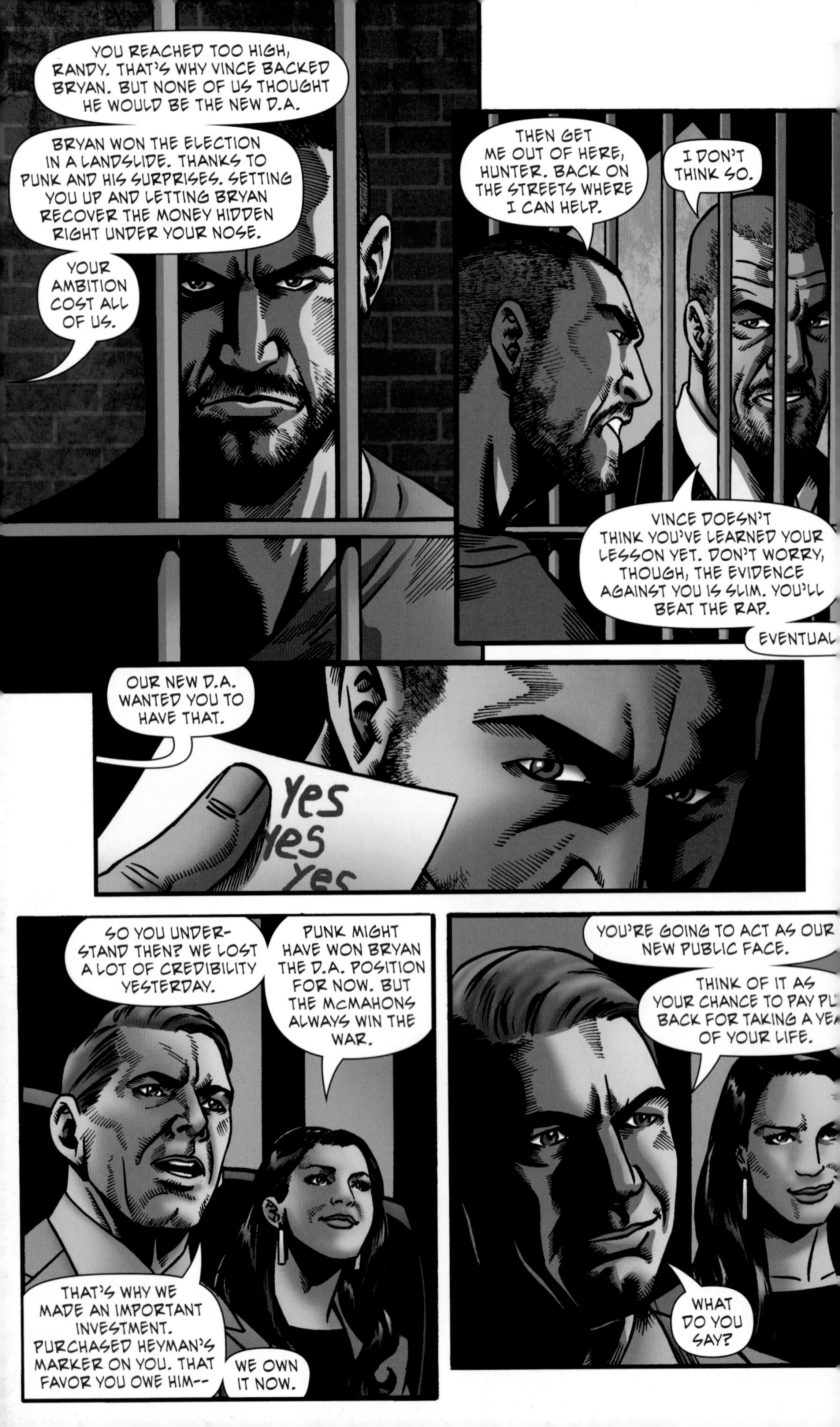
YOU REACHED TOO HIGH, RANDY. THAT'S WHY VINCE BACKED BRYAN. BUT NONE OF US THOUGHT HE WOULD BE THE NEW D.A.
BRYAN WON THE ELECTION IN A LANDSLIDE. THANKS TO PUNK AND HIS SURPRISES. SETTING YOU UP AND LETTING BRYAN RECOVER THE MONEY HIDDEN RIGHT UNDER YOUR NOSE.
YOUR AMBITION COST ALL OF US.
THEN GET ME OUT OF HERE, HUNTER. BACK ON THE STREETS WHERE I CAN HELP.
I DON'T THINK SO.
VINCE DOESN'T THINK YOU'VE LEARNED YOUR LESSON YET. DON'T WORRY, THOUGH, THE EVIDENCE AGAINST YOU IS SLIM. YOU'LL BEAT THE RAP.
EVENTUAL
OUR NEW D.A. WANTED YOU TO HAVE THAT.
Yes
Yes
Yes
SO YOU UNDER-STAND THEN? WE LOST A LOT OF CREDIBILITY YESTERDAY.
PUNK MIGHT HAVE WON BRYAN THE D.A. POSITION FOR NOW. BUT THE McMAHONS ALWAYS WIN THE WAR.
THAT'S WHY WE MADE AN IMPORTANT INVESTMENT. PURCHASED HEYMAN'S MARKER ON YOU. THAT FAVOR YOU OWE HIM--
WE OWN IT NOW.
YOU'RE GOING TO ACT AS OUR NEW PUBLIC FACE.
THINK OF IT AS YOUR CHANCE TO PAY PU BACK FOR TAKING A YE OF YOUR LIFE.
WHAT DO YOU SAY?

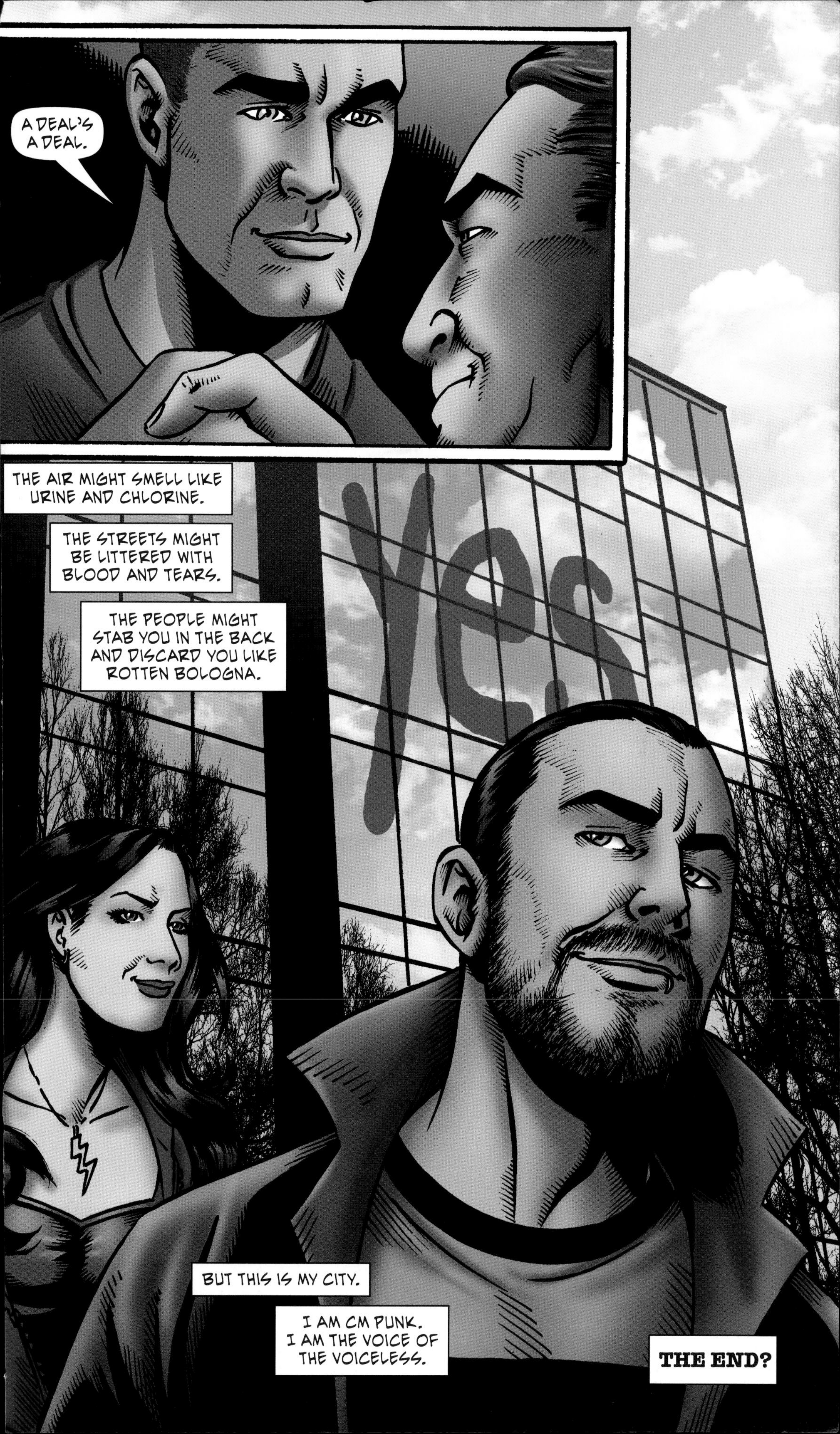
A DEAL'S A DEAL.
THE AIR MIGHT SMELL LIKE URINE AND CHLORINE.
THE STREETS MIGHT BE LITTERED WITH BLOOD AND TEARS.
THE PEOPLE MIGHT STAB YOU IN THE BACK AND DISCARD YOU LIKE ROTTEN BOLOGNA.
Yes
BUT THIS IS MY CITY.
I AM CM PUNK. I AM THE VOICE OF THE VOICELESS.
THE END?